Improving Urban Parks, Play Areas and Green Spaces

May 2002

May 2002

Nigel Dunnett, Carys Swanwick and Helen Woolley

Department of Landscape, University of Sheffield
Department for Transport, Local Government and the Regions: London

Further copies of this publication are available from:

Department for Transport, Local Government and the Regions
Publications Sales Centre
Cambertown House
Goldthorpe Industrial Estate
Goldthorpe
Rotherham S63 9BL
Tel: 01709 891318
Fax: 01709 881673

or online via the Department's web site.

ISBN 1 85112 576 0

Printed in Great Britain on material containing 75% post-consumer waste and 25% ECF pulp.

May 2002

Product Code 02HC000107

CONTENTS

Acknowledgements   6

Summary   7

    Introduction   7

    People and activities in urban green Spaces   10

    The ideal urban green space   12

    Adding up the benefits   12

    Structures and mechanisms   13

    Community involvement   14

    Making things happen   15

    A role in urban renewal   16

    Overview and conclusions   17

Chapter 1: Background   20

    Definitions and typology   22

    Research methods   26

    Content and organisation of report   28

Chapter 2: People and Activities   33

    Introduction   33

    Frequency of visits   38

    Patterns of visits   38

    Who are the users?   39

    Why do people use urban green spaces?   40

    Categorising users   45

Chapter 3: Barriers to use of Urban Green Spaces   46

    Introduction   47

    Definitions of non-users and infrequent users 47

    Previous research   48

    What are the barriers to use?   49

    Barriers for under represented groups   51

    Tackling the main barriers   54

    Revitalising urban green spaces   64

Chapter 4: The Ideal Urban Green Space   66

    Introduction   67

    Previous research   67

    The ideal urban green space   68

    Spaces for all   77

Chapter 5: Adding up the Benefits — 78

Introduction — 79
The range of benefits — 80
Social benefits — 80
Environmental benefits — 86
Economic benefits — 90
Quality of life capital — 90

Chapter 6: Structures and Mechanisms — 93

Introduction — 94
Institutional frameworks — 94
Action on the ground — 100
Tools for the task: strategic approaches to greenspace provision and planning — 113

Chapter 7: Communities and Involvement — 127

Introduction — 128
The range of community involvement — 128
Models for active community involvement — 131
Self management — 133
The role of friends and user groups — 136
Community engagement and development — 138
Encouraging involvement — 145
Costs and benefits of community involvement — 147
Conclusions — 152

Chapter 8: Making Things Happen — 154

Introduction — 155
Funding and budgets — 155
Making the most of resources: creative approaches to funding — 162
Partnerships — 166
Ownership — 173
Conclusions — 175

Chapter 9: A Role in Urban Regeneration — 180

Introduction — 180
Helping to attract inward investment — 182
Spin-offs from grassroots green space initiatives — 185
Parks as flagships in neighbourhood renewal — 189
Strategic, multi-agency area based regeneration, linking environment and economy — 193
Conclusion — 199

Chapter 10: Overview and Conclusions   **200**

    Introduction   200

    The Importance of urban green space   200

    Tackling the barriers   201

    It's all about design   202

    Working with others   203

    Breaking down organisational barriers   203

    Strategic approaches   204

    Establishing the information base   205

    Sharing good practice   206

References and Bibliography   **207**

Appendix 1: Detailed work Carried Out for Strand 1 and 2   **209**

    Telephone survey of non-users   209

Appendix 2: Using the typology as a basis for reporting on the extent of Urban Green Space   **212**

ACKNOWLEDGEMENTS

We would like to thank all the representatives of the case study local authorities, for providing us with such a wealth of assistance and information in the course of this research. We would also like to express our appreciation to all the other people, representing community groups, friends groups and other organisations in each area, who also gave so generously of their time to contribute. Thanks also go to all the participants in the focus groups, to the British Market Research Bureau for conducting the telephone survey, to the Urban Parks Forum for carrying out the telephone profiling survey and to the officers of all the local authorities who contributed to that survey. Ann Beer provided valuable material on experience of green space structure planning and community involvement in housing green space in Europe.

The research has been helped by the project Advisory Group of Peter Matthew, Sarah Fielder, Douglas Crockett and Michael Bach from DTLR, together with Alan Barber, Ken Worpole and Judy Ling Wong, who were members of the Urban Green Spaces Task Force, and Paul Bramhill of the Urban Parks Forum.

Particular thanks to Rachel Conner of DTLR, who provided overall supervision of the research, for all her hard work, help and support.

Authors
Nigel Dunnett
Carys Swanwick
Helen Woolley

Assisted by
Ian Baggott
Thom White
Frances Wells
Rebecca Hay
Ming Chia Lai
Shanti McAllister
Bruce Irvine

Department of Landscape
University of Sheffield
Third Floor
Arts Tower
Western Bank
Sheffield S10 2TN

Tel: 0114 222 0600
e-mail: landscape@sheffield.ac.uk

SUMMARY

Introduction

1. The vital importance of parks and other urban green spaces in enhancing the urban environment and the quality of city life has been recognised in both the Urban Taskforce report and the Urban White Paper. This report sets out the findings of research carried out to inform the work of the Urban Green Spaces Taskforce, set up to advise the government on proposals for improving the quality of urban parks, play areas and green spaces. It reflects the need for additional research identified in both the Urban White Paper and the report by the Environment, Transport and Regional Affairs Committee of the House of Commons on Town and Country Parks in 1999. The Department for Transport, Local Government and the Regions (DTLR) commissioned the work in April 2001 and appointed the Department of Landscape at the University of Sheffield to carry out the research. The brief divided the research into two strands, which ran in parallel.

2. **Strand 1** was designed to:

    *   Provide reliable identification of different categories of users of urban green spaces and how they use the range of types of such spaces, especially children and young people, the elderly, the disabled and people from an ethnic minority background.

    *   Determine the frequency and extent of use of urban green spaces and how this varies by different types of users and geographic location.

    *   Provide a comprehensive picture of the range and nature of activity in urban green spaces, and the facilities offered.

    *   Investigate what users want from urban green spaces and the extent to which the spaces meet these expectations.

    *   Develop a typology of open spaces and users that enables quick and useful reference.

    *   Examine the ways in which parks and urban green spaces contribute to enhancing the quality of life for people in urban areas and in particular the ways in which different groups of people benefit from the range of types of urban green spaces.

    *   Examine the barriers which deter different groups of people from using urban green spaces and play areas and identify the key factors that would encourage greater use.

    *   Examine how and to what extent parks and urban green spaces contribute to enhancing the quality and performance of urban environments in terms of their social, economic and environmental benefits.

3.   **Strand 2** was designed to:

- Assess current local authority practices for planning, providing, managing and maintaining urban green spaces and play areas, and identify strengths and weaknesses and areas where there may be potential for using other approaches to achieving improvements in standards.

- Identify and evaluate the range of innovative models which are developing or could be developed for creating, managing and maintaining urban green spaces and play areas.

- Develop new or innovative evidence based approaches and models for the management and maintenance of urban green spaces, which would: promote the effective involvement of local residents, user groups and business communities: extend and improve the 'capacity' of local user and for resident groups: and foster a greater sense of ownership and civic pride among the range of stakeholders

DEFINITIONS

4.   In this study the following definitions have been used:

- **Urban green space:** is defined as land that consists predominantly of unsealed, permeable, 'soft' surfaces such as soil, grass, shrubs and trees (the emphasis is on *'predominant'* character because of course green spaces may include buildings and hard surfaced areas); it is the umbrella term for all such areas whether or not they are publicly accessible or publicly managed. It includes all areas of parks, play areas and other green spaces specifically intended for recreational use, as well as other green spaces with other origins. The term 'urban green spaces' is used throughout this report as a short hand term for the parks, play areas and green spaces of the title, as it includes all these categories.

- **Open space:** should, it is suggested, be defined as that part of the urban area which contributes to its amenity, either visually by contributing positively to the urban landscape, or by virtue of public access. It is therefore defined as combining urban green spaces and civic spaces. This accords broadly with the Taskforce's own working definition of open space as encompassing *"a mixture of public (or civic) and green space, where public spaces are mainly 'hard' spaces such as squares, street frontages and paved areas."* It is also compatible with the approach proposed in Scotland, which defines open space as *"a mixture of civic spaces and green spaces"*.

- **Public open space** is defined as open space, both green spaces and hard 'civic' spaces, to which there is public access, even though the land may not necessarily be in public ownership. (This is different from the legal definition in the Town and Country Planning Act 1990 and the more traditional planning definition of 'public open space' (POS), still used by some local authorities, to mean publicly accessible green space without any formal facilities for recreation provision).

TYPOLOGY OF URBAN GREEN SPACES

5.   A typology of urban green spaces is suggested based on a classification of categories within which sit definitions of the different types of urban green space. Hierarchical division has the benefit of allowing the different categories to be either aggregated at a higher level or broken down further in a consistent way, depending on the level of detail required and the purpose of the classification. The typology reflects the full range of different types of urban green space which together form the green fabric of urban areas, including those that are publicly or privately owned and managed, and sites that may or may not be accessible for public recreation. The typology divides all urban green space into four main categories, which are further sub-divided into twenty six detailed sub-categories, although these can be grouped at an intermediate level. The four main categories are amenity green space, functional green space, semi-natural habitats and linear green space. The main emphasis in this research is on amenity green space (which is sub-divided into recreation green space, incidental green space and private green space) and particularly on the different types of recreation green space, that is parks and gardens, informal recreation areas, outdoor sports areas and play areas.

6.   It would be presumptuous to think that this typology is the only solution and consultation will undoubtedly be required before an agreed classification, and accompanying definitions, can be adopted for general use. The nature of a typology also depends to a great extent on the use to which it will be put and here the focus is primarily on a typology that could be used in providing a reporting framework for information about the extent of different types of green space.

RESEARCH METHODS

7.   The nature and breadth of the research objectives meant that several different approaches were required in addressing the two different strands of the research. The study was based on:

- A literature review

- A telephone survey of 50 local authorities

- More detailed examination of fifteen case study authorities, selected to cover a range of both regional locations and types and size of authority. This work involved:

  - structured interviews with managers and other staff;

  - collation and analysis of existing survey data on users and uses (Strand 1);

  - a telephone survey of 515 non- or infrequent users or urban green space and focus groups with users and non-users (Strand 1);

  - identification and review of a number of initiatives and projects in each area to demonstrate good practice, innovation and creativity (Strand 2).

The Case Study Local Authorities		
Strand 1 only	**Strand 2 only**	**Strands 1 and 2**
Ipswich	Basingstoke	Leicester
Bexley	Chelmsford	Newcastle
Lewisham	Cheltenham	Stockport
Milton Keynes	Wolverhampton	Oldham
Plymouth	Doncaster	Sheffield

People and activities in urban green spaces

8. Finding meaningful information about how many people actually use urban green spaces, who they are and when and why they use them, is hampered by the fact that survey information from local authorities is inevitably inconsistent. In recent years some data collection systems have been developed for funding bids to the Heritage Lottery Fund and other funding bodies, to identify local needs and more recently as part of the Best Value process. The standard questions in the Best Value User Satisfaction Survey are in themselves quite basic and more useful information has been available where local authorities have extended the scope of that questionnaire.

9. Findings from a telephone survey with the public can be used to estimate the number of urban green space users. It has been estimated that two and a quarter million people, across the ten locations of Strand1 for this research, make at least 184 million visits each year to urban green spaces. If the urban population of England is assumed to be 37.8 million (including only those areas with a population of 10,000 or more) a similar calculation suggests that some **33 million** people make over **2.5 billion visits** each year to urban green spaces, with this estimate considered to be on the low side.

10. Overall 46 per cent of people stated that they use urban green spaces more than once a week, with many using them several times a week, daily or several times a day. In terms of a daily pattern there appears to be a peak of use in the afternoons with weekends and holiday times also being key times for use of urban green spaces. Some people have seasonal patterns of use while others are affected by the weather. Men are confirmed as slightly higher users of urban green spaces than women, but there is no clear indication from the local authority surveys as to whether people from an ethnic minority background, or disabled people are under-represented among users.

11. The research has clearly confirmed that informal and passive activities are the main reasons that people visit urban green spaces. The information from the survey shows that people's reasons for using urban green spaces fall into seven broad categories of: enjoying the environment; social activities; getting away from it all; walking activities, including dog walking; passive or informal enjoyment; active enjoyment, including sport and specific activities; and attending events. These seven categories of primary use can be combined with a social typology, based on age, gender, physical and mental ability and ethnicity to create a categorisation of users. Such a framework could be of value in seeking to achieve greater consistency in surveys of users and uses in the future.

Non-users and barriers to use

12. Non-users have been defined as people who have used urban green spaces once in the last year, or less, or never, while infrequent users have been defined as those who have used these spaces less than once a month or only once in the last six months. The telephone survey suggested that 32% of people in the case study areas are either non-users or infrequent users of urban green spaces with 12% being non-users and 20% infrequent users.

13. People who do not use green spaces at all or only use them infrequently have less actual experience of using these spaces and so may have limited knowledge of how real, or otherwise, the perceived barriers may be. Their perceptions may therefore be quite different from users and the barriers that they identify could be imagined as much as they are real. Nevertheless, five main barriers have been identified that deter people from using urban green spaces. In approximate order of importance, and based on all three sources of information, they are:

     - Lack of, or the poor condition of, facilities – including play for children

     - Other users, including undesirable characters

     - Concerns about dogs and dog mess

     - Safety and other 'psychological' issues

     - Environmental quality issues such as litter, graffiti and vandalism.

14. In addition access issues are also of concern, particularly to the elderly and to people with disabilities. They relate to concerns about the proximity of and ease of access to urban green spaces, access to get into those spaces and ease of moving around safely within them. The access concerns of people with disabilities take on added significance in the light of the 1995 Disability Discrimination Act.

15. Most of these issues are resource issues that relate to the location, accessibility or environmental quality of urban green spaces and are therefore issues which could be overcome if the planners, designers and managers of these spaces could address them satisfactorily. Some of the secondary barriers to use are personal issues that cannot be addressed by those responsible for urban green spaces and include: not having enough time, working unsociable hours, poor health or mobility and other preferences.

16. The telephone survey revealed seven factors that are likely to encourage people to use urban green spaces more. In approximate order of mentions they are: dog mess, followed by improved safety, better maintenance, better facilities, more events/activities, more staff, making spaces easier to get to and having a space that is nearer. Similarly, in terms of facilities that would encourage more use if they were provided, non- and infrequent users particularly chose the provision of a café and toilets. The provision of dog litter bins, seating, litter bins, information centre/boards, children's play area and sports areas were also mentioned across all the under represented groups, but with the order of mentions varying to some extent.

17.　When asked what would improve their sense of safety in urban green spaces, the non- and infrequent users selected more lighting, followed by more rangers/staff, more things for young people to do, dogs being on a lead, no motor vehicles, dog-free areas, lower planting near paths and no cycling or roller skating. Again there was some variation in the order of these issues with respect to the different under represented user groups.

18.　Many of these barriers have been identified before and yet, despite the best efforts of many local authorities, there is still a deep concern that the problems remain and that to many people parks are simply not what they used to be. More steps need to be taken to overcome some of these barriers to use, to improve the image that people have of these important urban green spaces and to create the types of places that people want to visit.

The ideal urban green space

19.　The perception that someone has of an urban green space can significantly affect whether they use that space, contribute to the collective opinion that a community has of such a space and shape the wider community's image of urban green spaces. This image can be as important as the reality in deciding whether people will make use of these areas.

20.　Focus groups of both users and non-users from the under represented groups considered what would be in their ideal urban green space. The most frequently mentioned component was vegetation, followed by water, play opportunities, comforts like seating, toilets and shelters, good access – particularly an issue for people with disabilities – sport, and events. Refreshments of a good quality and reasonable price, environmental quality issues such as litter bins, lighting and vandalism, and specific features such as sculptures and mazes were also mentioned. Animals were considered to be important for children, opportunities for wheeled activities were desired by women and young people while the presence of identifiable and approachable staff, was also a feature of the ideal urban green space. People with disabilities mentioned sensory stimulation and dog issues were also mentioned, but far less than in the telephone survey of non-users.

21.　Overall it is clear that the improvements that people want to see in urban green spaces are related to: good design and management, focused on meeting people's needs, overcoming barriers to use and providing a high quality and varied experience for the whole range of different groups in the community as a whole. People showed considerable awareness of the needs of others and wanted the ideal green space to be inclusive – a space for all.

Adding up the benefits

22.　Many studies refer to the social benefits of urban green space. It has both an existence value, because people know it is there, and a use value for a wide range of different activities. In particular it:

- contributes significantly to social inclusion because it is free and access is available to all;

- provides neutral ground available to all sectors of society and can become the focus of community spirit through the many and varied opportunities provided for social interaction;

- contributes to child development through scope for outdoor, energetic and imaginative play and may positively influence the behaviour of both individuals and wider society.

- offers numerous educational opportunities.

In addition the health benefits of urban green space are extremely important and merit separate attention. They stem both from the opportunity to engage in healthy outdoor exercise and from the psychological effects arising from the way that they allow escape to a less stressful, more relaxing environment.

23. The main environmental benefits of urban green space are:

- contributions to maintaining biodiversity through the conservation and enhancement of the distinctive range of urban habitats;

- contributions to landscape and cultural heritage;

- amelioration of the physical urban environment by reducing pollution, moderating the extremes of the urban climate, contributions to cost-effective sustainable urban drainage systems and some influence as sinks for carbon dioxide;

- provision of opportunities to demonstrate sustainable management practices.

24. Economic benefits include both on-site benefits, such as direct employment and revenue generation, and less tangible off-site benefits, including effects on nearby property prices, contributions to attracting and retaining businesses in an area and an important role in attracting tourists. There have been few studies in the UK of these wider economic benefits and this is an area where additional research would be valuable in informing understanding of the role that green space plays in sustaining vibrant urban economies. Previous economic evaluations of environmental improvement initiatives do, however, demonstrate the difficulties of clearly linking cause and effect.

25. Demonstrating how parks and other green spaces meet wider council policy objectives linked to other agendas, like education, diversity, health, safety, environment, jobs and regeneration, can raise the political profile and commitment of an authority to green space issues. There may be merit in local authorities using an adapted version of the Quality of Life Capital approach to provide a framework for presenting consistent arguments about the important benefits offered by urban green spaces and also for evaluating individual sites and features.

Structures and mechanisms

26. It is clear that a diversification of urban green spaces, (in terms of their form, content and range of users, as well as who is involved in their management and who owns them) is

taking place and that that the best examples of innovation and creativity are associated with this.

27. Institutional structures are important. There is some evidence that urban green space service delivery from within a local authority's environmental directorate, rather than from leisure and education or equivalent directorates, may have benefit in terms of both budget protection and policy implementation and a holistic approach to urban green space. Certainly fragmentation of responsibility for and ownership of, urban green spaces across different departments or directorates within a local authority is a barrier to efficiency and innovation, but also to community involvement. Unified divisional structures, bringing all aspects of green space service delivery together, as well as clear "one-stop-shops" for public contact, all appear effective approaches to overcoming the problems.

28. On matters of staffing it is clear that greater emphasis on community involvement and support requires a change in the skills base and the structures of parks and open spaces services. A community development approach is greatly aided by a departmental structure that is based upon geographical area, tied into other area-based service boundaries, and related to the hierarchy of area based community consultation. Re-instatement of site-based gardeners /wardens /park keepers is very well received by site users. Similarly breaking down demarcated site based roles (rangers, gardeners, security staff inspections, cleansing) can promote ownership and initiative by site-based personnel and also produce savings sufficient to introduce more 'static' personnel. Enabling a ranger service, with their people orientated skills, to be responsible for all aspects of the management of a mainstream urban park, can also successfully bring in low cost, low maintenance non-urban or "countryside" management techniques into a mainstream urban inner city park, usually with full public acceptance.

29. The principles of good practice in strategic management of parks are now reasonably well established. Innovation now lies in extending these principles to take a more holistic view of the place of parks in the wider network of urban green spaces and explaining how this network can meet the needs and aspirations of urban populations. Producing green space audits that incorporate qualitative as well as quantitative information; formulating green space categorisation systems and typologies that drive policy; and producing holistic green space strategies and green structure plans that consider parks as just one element in a larger environmental network; are all examples of important emerging developments in strategic approaches to urban green space. In addition developing local standards, rather than simply relying on national standards for provision, enables planning of all types of green space to be matched to local social, economic and environmental need.

Community involvement

30. The Urban White Paper stresses the need to identify opportunities for both building and supporting partnerships for managing open space in and around towns, particularly where this involves businesses and local communities. Community involvement in urban parks and green spaces can lead to increased use, enhancement of quality and richness of experience and, in particular, to ensuring that facilities are suited to local needs. There are two basic and different objectives for community engagement: one involves communication, information exchange and consultation, and the other takes the process

forward into active collaboration in decision making, design, planning and management. In this spectrum the development of self-management activity can be the ultimate expression of community involvement.

31. A small number of parks services in this study have changed the way they operate, shifting the focus from direct service delivery to supporting and developing community groups. From these and other examples it is clear that developing a community focus requires a new skills balance within parks services. It is also clear that it is possible to actively and strategically manage groups into the more advanced stages of partnership, and that this can happen in the more deprived areas of a town or city as well as the more affluent. It is also apparent that the importance of a group being representative of a local community varies according to the objectives of the group. At a wider level, beyond individual sites, promoting networking and co-ordination of friends group activities promotes good practice across a town or city.

32. The potential for successful involvement of local communities in urban parks and green spaces is related to several factors but most importantly to: the culture of the local authority and parks service; the resources available; the type of site and local capacity. Both local authorities and community groups in the case study areas saw increasing a local sense of ownership, accessing additional funding and promoting communication and understanding as the main advantages of community involvement. There is, however, a need to explore mechanisms to recognise and in some way to reward local voluntary input.

Making things happen

33. The acknowledged decline in the quality of care of the urban green space resource in England can be linked to declining local authority green space budgets over the past 10 – 15 years. The majority of the case study authorities had witnessed budgetary reductions over this period and reduced budgets force hard choices, which have manifested themselves in lower maintenance standards and failing infrastructure. However, the creative approaches found to resourcing urban green space management result from more than an increase in funding alone. The examples given (including private finance arrangements, creative redirection of existing spending, partnership working) make creative use of funding to lever in additional resource, or make better use of existing resource.

34. There are wide variations in spend per head of population across the authorities in the survey (although the figures are not necessarily easily compared). There does not, however, seem to be any clear correlation between levels of spending and the extent of good or innovative practice. There are certainly cases where higher spending authorities are performing at a high-level and appear to have a highly innovative culture but there are also good examples of innovation in less well funded authorities. An agreed typology of green spaces and associated costs would enable more direct comparison of spend between authorities.

35. The lack of resources for capital spending was identified by all the local authorities as a major problem. In terms of the importance of different external sources for capital development, two were consistently named as the most valuable. They were the Heritage Lottery Fund and Section 106 Agreements under which developers may be required to

meet certain planning obligations when they are given permission to develop, including funding of green spaces. In most cases private sponsorship cannot really be counted as a significant contribution in terms of overall budgets, but it can enable features or facilities to be created or operated that would otherwise not be viable.

36. Effective partnerships between a local authority and community groups, funding agencies and business can result in significant added value, both in terms of finances and quality of green space. However, time and resources have to be put into forming and supporting partnerships. There is therefore a potential short and medium term financial cost associated with what might be a longer term financial gain

37. Several approaches were encountered that either increased the financial resources available, or made better or more efficient use of existing resources. These included:

   ●   Private Finance Initiatives

   ●   Partnership with grant-making organisations, business and community groups

   ●   Creative re-direction of revenue spend

   ●   Opportunistic use of targeted grant funding to achieve wider strategic aims

   ●   Flexible use of Section 106 funds

38. Self-management and trust status is becoming a valuable means to create and manage mainstream urban parks. There is a reduced financial and administration cost to the local authority in the long-term involved in transfer of a park to a self-managing trust. The main advantages spring from the benefits associated with a high degree of community involvement. There is also potential for creation of city-wide partnerships for parks and green space, not just to increase use and activity in a single park or green space, but also to raise the level and quality of open space and parks in an entire city, through neighbourhood organizations and park partnerships.

A role in urban renewal

39. The case studies presented in this research begin to build an alternative picture of the contribution of urban green space to urban renewal. Evidence has been put forward to suggest that environmental enhancement not only makes places more attractive and pleasant (thereby promoting inward investment and increase in land values), but that green space initiatives can result in community strengthening and local economic stimulation as well as improvement to local environmental quality.

40. It is suggested that urban green spaces can, uniquely, be the catalysts for wider community and economic spin-offs in a way that other neighbourhood facilities or buildings are unable to achieve. The fact that parks in particular offer free, open, non-discriminatory access all day, every day and are visible representations of neighbourhood quality were identified as important reasons for their special role.

41. Four levels of integration of urban green space into urban renewal can be identified, characterised by an increasing strategic synergy between environment, economy and community. They are:

   • attracting inward economic investment through provision of attractive urban landscapes;

   • unforeseen spin-offs from grassroots green space initiatives;

   • parks as flagships in neighbourhood renewal;

   • strategic, multi-agency area based regeneration, linking environment and economy.

42. Case studies in the research demonstrate a wide range of social, educational and economic benefits associated with community led green space renewal. As a result it is concluded that green space action plans should be inextricably bound into processes of economic, environmental and social regeneration. Raising awareness of the value of urban green space and its potentially key role in urban renewal represents perhaps the best argument for a significant increase in resources, investment and political attention for urban parks and other green spaces.

Overview and conclusions

43. This research has confirmed the exceptional importance of urban green space to the future of towns and cities in England. It reaffirms and elaborates on the findings of earlier studies on the role that urban green space plays in the day-to-day life of urban dwellers, by virtue both of its existence – that is people simply knowing that it is there and seeing the contribution that it makes to the urban landscape – as well as its use for recreation and enjoyment.

44. The research has shown that urban green spaces can act as catalysts for wider community initiatives in ways that no other public facility seems able to achieve in similar circumstances. Again and again, people involved in these initiatives said that if it wasn't for the park (or other green space) nothing would have happened. This social, community and economic role goes well beyond the normal, somewhat blinkered view of the contribution of urban green space to the future of our cities. It needs to be given much greater prominence in promoting a higher profile for urban green spaces and in supporting the case for funding at both local and national levels.

TACKLING THE BARRIERS

45. Social exclusion in society is mirrored by the under representation of some groups of people among users of urban green spaces. There is often lack of awareness and understanding within mainstream organisations, which can, for example, lead to failure to recognise fully, or to address, the particular needs of those groups who are most likely to be excluded in society. The research suggests that issues such as access for the disabled and the elderly, the

cultural needs of different ethnic groups, and the changing lifestyles and needs of children and young people may all contribute to low levels of engagement with urban green spaces

46.   The specific barriers to use, and changes that could be made to overcome them, are generally well recognised. Tackling them and, equally importantly, letting people know that they are being tackled and publicising the resulting improvements, will do much to increase the willingness of people to use the green spaces which they may currently turn away from. Several of the case study authorities, and no doubt others elsewhere, are seeking to tackle these barriers in imaginative ways. Everything possible needs to be done to share and spread such good practice. Some form of central agency to deal with urban green spaces could provide an ideal focus for such exchange.

THE IMPORTANCE OF DESIGN

47.   Ordinary people, as well as many professionals, recognise that design often lies at the heart of what makes a successful urban green space. Design is also a key part of tackling many of the barriers to use of urban green spaces. It is not just a one-off thing that happens when a new park or green space is created, but an attitude of mind and an approach to solving problems that should also be an integral part of the ongoing management of urban green spaces (in the same way that thinking about management should also be a key part of the design process).

48.   Approaches to design have to vary to suit individual circumstances – from facilitating community design at one level, to high-level innovative approaches to creating new urban green spaces at the other. Quality in design must always be the aim and designers need to find the right balance for each particular situation. 'Flagship' sites of citywide importance are likely to merit the highest level of design input and a highly creative approach dedicated to achieving the highest possible quality in either restoration or creation of new open spaces. This takes significant capital and the perceived lack of capital funds in local authorities in England is often an obstacle to developments of this type and needs to be addressed.

WORKING WITH OTHERS

49.   Community involvement of some form is now a part of mainstream activity in most places. Some of the most successful approaches seem to occur where there has been a real change in culture in the local authority parks service so that the emphasis on community involvement is core rather than partial or token.

50.   Many of the issues come down in the end to questions of 'ownership', whether real or perceived. Creating greater 'ownership' by communities using urban green spaces results in greater levels of innovation, creativity, involvement, care and resourcing. Delegating responsibility to community groups and supporting their activities and decisions, can result in a high degree of initiative. Beyond communities, the search for partner individuals, organisations and institutions seems less well developed in England than in some other countries, and notably the United States.

BREAKING DOWN BARRIERS

51.   Fragmentation of responsibility for different aspects of urban green space management is a major hindrance to efficiency and community involvement. Bringing together all responsibilities for green space strategy, management and maintenance within one section will foster a holistic view of the urban green space resource, of which parks are but one part. Breaking down barriers between different groups of staff and instilling a sense of 'ownership' in everyone involved can not only be cost effective, potentially allowing more staff to be employed on-site, but can also encourage individual initiative and a culture of innovation in tackling problems. Changing roles does, however, require new skills and there is increasingly a need for a new breed of modern green space professional.

STRATEGIC APPROACHES

52.   Local authorities need to take a broad integrative view of the whole urban green space resource, which recognises its vital contribution to the quality of life of urban dwellers. Producing 'green space audits' which incorporate qualitative as well as quantitative information; formulating green space categorisation systems and typologies that drive policy; and producing holistic green space strategies and green structure plans that consider parks as just one element in a larger green space network, are examples of these developments. This approach is given much greater emphasis elsewhere in Europe and current European initiatives demonstrate the importance attached to this area.

ESTABLISHING THE INFORMATION BASE

53.   It is already well-recognised that information on urban green spaces needs to be improved. This research has made suggestions about a typology for urban green space that could, albeit possibly with some modification, provide a basis for developing consistent records and estimates of the extent of different types of green space both locally and nationally. Similarly a typology of users of urban green space by type of activity and type of person has been suggested as a result of the research. This too might usefully be taken forward as a starting point for model surveys of the use of the spaces and people's satisfaction with them. Both of these need to be further developed through consultation and pilot studies so that local authorities can be given guidance on a preferred approach.

CHAPTER 1

Introduction

Background

1.1 The vital importance of parks and other urban green spaces in enhancing the urban environment and the quality of city life has been recognised in both the Urban Taskforce Report[1] and the Urban White Paper[2]. This Report sets out the findings of research carried out to inform the work of the Urban Green Spaces Taskforce, set up to advise the government on proposals for improving the quality of urban parks, play areas and green spaces. It reflects the need for additional research identified in both the Urban White Paper and the report by the Environment, Transport and Regional Affairs Committee of the House of Commons on Town and Country Parks in 1999. The Department for Transport, Local Government and the Regions (DTLR) commissioned the work in April 2001 and appointed the Department of Landscape at the University of Sheffield to carry out the research.

OBJECTIVES

1.2 The brief divided the research into two strands, which ran in parallel:

- **Strand 1** has examined the ways that urban green spaces are used and by whom, what users want from them, what they currently provide and the benefits they bring to the quality of life for people in the urban environment.

- **Strand 2** has identified and examined innovative and alternative approaches to creating, managing and maintaining urban green spaces, especially those that involves the community.

1.3 Work on **Strand 1** was intended to address a number of objectives, namely to:

- Provide reliable identification of different categories of users of urban green spaces and how they use the range of types of such spaces, especially children and young people, the elderly, disabled people and those from an ethnic minority background.

- Determine the frequency and extent of use of urban green spaces and how this varies by different types of users and geographic location.

1 *Towards an Urban Renaissance:* Report of the Urban Taskforce. DETR/Spon Press. (1999)
2 *Our Towns and Cities: Delivering an Urban Renaissance.* The Stationery Office (2000)

- Provide a comprehensive picture of the range and nature of activity in urban green spaces, and the facilities offered.

- Investigate what users want from urban green spaces and the extent to which the spaces meet these expectations.

- Develop a typology of open spaces and users that enables quick and useful reference.

- Examine the ways in which parks and urban green spaces contribute to enhancing the quality of life for people in urban areas and in particular the ways in which different groups of people benefit from the range of types of urban green spaces.

- Examine the barriers which deter different groups of people from using urban green spaces and play areas and identify the key factors that would encourage greater use.

- Examine how and to what extent parks and urban green spaces contribute to enhancing the quality and performance of urban environments in terms of their social, economic and environmental benefits.

1.4   Work on **Strand 2** was similarly intended to address a number of objectives, namely to:

- Assess current local authority practices for planning, providing, managing and maintaining urban green spaces and play areas, and identify strengths and weaknesses and areas where there may be potential for using other approaches to achieving improvements in standards.

- Identify and evaluate the range of innovative models which are developing or could be developed for creating, managing and maintaining urban green spaces and play areas, taking account of:

    – approaches which are in themselves sustainable in the long run and would lead to the long-term management and maintenance of green spaces;

    – different types of partnerships and organisation structures, including those which are led by local authorities, where community groups play a leading role and where the private sector is instrumental:

    – the characteristics of sound community-based approaches and partnerships and the timescale is involved in developing such partnerships and 'making things happen';

    – the resource streams relied on by such approaches and partnerships and the accessibility of such resources to the various approaches.

- Develop new or innovative evidence based approaches and models for the management and maintenance of urban green spaces, which would: promote the effective involvement of local residents, user groups and business communities: extend and improve the 'capacity' of local user and for resident groups: and foster a greater sense of ownership and civic pride among the range of stakeholders.

PREVIOUS RESEARCH

1.5 In the last decade two key documents have been instrumental in bringing recognition of the vital importance of urban parks and green spaces as key components of urban environments. *'Park Life'*, the seminal report on urban parks and their role in social renewal, produced in 1995[3], and the detailed examination of good practice in management in *People, Parks and Cities*, published in 1996[4], both had a profound effect in focusing attention on the declining quality of parks and their low priority in the political agenda at both national and local levels. At about the same time as the publication of these reports the Heritage Lottery Fund launched its Urban Parks Programme, providing substantial new funds for the restoration of historic parks. Together these were key events in the recent history of parks and green spaces, and marked the beginning of a turnaround in attitudes as well as contributing to new policy initiatives. They paved the way for the House of Commons Select Committee Report on Town and Country Parks, the coverage of the issue in the Urban Taskforce Report and, ultimately, the Urban White Paper.

1.6 Together these previous pieces of research were similar in their scope and objectives to this new research. However, this study seeks to extend the scope of investigation and to fill gaps where possible. In particular it seeks to: broaden the focus beyond parks alone and place them in the wider context of the whole range of urban green spaces, including children's play areas; look particularly at those who are non- or infrequent users of these spaces; explore people's aspirations for them; and provide up to date information to assist the Taskforce.

Definitions and typology

1.7 The project brief requested that a typology of urban green space should be developed as part of the research. This is discussed here since it helps to establish both the scope of the research and the definition of urban green space that is used throughout this report. Two main issues need to be considered: firstly the meaning of urban green space, particularly in relation to other terms such as open space or public open space; and secondly the types of urban land included under the umbrella of urban green space.

GREEN SPACE AND OPEN SPACE

1.8 At present both these terms seem to be used loosely and interchangeably. Green space is a more recent term. It seems to have its origins both in the urban nature conservation movement, and in the arrival in the UK of some of the European thinking about green space planning. It is particularly used to emphasise that the green environment of urban areas is about more than just parks, gardens and playing fields. Open space is increasingly used to refer to the whole of the external environment outside buildings in urban areas. The term does, however, also have a formal meaning, at least in the planning context, because it is defined in the Town and Country Planning Act 1990 (Section 336) as *"land*

1   *Park Life: Urban Parks and Social Renewal.* Comedia and Demos (1995).

2   *People, Parks and Cities: A guide to current good practice in Urban Parks.* Department of the Environment, (1996).

laid out as a public garden, public recreation area or a burial ground". With this meaning it can be considered to be a subset of green space. Certainly those responsible for the planning and management of parks and open spaces in Local Authorities appear to use the term open space or public open space to refer to publicly accessible land whose management is usually the responsibility of the local authority.

1.9 In this research it has been considered that urban areas are made up of the built environment and the external environment between buildings. The external environment consists of: **'green space'**, which is land that consists predominantly of unsealed, permeable, 'soft' surfaces such as soil, grass, shrubs and trees; and what can usefully be termed **'grey space'**, which is land that consists predominantly of sealed, impermeable, 'hard' surfaces such as concrete, paving or tarmac[5]. The emphasis is on 'predominant' character because of course green spaces may include buildings and hard surfaced areas and grey spaces may contain trees. The distinction between the two is nevertheless important.

1.10 **Urban green space** is therefore the umbrella term for all areas of land covered by this definition of green space, whether or not they are publicly accessible or publicly managed. It includes, as shown below, all areas of parks, play areas and other green spaces specifically intended for recreational use, as well as other green spaces with other origins. For this reason the term 'urban green spaces' is used throughout this report as a short hand term for the parks, play areas and green spaces of the title, and embracing all these categories.

1.11 Grey space can be further subdivided into functional spaces, which serve a particular practical purpose, such as roads, pavements, car parks and other hard surfaced areas associated with different types of built development, and **civic spaces**, which are publicly accessible areas designed primarily for public enjoyment, including town squares, plazas, pedestrianised streets and esplanades. **Open space** should therefore, it is suggested, be defined as that part of the urban area which contributes to its amenity, either visually by contributing positively to the urban landscape, or by virtue of public access. It is therefore defined as combining urban green spaces and civic spaces. This accords broadly with the Taskforce's own working definition of Open Space as encompassing *"a mixture of public (or civic) and green space, where public spaces are mainly 'hard' spaces such as squares, street frontages and paved areas."* It is also compatible with the approach proposed in Scotland[6], which defines open space as *"a mixture of civic spaces and green spaces"*.

1.12 Finally, **public open space** can therefore be defined as open space, both green spaces and hard 'civic' spaces, to which there is public access, even though the land may not necessarily be in public ownership. This is different from the legal definition in the Town and Country Planning Act 1990 and the more traditional planning definition of 'public open space' (POS), still used by some local authorities, to mean publicly accessible green space without any formal facilities for recreation provision[7].

---

5 *Managing Urban Spaces in Town Centres.* Department of the Environment and the Association of Town Centre Managers (1997).

6 *Rethinking Open Space: Open Space Provision and Management.* Research Report for the Scottish Executive Central Research Unit. Kit Campbell Associates (2001).

7 Open Space Terminology. ILAM Fact Sheet 00/99 (1999).

TYPES OF URBAN GREEN SPACE

1.13   A typology of urban green spaces means developing a classification of categories within which sit definitions of types of urban green space. Hierarchical division has the benefit of allowing the different categories to be either aggregated at a higher level or broken down further in a consistent way, depending on the level of detail required and the purpose of the classification. The typology needs to reflect the full range of different types of urban green space that occur and which together form the green fabric of the urban area. They may be publicly or privately owned and managed, and may or may not be accessible for public recreation. The typology developed in this research is shown in **Table 1.1** and definitions of the categories are included in **Table 1.2**, both at the end of this chapter. This typology is not radically different from the one used by the Taskforce in its work.

1.14   It would be presumptuous to think that this typology is the only answer to the problem and consultation will undoubtedly be required before an agreed classification, and accompanying definitions, can be adopted for general use. It is also important to recognise that the nature of a typology depends to a great extent on the use to which it will be put. In discussion with the project Advisory Group it was agreed that in this study the focus would be primarily on a typology that could be used in providing a reporting framework for information about the extent of different types of green space. The problems currently experienced in gaining a clear picture of how much green space of different types actually exists in our urban areas have been outlined elsewhere[8]. Key issues are lack of consistency in definitions and the risk of double counting where certain types of green space overlap, especially children's play areas, outdoor sports areas and woodland all of which may occur in more broadly defined parks and recreation spaces. There are also concerns about the accuracy of returns and about lack of comparability between different local authorities. More detailed discussion of the way that the suggested typology could be used for this purpose is included as **Appendix 2**.

RELATIONSHIP TO OTHER TYPES OF CLASSIFICATION

1.15   A typology of green space based on type of space alone does not give a complete picture and other approaches also need to be considered for other purposes. Most local authorities base their strategies for open space provision and management on either the standards set by the National Playing Fields Association[9] or on a hierarchy of provision based on the London Planning Advisory Committee (LPAC) accessibility/catchment hierarchy[10] or a variation of this. In addition there are also English Nature's recommendations on standards for accessible natural green space[11], which some local authorities are also using.

8   *Green Spaces, Better Places.* Interim Report of the Urban Green Spaces Taskforce. DTLR 2001 and the accompanying Report from the Taskforce's Working Group One on the Information Base.

9   *The Six Acre Standard: Minimum Standards for Outdoor Playing Space.* National Playing Fields Association, (1992).

10   *Open Space Planning in London.* Llewelyn-Davies/London Planning Advisory Committee (1992).

11   *Accessible Natural Green Space in Towns and Cities: A review of Appropriate Size and Distance Criteria.* Harrison, Burgess, Millward and Dawe. English Nature (1995)

1.16   The hierarchy approach introduced by LPAC and further developed by others, is in effect a typology of public open space (as defined above) based on the importance of each space in terms of its extent, the size of its catchment area, the nature of the resource, and the type of facilities provided. The categories adopted vary between authorities but the Institute of Leisure and Amenity Management (ILAM) terminology paper (see Footnote 7) usefully defines a four level hierarchy of parks as shown below, although these are often combined or amended:

- **Principal/City/Metropolitan Parks** of more than 8.0 hectares, with a Town/City wide catchment, a varied physical resource and a wide range of facilities, which would generally be recognised as a visitor attraction in its own right;

- **District Parks** up to 8.0 hectares in extent with a catchment area from 1500 to 2000 metres, with a mixture of landscape features and a variety of facilities such as sports field/playing fields and play areas;

- **Neighbourhood Park** up to 4.0 hectares in extent serving a catchment area of between 1000 to1500 metres with both landscape features and a variety of facilities;

- **Local Park** up to 1.2 hectares in extent serving a catchment area of between 500 and 1000 metres, usually consisting of a play area and informal green area and landscape features but lacking other facilities.

1.17   This type of hierarchical classification can only be usefully applied to publicly owned and managed green space that is accessible for some form of recreation and there are also separate hierarchies that can be applied to children's play areas. Whatever the approach used, this form of hierarchy can be combined with the typology suggested above to provide a framework for categorising individual sites. **Table 1.3** is a hypothetical worked example of this based on sites from the Sheffield City Council Site Categorisation. This type of matrix approach to categorisation can also be applied to other 'overlays' of information about the status of green spaces, for example the quality of provision, types of facilities or resource value.

RELATIONSHIP TO STRATEGIC DESIGNATIONS

1.18   Many local authorities apply a range of strategic or planning designations to their green spaces. These include greenways, green corridors, green links, and green wedges, all of which have been actively promoted recently by the Countryside Agency as a means of linking town and country. Some of these designations, or variations on them, are often included in Development Plans and Local Authority green space or parks strategies. Such 'designations' will often embrace several different types of green space – for example, a town park may be linked to the urban edge by a green corridor combining woodland, semi-natural grassland, a cemetery, a linear green space along a river or canal and an area of encapsulated farmland. As a whole the corridor will function both as a wildlife corridor, a recreation resource, a landscape feature and a strategic break between adjacent areas of development. It may also contain a linked series of footpaths or private parks which may be further designated as a walk, trail or nature trail.

1.19   Strategic approaches to urban green space planning require a different and more comprehensive approach to classifications and definitions than the more traditional approach that has evolved in the field of park and open space management. They need to recognise the vital importance of the whole range of different green spaces within urban environments, whether or not they are publicly accessible or publicly managed. The ideal is a system that categorises the physical green space resource in its entirety using a typology like the one proposed here, and bases a quantitative inventory on this. This information can then also be combined with other information, such as a classification according to, for example, function as a recreational resource or evaluation of site quality or environmental value, as well as using planning designations such as green corridors, links or wedges as a further overlay.

Research methods

1.20   The nature and breadth of the research objectives has meant that several different approaches have been required in addressing the two different strands of the research. The work has involved collection and analysis of information at four different levels.

LITERATURE REVIEW

1.21   A review of literature and other relevant material has informed both strands of the study. Material has been drawn from a wide range of academic and professional publications and from local and national policy documents relating to urban green space. A limited selection of literature from North America and from Europe has been included and some additional investigation of European approaches has been incorporated by contact with the European Union funded Cost Action 11 Programme on planning urban green space. A separate report on the literature review was prepared at the end of Stage One of the work in July 2001 but the content has been drawn on throughout this report.

PROFILING SURVEY

1.22   To collect sufficient information to both illuminate understanding of current practice and also to enable selection of case study areas, a short, sharp telephone questionnaire survey was carried out to provide a profile of 50 local authorities. Local authorities were selected on the basis of census information on the population of partly or wholly urban local authority areas, settlement type (cities/large towns/town and country), Government Office region; and by category (larger and smaller metropolitan areas, larger and smaller regional urban centres, inner London and outer London authorities, historic towns or cities, new towns, coastal ports, and coastal resorts). A short questionnaire was used to collect basic information about: the records that authorities kept of users and uses; their approach to community participation and involvement; strategic approaches to green space planning; approaches to site maintenance and management; involvement in partnerships; and potential availability of innovative or good practice examples.

CASE STUDY LOCAL AUTHORITIES

1.23 In this research the aim was to take a structured approach to try and identify a varied group of local authorities that would be representative of the range of types of authority and their regional locations. On the basis of information compiled from the profiling survey, fifteen case study local authorities were selected to provide more detailed information relevant to both strands of the research. Authorities were selected to give good regional coverage and good representation of different types of urban area, ranging from the largest metropolitan area to smaller regional centres or coastal towns. In the sample of fifteen case study areas, five were used for the Strand 1 research only, five for Strand 2 only, and five for both Strand 1 and Strand 2, as below:

The Case Study Local Authorities		
Strand 1 only	**Strand 2 only**	**Strands 1 and 2**
Ipswich	Basingstoke	Leicester
Bexley	Chelmsford	Newcastle
Lewisham	Cheltenham	Stockport
Milton Keynes	Wolverhampton	Oldham
Plymouth	Doncaster	Sheffield

1.24 In each of the fifteen case study authorities structured interviews were held with senior policymakers and managers covering: organisation and structure, finance, the nature of the urban green space resource; strategic approaches to green space planning; maintenance and management, including use of GIS as a management tool; approaches to community involvement; involvement in partnership working; and involvement in awards or other schemes designed to recognise good practice. A further round of follow up interviews for each area were specific to the two strands of the research and also resulted in the assembly of a wide range of published and unpublished material on many different aspects of urban green space provision and management in each area.

DETAILED WORK ON STRANDS 1 AND 2

1.25 The work described so far was common to both of the research strands but at the detailed level more focused survey work was tailored to meeting the requirements of the two individual strands.

- In **Strand 1** the detailed work consisted of collation and analysis of existing data from the case study authorities on surveys of users and uses, a telephone questionnaire of people defined as non-users or infrequent users of urban green space, and a series of 43 focus groups in the ten Strand 1 case study areas with sectors of the population previously identified as under represented as users of urban green space.

- In **Strand 2** the detailed work in each of the ten case study areas involved identification and review of examples of good practice in urban green space management and review of three selected examples of innovation and good practice in projects demonstrating partnership or community involvement or other innovative area of current practice.

Fuller details of the work carried out are in **Appendix 1**.

Content and organisation of report

1.26   This report is structured around the two main strands in the research brief:

- **Chapters 2 to 5** focus on **Strand 1** and cover: people and activities (Chapter 2); non-users and barriers to use (Chapter 3); the ideal green space (Chapter 4); and adding up the benefits (Chapter 5).

- **Chapters 6 to 9** focus on **Strand 2** and cover: structures and mechanisms (Chapter 6); community involvement (Chapter 7); making things happen (Chapter 8); and a role in urban renewal (Chapter 9).

1.27   The main purpose of this research is to provide evidence about the issues surrounding urban green space. All the components of the research – that is the literature review, the profiling survey, the interviews with local authorities, examination of local authority reports and surveys, the focus groups and the detailed assessments of individual initiatives and projects – have contributed to each chapter.

Table 1.1: A Typology of urban green space

Main types of Green Space

ALL URBAN GREEN SPACE	**Amenity Green Space**	**Recreation Green Space**	Parks and Gardens
			Informal Recreation Areas
			Outdoor Sports Areas
			Play Areas
		Incidental Green Space	Housing Green Space
			Other Incidental Space
		Private Green Space	Domestic Gardens
	Functional Green Space	**Productive Green Space**	Remnant Farmland
			City Farms
			Allotments
		Burial Grounds	Cemeteries
			Churchyards
		Institutional Grounds	School Grounds (including school farms and growing areas)
			Other Institutional Grounds
	Semi-natural habitats	**Wetland**	Open/Running Water
			Marsh, Fen
		Woodland	Deciduous woodland
			Coniferous woodland
			Mixed woodland
		Other Habitats	Moor/Heath
			Grassland
			Disturbed Ground
		Linear Green Space	River and Canal Banks
			Transport Corridors (road, rail, cycleways and walking routes)
			Other linear features (e.g. cliffs)

Table 1.2: Definitions of types of urban green space

AMENITY GREEN SPACE All land which is designed primarily for amenity, both visual amenity and enjoyment for access and recreation. It consists mainly of publicly owned land but also includes private land, such as domestic gardens, which can contribute greatly to the green fabric of towns and cities. Sub–types of amenity green space are:	**Parks and Gardens** Areas of green space specifically designed for public access and enjoyment and combining a variety of landscape and horticultural elements (sometimes including semi-natural habitats) and facilities for the public (including buildings) and in some cases incorporating sports facilities and/or play areas. At the smaller scale may include community gardens.
	Informal Recreation Areas Areas of green space available for public access and enjoyment but with only low key provision of facilities. Usually consist mainly of grass areas for informal recreation, but may also have trees, a play area, paths and sometimes toilets and parking area.
	Outdoor Sports Areas Green space designed to accommodate sports; including sports pitches, playing fields, golf courses, and other outdoor activities. Often occur within parks, but may also be separate, especially in the case of golf courses.
	Play Areas Green space designed specifically for children's play, with various levels of provision of equipment and facilities. May occur separately but also often incorporated within parks, informal recreation areas and outdoor sports facilities.
	Incidental Green Space Areas of green space that, although publicly owned and managed, and accessible for public enjoyment, have no clear recreation function, and little significant value as habitat. Their function is usually as a green 'landscape backdrop' but their landscape value can sometimes be minimal because of poor design. They include the 'left over' green spaces within housing and other forms of development.
	Domestic Gardens Green space within the curtilage of individual dwellings, which is generally not publicly accessible, but which often makes a significant contribution to the green fabric of urban environments.
FUNCTIONAL GREEN SPACE Green space which has a primary function other than amenity or recreation, although some of these areas may also be publicly accessible and available for people's enjoyment. The primary functions include farming, horticulture, burial grounds and educational and other institutional use. Access to these green spaces may go hand in hand with the primary function (for example cemeteries, churchyards and allotments) or be by public right of way, or by agreement, for example where school grounds are made available for public use.	**Farmland** Green space under agricultural management. Includes farms which also have a recreation and education function such as City Farms.
	Allotments Green Space available for members of the public who occupy them to cultivate vegetable or fruit crops for their own use.
	Burial Grounds Land used as burial grounds, including cemeteries and churchyards.
	School Grounds Green space in the grounds of schools including sports pitches, other outdoor sports facilities, play areas, gardens, nature areas, school farms and growing areas and incidental green space.
	Other Institutional Grounds Green space in the grounds of institutions such as universities and colleges, hospitals and nursing homes, and associated with commercial and industrial premises, including gardens, sports pitches, other outdoor sports facilities, play areas, semi-natural habitats and incidental green space.

Table 1.2: Definitions of types of urban green space (continued)

SEMI-NATURAL GREEN SPACE

Green space that is made up of semi-natural habitat. These habitats may be encapsulated areas of the countryside that existed before the urban area expanded. Alternatively they may have been formed by the natural processes of colonisation and succession on abandoned or disturbed ground or by deliberate creation of new habitats through initiatives such as urban forestry and reclamation of derelict land. All these habitats make a vital contribution to the urban landscape but may or may not be accessible for public enjoyment. In some cases where there is access it may be unofficial, but still extremely important to local people.

Wetland

Green space dominated by wet habitats, including water bodies, running water and fen, marsh, bog and wet flush vegetation.

Woodland

All forms of urban woodland including deciduous woodland (both ancient semi-natural and woodlands of more recent origin) and mixed and coniferous woodland (including plantations and shelterbelts). Includes newly planted woodland.

Moor and Heath

Areas of moorland and heathland vegetation consisting mainly of ericaceous species, and including moorland grass, shrub moor, shrub heath and bracken. Likely to include some Commons within urban areas.

Grassland

Grassland which is not agriculturally improved and not formally part of an amenity greenspace, including calcareous grassland, acidic upland grassland and unimproved meadows. Could include established vegetation on reclaimed derelict land which is not part of a formal recreation green space.

Disturbed Ground

Land which has been disturbed by previous development or land use but is now abandoned, waste or derelict and is becoming re-colonised by processes of colonisation and natural succession.

LINEAR GREEN SPACE

Green space that occurs in association with linear features, especially transport routes such as roads, railways and canals, but also rivers and streams. It is a matter for debate whether this category should be considered separately, since these spaces might also be defined as either semi natural habitat, or functional green spaces whose primary function is transport, or incidental green space with a visual amenity function. These spaces are, however, distinguished by their linear character and are often an important part of strategic green space designations such as green links and green corridors and for this reason we suggest that they should be considered separately.

River and Canal Banks

Green space occurring along the margins of canals or rivers and forming part of the river or canal corridor.

Transport Corridors

The often substantial areas of green space associated with transport. Includes: the variety of habitats, associated with railways, which are often inaccessible but when they fall into disuse can become an important part of an open space network; green space associated with roads, and especially the large areas of grassland, scrub, trees and woodland found along major roads and motorways; and green space along cycleways and walking routes.

Other Linear Features

Cliffs and other natural areas of linear green space.

Table 1.3: Hypothetical example of classification of publicly accessible urban green spaces

Hierarchy of Importance ⇨ Type of Greenspace ⇩	Principal/City/ Metropolitan	District	Neighbourhood/ Local
GREEN SPACE SPACES WHERE RECREATION IS THE PRIMARY USE			
Parks	Norfolk Heritage Park Weston Park Rivelin Valley Park Porter Valley Parks Millhouses Park Firth Park Concord Park	Bingham Park Chapeltown Park Crookes Valley Park Meersbrook Park *(and 16 others)*	
Gardens	Sheffield Botanical Gardens Peace Gardens Hillsborough Walled Garden	Beauchief Park Whinfell Quarry Garden Stocksbridge War Memorial Garden	Barkers Pool Garden Bocking Lane Garden Monument Ground
Outdoor Sports Areas	Beauchief Golf Course	Beighton Sports Ground Steel City Sports Ground Redmires Road Playing Field	Arbourthorne Playing Field Ellesmere Park Manor Sports Ground *(and 46 other spaces)*
Play Areas (Outside Parks)			Grammar Street Playground Errington Avenue Playground Motehall Playground *(and 63 others)*
Informal Recreation Spaces			Abbey Lane Catcliffe Road Meadowgate Lane *(and 170 other spaces)*
2. OTHER GREEN SPACES WHERE RECREATION MAY BE A SECONDARY USE			
City Farms	Graves Park Animal Farm Heeley City Farm		
Allotments			Bowstead Allotments Manor Allotments Shirecliffe Allotments *(and 71 others)*
Cemeteries	General Cemetery		Attercliffe Common Burial Ground Oughtibridge Cemetery
Churchyards	St Peter and St Pauls Cathedral		Dore Church Yard St George's Church
Woodland	Ecclesall Woods	Gleadless Valley Woodland Park Limb Valley *(and 13 others)*	Abbeydale Wood Crabtree Wood Poggs Wood Rivelin Lodge *(and 107 Others)*
Moor/Heath		Loxley/Wadsley Common Blacka Moor	

Note: This example is hypothetical but uses site names from the Sheffield City council site categorisation for illustrative purposes.

CHAPTER 2
People and Activities

SUMMARY OF KEY POINTS

- The task of compiling information on urban green spaces is hampered by the fact that survey information from local authorities is inevitably inconsistent. In recent years some data collection systems have been developed for funding bids to the Heritage Lottery Fund and other sources, to identify local needs and more recently as part of the Best Value process. The two standard questions in the Best Value User Satisfaction Survey are in themselves quite basic and more useful information has been available where local authorities have extended the scope of that questionnaire.

- A telephone survey was used to estimate that two and a quarter million people, across ten case study areas, make at least 184 million visits each year to urban green spaces. If the urban population of England is assumed to be 37.8 million a similar calculation suggests that some 33 million people make more than 2.5 billion visits each year to urban green spaces.

- Overall 46 per cent of people stated that they use urban green spaces more than once a week, with many using them several times a week, daily or several times a day. Men are confirmed as slightly higher users of urban green space than women but there is no clear indication from the local authority surveys as to whether people from an ethnic minority background, or disabled people are under-represented among users.

- People's reasons for using urban green spaces fall into seven broad categories: enjoying the environment; social activities; getting away from it all, walking activities, including dog walking; passive or informal enjoyment; active enjoyment, including sport and specific activities; and attending events.

- These seven categories of primary use can be combined with a social typology, based on age, gender, physical and mental ability and ethnicity, to create a categorisation of users. Such a framework could be of value in seeking to achieve greater consistency in surveys of users and uses in the future.

Introduction

2.1   How many people actually use urban green spaces and who are they? And when and why do they use them? These are the questions that this chapter seeks to address. In order to find the answers four sources have been used: the literature review and particularly reports of previous user surveys; information from surveys provided by the case study local authorities; the responses from the telephone survey and the focus group discussions. The local authority surveys includes a mix of users and non-users of urban green spaces, the initial contacts made in the telephone survey to identify non- or infrequent users provide information about frequency of use of urban green spaces across ten local authority areas, while the focus groups provide detailed insights that will help to answer some of the questions about why people go to these areas. At the outset of this research it was agreed that no new surveys of users and activities within parks and green spaces would be carried out because this would duplicate the work carried out in the 'Park Life' study in 1995. This time the emphasis has been on non- or infrequent users and under represented groups in the population.

2.2   Survey information from local authorities is inevitably inconsistent. Reasons for collecting the information vary, as do approaches to sampling and the detailed design of survey methods. For most, recording user information has not been part of the normal regime although during recent years many authorities have begun to introduce regular survey and monitoring schemes for some urban green spaces. Some of these have been related to the development of parks strategies, to bids for funding to Heritage Lottery Fund or other bodies, and are designed to identify local needs or to investigate people's reactions to specific events and festivals. In addition citizen's panels, or their equivalents, people counters at entrances, visitor and user surveys and focus groups have been used in some locations. The initiation of Best Value has introduced the User Satisfaction Survey, BV 119, which the DTLR requires to be undertaken every three years. The first of these were undertaken in 2000/2001. Of the fifteen case study areas 2 had completed their Best Value review at the time of the study, 6 were in progress and 7 had yet to be started (of which 2 had been piloted with 1 of these still in progress). The information base is therefore improving but the picture is still fragmented and it is difficult to aggregate local information to produce a national picture. This is particularly so because local circumstances vary widely in terms of the nature of the communities using urban green spaces and the nature of the spaces themselves. The surveys that have been drawn upon are summarised in **Table 2.1**.

Table 2.1: Sources of information about users from twelve case study areas	
Location	**Information used**
Wolverhampton	Parks User Survey 2000 (732 responses to 8 locations) and market review of sports
Milton Keynes Park Trust	1995 (1178 people) and 1996 surveys
Doncaster	Greenspace Audit 2001 68 organisations, 723 individuals and 690 school children
Lewisham	Parks Survey and Best Value Survey (15 and 23 groups represented). Both March 2001 and Lewisham Junior Citizen Event (312 attendees) Nov 2000
Newcastle	Survey of residents 1996 and 100 residents around a specific site
Plymouth	City Parks Survey (144 people) 2001
Cheltenham	View Point Cheltenham (510) respondents
Sheffield	Talkback 2000 (1551 responses), estimated attendance at events (2000/2001) and Assessment of playing pitches in Sheffield
Bexley	1998 and 2001 surveys (532 responses to the latter)
Stockport	Land Services Annual Report and Best Value Performance Indicators 2000
Leicester	List of events/sports and Blueprint Leicester
Ipswich	Expected attendance at events (2000/1)

NUMBER OF VISITS TO URBAN GREEN SPACES

2.3   At a national (UK) level one of the most recent (and indeed one of the few) estimates of the total number of visits to urban parks and green spaces comes from the Public Parks Needs Assessment . This estimates that there are some 400 million visits a year to historic parks in the UK and extrapolates this figure to suggest that there may be between 922 million and 4 billion visits to parks and open spaces as a whole, with 'a figure of 1.5 billion visits suggested as an appropriate estimate' in this range. This estimate is based on responses from approximately three-quarters of the local authorities in the country and their estimates of visitor numbers.

2.4   In this research an estimate can be made in a different way, based on the initial question in the telephone survey, which was designed to find out how often people use urban green spaces and therefore to determine whether a respondent was a regular user, an infrequent user or a non-user. The initial question about frequency of use was put to 1588 people. Using these figures (**as in Table 2.2**), together with the population of each of the relevant case study areas, it is possible to calculate the number of people in each of the ten location who use urban green spaces and also to calculate the total number of visits made to green spaces, each year in each location.

2.5   Such calculations have some limitations in that the percentage of visits for each frequency may, in reality, vary between urban locations but nevertheless they can give an insight into the numbers of users and visits made each year. On the basis of these calculations the number of people using urban green spaces regularly across the ten Strand 1 areas (**Bexley, Ipswich, Leicester, Lewisham, Milton Keynes, Newcastle, Oldham, Plymouth, Sheffield,** and **Stockport**), with a total population of more than 2.6 million people is indicated as well over **2.25 million**. The estimated number of visits per year across these ten locations is indicated as being over **184 million**. If anything this figure for the number of visits may be on the conservative side because the calculation has assumed that those who said they use urban green space more than once a week use them twice a week, whereas in fact it may be more. In addition it is known and accepted that many dog walkers use urban green spaces more than once a day and yet daily has been taken to mean only once a day in the calculation, not twice, three or four times a day.

2.6   If a similar calculation is undertaken using the whole urban population of England, estimated to be 37.8 million in urban areas with a population of over 10,000, then it can be roughly estimated that the total number of people in England who use urban green spaces is **32.9 million** and the number of visits per year in England adds up to **2.6 billion**. Interestingly this estimate falls in the middle of the range of estimates made in the Public Parks Needs Assessment study. It is impossible to claim precision in any of these estimates but they do, nevertheless, indicate the enormous scale of use of urban green spaces at the national level and therefore their exceptional importance as a resource for urban communities.

---

1   *Public Park Assessment – A Survey of Local Authority Owned Parks, focusing on Parks of Historic Interest.* Urban Parks Forum. DTLR, Heritage Lottery Fund, Countryside Agency and English Heritage. May 2001.

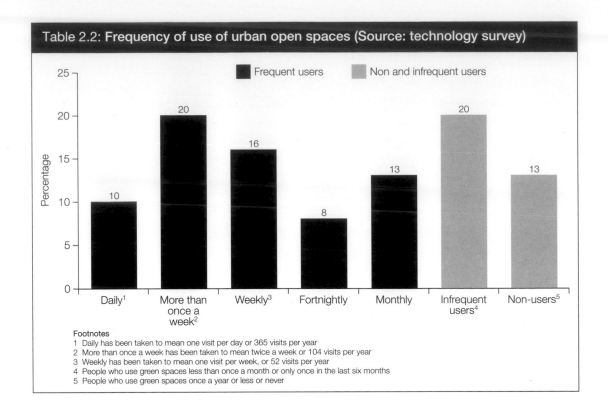

Table 2.2: Frequency of use of urban open spaces (Source: technology survey)

■ Frequent users   ■ Non and infrequent users

Footnotes
1 Daily has been taken to mean one visit per day or 365 visits per year
2 More than once a week has been taken to mean twice a week or 104 visits per year
3 Weekly has been taken to mean one visit per week, or 52 visits per year
4 People who use green spaces less than once a month or only once in the last six months
5 People who use green spaces once a year or less or never

THE PICTURE OF USE AT THE LOCAL LEVEL

2.7   At the local authority level accurate information about the number of people who use
urban green spaces is hard to come by because, unlike sports centres, people do not pay to
enter and are therefore not counted at the point of entry. During recent years, however,
some authorities have made estimates of total annual visits to urban green spaces from the
databases that they have been developing. For instance in **Sheffield** the 1551 responses
from the Citizen's Panel, Talkback 2000, have been used to calculate an estimated number
of visitors to the city's parks and woodlands of 25 million people a year, excluding children
or visitors to the city. **Doncaster's** questionnaire survey of 732 individual residents revealed
that 85.6 per cent used green space, equating to 252,520 people within the borough. From
the percentages of people in this survey stating that they use different types of green space
at particular frequencies, annual use figures have been estimated of over 43 million for parks
and woodlands and nearly 7 million for children's play.[2]

NUMBERS ATTENDING EVENTS

2.8   Events are one activity that take place in urban green spaces where numbers are sometimes
recorded, often for market research reasons but also for Health and Safety purposes. *'Park
Life'* (1995) identified a wide range of events taking place in parks from a 'Bird Box Update'
involving 26 people, through May Day festivals, Hindu prayer meetings, Shows, Fun Runs,
attracting thousands of people, to events such as the International Kite Festival in Bristol
attracting 100,000.

2   The responses to the Sheffield Citizen's Panel should have minimal bias because the panel regularly
respondes to a range of issues. It is possible that responses to Doncaster's surveys may have had
some bias towards users, but the extent of any such bias can not be easily measured in this situation.

2.9 The current research shows that a great variety of events continue to take place across many different types of urban green spaces, with some being small educational events, some community events and others large events such as a 'Mela'. Many local authorities now have programmes of events and an officer to support this programme. These events can, however incur significant costs and only one local authority was found that was able to make enough money from events in order to re-invest in some area of the urban green space service.

2.10 **Leicester** runs a programme over the ten month period March to December and estimates that 400,000 people attend its range of events, including orienteering, an historic transport pageant, a pets fair, hot air balloon launches, and fireworks for a Diwali celebration and Guy Fawkes night. Events in **Ipswich** in 2001 attracted some 90,000 attendees, despite some having to be cancelled due to foot and mouth disease. These events included drama, a 'Walk for Whales', May Day celebrations, concerts, religious services and Remembrance Sunday and were held between May and November. **Sheffield** has three 'levels' of events. About 150 are arranged by the rangers and include activities, games, and educational events, attracting a total of 32,000 people in 2000/2001 with two thirds being young people and one third adults. The second level of events are those which are organised by communities and include fun runs, galas, fetes, festivals and club regattas. In addition about 50 'commercial' activities take place which include funfairs, circuses, shows, outdoor theatre and large fundraising partnerships such as the After Dark Bonfire and Sheffield May Fest. The latter attracts 20,000 people while the Sheffield Show attracts 30,000. It is conservatively estimated that a total of 250,000 people attend events overall.

2.11 In **Stockport** 357 organised events took place in 2000/2001 and in addition 683 children from 14 different schools took part in formally organised visits to urban green spaces for educational purposes. **Lewisham** has recently put the organisation of events out to contract, along with its grounds maintenance (see **Case Study 8.1** in **Chapter 8**) where one off events such as jazz in the park, classics in the park, jungle road shows Sydenham Wells 100, the Easter egg hunt and 'Keep on the Grass' each attracted between 50 and 500 people. In addition regular events such as a One o'clock club, sports scheme and gardening afternoons have attracted up to 300 people at a time.

NUMBERS INVOLVED IN SPORT

2.12 The profiling survey of 50 local authorities showed that they are particularly likely to keep records of people involved in active sport, either through pitch bookings, payment records or records of club involvement. While this is useful it gives a very limited picture of the use of urban green space. For example, according to the Landscape Institute[3] only 6 % of users of parks are involved in sports activities, and most of these are male, meaning that statistics are far from representative. Nevertheless available records show that, for example, Leicester's urban green spaces support 1985 team games a year involving 54,249 men and 1,136 women. **Sheffield** has 8,000 to 9,000 regular football players, who are predominantly male with more than half of them being adults. There are also 100 male adult/youth cricket teams representing an estimated 1,500 players. Rugby, rounders and hockey are also played, but figures are not available for these sports. A market review in **Wolverhampton**, in 1998, revealed the involvement of 17,500 footballers with 129 adult and 28 junior teams. In addition there were estimated to be 15,000 tennis players, 10, 000 bowlers, 8,000 cricket players and 6,000 rugby players. Data from **Stockport** reveals 18,000 playing golf, 1,700 football, 2,300 bowls and 300 cricket.

3 *Urban Parks: A Discussion Paper.* Holden, R, Merrivale, J and Turner, T. Landscape Institute, 1992.

Frequency of visits

2.13   'Park Life' found in 1995, from household surveys and user questionnaires (in ten different parks in Bristol, Cardiff, Greenwich, Hounslow, Leicester, Middlesbrough, Sutton and Southwark), that about 40 per cent of existing users claimed to use their urban parks at least daily, with many of those using parks more than once daily being dog walkers. Information from the local authority data for this research is not fully comparable due to the variety of survey methods used but such information can give an insight into some of the use patterns, in terms of frequency of use in the different locations.

2.14   Overall 46 per cent of the respondents state that they use their urban green spaces daily, several times a week or weekly. This roughly agrees with the findings of surveys in the London Royal Parks, which found that around 50 per cent of the visitors go at least once a week. The exceptions to this are **Milton Keynes**, where only 38 per cent said that this was the frequency with which they visit urban green spaces, **Sheffield** where only 37 per cent stated that this was their level of use and **Stockport** where the figure was 29 per cent. Monthly use appears to be the pattern for about a quarter of the respondents, but it is noticeable that this figure is much higher, at 50% of the respondents, in **Lewisham** and may possibly relate to the different use patterns of the higher proportion of people from an ethnic minority background who live there. Where there are figures for those using urban green spaces very infrequently (less than once a year), they indicate that this is generally the pattern for approximately a fifth of the population of the respondents, except in **Milton Keynes** where the figure is higher at nearly a third (although this may be a function of the particular sample used).

Patterns of visits

2.15   There are only a few indications from the local authority survey information about the times at which people use urban green spaces. In **Lewisham** early to late afternoon are the most frequent use times while in **Bexley** over half of the respondents said they visit urban green spaces on a weekend afternoon, more than a fifth on weekday evenings and nearly a sixth on weekday afternoons. In **Wolverhampton** the pattern of use of urban green spaces in the summer is that of low use in the early morning, followed by higher levels in the late morning, with a slight drop in the early afternoon before the peak in late afternoon and another decline in the evening. In the winter months the overall levels of use fall (reflecting the findings of Llewelyn-Davies[4]) who identified lower levels of use in the winter months) but the pattern is otherwise similar except for an increase in the late morning use.

2.16   The focus groups across ten urban locations consisted of a mixture of people who both do and do not use urban green spaces. Across all types of groups the discussions revealed that most of the participants who were users visited urban green spaces on a daily or weekly basis with less people reporting fortnightly or monthly use. Women and young people's groups suggested that they made higher use of these spaces at weekends and many people reported that they use urban green spaces more in the summer. A few pointed out that the weather

---

4   *Open Space Planning in London: Final Report.* Llewelyn Davies Planning and Environment Trust Associates Limited. London Planning Advisory Committee (1992).

influenced their use of urban green spaces. In addition there were many people across the groups who said that they only used these spaces very occasionally or in fact never use them.

WAYS OF REACHING URBAN GREEN SPACES

2.17   Previous research (see literature review) found that the large majority of visitors to urban green spaces travel to them on foot (41% in the Royal Parks surveys, and 69% in the 'Park Life' surveys). In the focus groups most people similarly reported that they walk to their park, play area or green space. Bus and car were the second most frequently mentioned methods of getting to parks, play areas and green spaces. Only people with disabilities reported using taxis and two people with disabilities said that their lives had changed with the ability to go to a park on an electric scooter.

Who are the users?

2.18   Previous research provides a variety of evidence about who uses parks and urban green spaces. In terms of **age**, the observation exercises reported in 'Park Life' (1995) revealed that young adults and middle aged people constituted more than 50 per cent of all park users. Teenagers and young adults were also identified as significant users of parks. Elderly people were identified as significant under users of urban parks reflecting other research that has identified this, and suggesting that the reasons for this include lack of opportunities for passive activities, unfamiliarity with other park users, with a particularly negative perception of young people and environmental issues such as vandalism and dog mess. The earlier research by Llewelyn Davies (see Footnote 15) that compared different surveys of users in the different locations across the country between 1972 and 1991 found that the large majority of users tended to be young people up to 15 years old, which somewhat contradicts the 'Park Life' findings.

2.19   It is clear that there does not appear to be any consistency in the characteristics of urban green space users according to age, which almost certainly reflects the great variety both of spaces and of people in different locations. People aged 40-59 have been identified as the dominant user group in **Cheltenham** and a similar age group of over 45 year olds have been identified as the dominant age group of users in **Milton Keynes**. In **Sheffield**, on the other hand, the dominant age for use of urban green spaces is revealed to be younger, at 25 to 39, with the council assuming that this is because this is the age group with children to take to such spaces. This younger aged group was also the most frequent age group of users in **Wolverhampton** with those aged 55 or over being the second most frequent group of users.

2.20   In terms of the **gender** of those who use urban green spaces, 'Park Life' indicated that there were slightly less female than male users of urban parks. This appears to be confirmed by the few case study local authorities that were able to provide data relating to the gender of their users, with **Sheffield** stating that 'there is little difference between genders', and **Milton Keynes** and **Wolverhampton** recording male use as 53 and 52 per cent respectively and female use as 47 and 48 per cent respectively.

2.21 There is only very limited information on the **ethnicity** of those using urban green spaces. According to *'Park Life'* use of urban parks by people from an ethnic minority background generally reflected the local demography of the ethnic minority population. In this research only a few local authorities held any information about the ethnicity of users. **Cheltenham** and **Milton Keynes** both reported a 4 per cent level of use by people from an ethnic minority background while **Wolverhampton** reported 7 per cent use, although having set itself a target of 20 per cent. In the population as a whole the percentage which is from an ethnic minority background in each of these locations is 4 per cent for **Cheltenham**, 8 per cent for **Milton Keynes** and 19 per cent for **Wolverhampton**.

2.22 It is estimated that about 10% of the population nationally have some sort of **disability**, although as the population ages the proportion with a disability is naturally likely to increase. And yet *'Park Life'* found from observations of those using parks that only 0.5 % were disabled people, although as not all disabilities are visible to an observer this figure may well be an underestimate. In comparison this study has found that in **Cheltenham** and **Wolverhampton** 10 per cent of users were identified as having an impairment, which is certainly much more a reflection of the representation in the wider population.

Why do people use urban green spaces?

2.23 The focus group discussions for this research, together with available information from the case study local authorities, reveal many different expressions of reasons for people using urban green spaces. They fall broadly into seven groups, which are discussed below, roughly in the order that they were mentioned in the focus groups. The groups are: enjoying the environment; social activities; getting away from it all, walking activities, including dog walking; passive or informal enjoyment; active enjoyment, including sport and specific activities; and attending events. Cross-reference to **Chapter 5** will show that these uses of urban green space are closely linked to the benefits that they bring to society.

ENJOYING THE ENVIRONMENT

2.24 Most of the focus groups gave a range of environmental reasons for visiting parks, play areas and green spaces – except groups of young people who barely mentioned this as a reason for using these spaces. The elements of the environment that people go to enjoy include the trees and flowers, particularly mentioned by disabled people and women, while the fact that these open spaces remind people of the countryside or nature and provide a 'green' and sometimes 'wild' experience was mentioned by all groups. As one woman in **Sheffield** expressed it *"you can create the perception that you are in a rural area by visiting green areas"*. The information from the Sheffield Talkback survey confirmed that nearly half of the respondents go to urban green spaces for trees and flowers and, as one of the elderly people's groups in Sheffield said "we enjoy the greenery and beauty". Many people in **Milton Keynes** reported that they went to enjoy the wildlife and in **Bexley** over a quarter of respondents stated that they visit for the garden displays. As a woman in **Ipswich** said *"I use the park as an educational tool to teach children about nature, seasonality and curiosity"*.

2.25 The fact that there is perceived to be 'no pollution' together with the opportunity for experiencing 'fresh air' were also important for some, particularly disabled people and people from ethnic minority backgrounds. The existence of wildlife, including ducks and squirrels, together with educational opportunities that such spaces afford were identified as being especially important for children and were specifically mentioned by women, disabled people and people from ethnic minority groups. The smell of freshly cut grass and flowers was mentioned by disabled people. It is, however, clear that although these were the most mentioned reasons for visiting urban green space in the focus group discussions, this was not always the case in the information available from the local authorities.

SOCIAL ACTIVITIES

2.26   Across all the focus groups the dominant social reason for going to a park, play area or green space was that of taking children to play: whether ones own children, grand children, siblings or nephews and nieces. The **Sheffield** local authority survey also showed that 41% of the respondents go to urban green spaces to take children with 29% saying that they go to take children to a playground – the same percentage in **Bexley** also stated that this was the main reason for a visit. In **Milton Keynes** taking children was the second most frequently mentioned reason for visiting urban green spaces. As a disabled person in Sheffield said *"children need somewhere to play and need to explore – to let off steam in a green environment"*.

2.27   The use of urban green spaces for social interaction is also extremely important – *"the field is somewhere to go, a place to talk, somewhere to sit on the grass"* (young person in **Bexley**) – and going to these spaces with other family members was felt to be particularly important, especially if it involves having a picnic. The focus groups involving disabled people, women and people from an ethnic minority background particularly mentioned this function for urban green spaces. In the **Sheffield** survey one tenth of the respondents said that they go to urban green spaces to meet family or friends and in **Bexley** one tenth of the respondents visit for picnics. Meeting people, either casually bumping into them – perhaps when walking a dog – or specifically meeting friends was mentioned across all types of focus groups but was especially important for young people and a woman from an ethnic minority background in **Leicester** pointed out the value of parks for older people to meet.

GETTING AWAY FROM IT ALL

2.28   **Chapter 5** discusses the health and psychological benefits of urban green spaces and identifies this as an area that requires separate consideration from the other social benefits. This became clear in the focus group discussions and 'getting away from it all' is to many people a reason in itself for visiting urban green spaces even though it is also linked with walking or passive activities. It was mentioned so much that it seems that those wishing to escape from aspects of urban life merit consideration as a separate category of users. These 'psychological reasons' for visiting urban green spaces were mentioned to a greater or lesser extent across all types of focus groups. There were two main elements to this, one relating to the need to escape – from the city, from the pollution and from people – and the other relating to the restorative effects of urban green spaces. The survey data from the case study local authorities supports the importance of these reasons for visiting urban green spaces. For example, going to parks for relaxation was mentioned by over half of the respondents in **Bexley**, while over a third in **Sheffield** said that they went for the peace and quiet as did many in **Milton Keynes**. The local authority data from **Plymouth** revealed that looking at a view was the main reason that people visited urban green spaces, although this needs to be seen in the context that 74% of the Plymouth respondents were referring to visiting The Hoe, an open space on the sea front with sea views.

What the focus groups said about 'getting away from it all'

"it's a good way for getting away
from the hustle and bustle..
better than tranquillizers any day"
Disabled person, Ipswich

"brothers and sisters-
want to get away from them because they argue a lot"
Young person, Bexley

"Like the space, it's good to get away
from the people who tell you what to do"
Disabled person, Ipswich

"I love nature. I can't see nature
but it is like another world when I go to open spaces
I can feel the open space around me.
I love to listen to water and meditate on it
and think about where it is going.
I take my tape recorder to record the sounds
and take it home to listen to it"
Disabled man, Oldham

"I go to feel inspired.
Parks improve your health,
education and social behaviour.
Health problems are directly related to stress,
therefore you go to parks to feel relaxed"
Man from ethnic minority background, Lewisham

WALKING ACTIVITIES

2.29 Walking a dog, or dogs, has long been accepted as a major reason that many people visit their urban park, play area or green spaces. It was estimated in 'Park Life' (1995) that one in eight people visit urban parks for the purpose of walking a dog. Information from **Bexley** and **Sheffield** revealed that 16 and 18% (slightly more than 1 in 8) of respondents said that they visited urban green spaces in order to walk their dogs. In Plymouth the figure was somewhat lower at 9%. It should be noted, in passing, that it is possible that during the timescale of this research the numbers of dogs being walked in urban green spaces was higher than normal due to foot and mouth disease with many areas of countryside, even within city boundaries, being closed to the public. Nevertheless all types of focus groups, except the ones with people from ethnic minority backgrounds, mentioned this as a reason for using these spaces. A disabled person in **Newcastle upon Tyne** showed the importance of dogs by saying *"I go for dog walking, the dog dictates which park to go to and how to get there, either by walking or by car"*.

2.30 Even more frequently mentioned across all types of focus groups, except young people, was that of walking in itself. Sometimes this was associated with health, exercise or fresh air – *"To walk, part of the healthy walking campaign"* (woman from an ethnic minority background, **Oldham**).

2.31 Walking socially, as part of a group, with friends or as part of an organised group, was also very popular and organised wheelchair walks were also mentioned in groups of disabled people. Visiting urban green spaces for walking was the reason given most by respondents in **Bexley** and **Sheffield**. Over half of the people in **Bexley** said that going for a walk was their main reason to visit while in **Sheffield** the figure was nearly three quarters. *'Park Life'* revealed that taking a short cut was the third most frequently mentioned reason for using urban parks and this reason was confirmed in many of the focus groups when people admitted to using a green space as a short cut, perhaps to get into town or to the shops. This was so for all types of groups except those with young people. In **Bexley** surveys suggest nearly one tenth of people use urban green spaces as a through route.

PASSIVE ENJOYMENT

2.32 Many people enjoy urban green spaces passively – groups of young people particularly mentioned the importance of sitting, either on grass or on seats and also mentioned just 'hanging out' and 'messing about on swings', activities also identified by *'Park Life'*. The focus groups also revealed that people visit urban green spaces for watching sport, or watching life go by, as well as for reading, smoking, photography and sunbathing. Informal pursuits like fishing and flying kites were also mentioned in some focus groups, though to a lesser extent.

2.33 The existence of cafes, or restaurants or somewhere to eat or drink were mentioned across focus groups with disabled people, the elderly, and women as reasons for going to an urban green space. For some of the younger elderly people this was the main reason for their visit – as one elderly man in **Bexley** said *"I go for refreshment, food and drink"*. Some people said that they visited certain urban green spaces because they were visiting a particular building that was located there, for example a library, environmental centre or museum. This is epitomised by one park in **Sheffield** where a woman stated that *"the Centre in The Park has become a reason to go"*.

ACTIVE ENJOYMENT AND SPORT

2.34 Previous research has identified that 6% of urban green space users go for activities and sport (see Footnote 14) and this figure appears to be confirmed by the information available from the case study local authorities. Among the respondents to surveys in **Bexley** 7% said that they visited urban green spaces for sport while in Sheffield the figure was slightly higher at 10 per cent. Sport was the most mentioned type of active enjoyment mentioned across all types of focus groups. Although football was mentioned most other sports were felt, by some, to be under-represented in their provision and bowls, tennis, cricket and rounders were mentioned. In several locations the lack, or perceived lack, of free and easy access to courts and pitches was of concern. Other forms of activity and exercise were also mentioned as reasons for going to urban green spaces and were particularly mentioned by disabled people, elderly people and people from ethnic minority backgrounds. Skateboarding and BMX biking were exclusively mentioned by young people as a reason for using these spaces while women and young people spoke of using these spaces for cycling.

What the focus groups said about passive enjoyment

"Exercise, walking and to look at the lake.
Sitting, reading watching the ducks, the deer and the children"
Elderly people, Bexley

"Lots of places to sit and shelter along the riverside walk"
Disabled person, Ipswich

"Go to walk, meet friends, to relax, or when I'm bored"
Young person, Leicester

"I go to The Hoe to chill out, to watch the sea and to smoke"
Young person, Plymouth

"I go to watch skateboarding"
Young females, Bexley and Sheffield

EVENTS

2.35   As the figures quoted earlier indicate, attending events is a very significant reason for people to use urban green spaces. One fifth of respondents to the **Bexley** survey stated that this was why they visit urban green spaces and events were mentioned as a reason for visiting across all types of focus groups. In the focus groups music events were mentioned most but craft fairs, fun fairs and firework displays were amongst other types mentioned. An elderly person in **Bexley** spoke of going for all "*events, Christmas carol concert, jazz etc*", while a woman in **Ipswich** said that she goes for "*Bonfire night, the opera, orchestral performances and the circus*". Some elderly people held fond memories of bands playing on bandstands and treasured these, some wanting to see their return. "*I used to like bandstands where bands played every day. They were in many parks, but there are not many left now*", was a comment from someone in **Plymouth** while others reminisced that they "*used to dance up and down The Hoe with music in the bandstand*".

Categorising users

2.36   One of the objectives of this research was to *"provide reliable identification of different categories of users of urban green spaces and how they use the range of types of such spaces, especially children and young people, the elderly, disabled people and ethnic minority groups"*. Much previous research has focused solely on parks and it is important to recognise that this research has extended the discussion to parks and other forms of urban green space, with people in the focus groups making clear that they use river walks, canal walks, and small areas of incidental green space as well as urban parks. The typology of urban green spaces discussed in **Chapter 1** needs to be used together with any categorisation of users to build up a consistent picture of the users and uses of different types of site.

2.37   Despite the emphasis often given by service providers to meeting the needs of those involved in sport and other active pursuits this research has clearly confirmed that passive activities are the main reasons that people visit urban green spaces – something clearly indicated by the *'Park Life'* surveys. The information summarised above shows that people's reasons for using urban green spaces fall into the seven broad categories of enjoying the environment, social activities, getting away from it all, walking activities, including dog walking, passive or informal enjoyment, active enjoyment, including sport and specific activities, and attending events. These categories are generally discreet but there is inevitably some overlap, for instance those using green spaces to get away from it all may also be involved in passive enjoyment. But it does seem possible to define the *primary* reason for using urban green spaces although individuals may of course go for different reasons at different times and the reasons may change during a person's lifetime, from predominantly active enjoyment in youth to more relaxing passive enjoyment in later life.

2.38   These seven categories of primary use can be combined with a social typology, using age (children up to 10, young people from 11-15 and 16-19, adults from 20-25, 26-45 and 46-55, and older people from 56-65, 66-75 and over 75), gender, physical and mental ability and ethnicity, (based on the Office of National Statistics recommended categories) to create a categorisation of users. Such a framework could be of value in seeking to achieve greater consistency in surveys of users and uses in the future.

CHAPTER 3

Barriers to use of Urban Green Spaces

SUMMARY OF KEY POINTS

- The telephone survey suggested that 32% of people in the case study areas are either non-users or infrequent users of urban green spaces with 12% being non-users and 20% infrequent users.

- People who do not use urban green spaces at all or only use them infrequently have less actual experience of using these spaces and so may have limited knowledge of how real, or otherwise, the perceived barriers may be.

- Five main barriers have been identified that deter people from using urban green spaces. In approximate order of importance they are: lack of, or the poor condition of, facilities, including play for children; other users, including undesirable characters; concerns about dogs and dog mess; safety and other 'psychological' issues; environmental quality issues such as litter, graffiti and vandalism.

- Access issues are also of concern, particularly to the elderly and to disabled people. They relate to concerns about the proximity of and ease of access to urban green spaces, access to get into those spaces and ease of moving around safely within them. The access concerns of disabled people take on added significance in the light of the 1995 Disability Discrimination Act.

- Most of these issues are resource issues, which relate to the location, accessibility or environmental quality of urban green spaces and are therefore issues that could be overcome if the planners, designers and managers of these spaces could address them satisfactorily.

- Some of the secondary barriers to use are personal issues that cannot be addressed by those responsible for urban green spaces and include: not having enough time; working unsociable hours; poor health or mobility; and other preferences.

- Less dog mess, improved safety, better maintenance, better facilities, more events/activities, more staff, making spaces easier to get to and having a space that is nearer are all factors mentioned by non-users and infrequent users when asked what would encourage them to use urban green spaces more frequently.

- When asked what specific facilities would particularly encourage them to use urban green spaces, the non- and infrequent users, across all the under represented groups, particularly chose the provision of a café and toilets. The provision of dog litter bins, seating, litter bins, information centre/boards, children's play area and sports areas were also mentioned.

- Changes that would improve the sense of safety in urban green spaces for non- and infrequent users are more lighting, mentioned most frequently, followed by more rangers/staff, more things for young people to do, dogs being on leads, no motor vehicles, dog-free areas, lower planting near paths and no cycling or roller skating.

Introduction

3.1   This chapter is concerned with the reasons why some people either do not use urban green spaces, or use them only infrequently. It also considers some of the improvements that would encourage such people to use urban green spaces more frequently. Of course it is unrealistic to expect that everyone will want to use urban green spaces, or that everyone will be a regular user. But, on the other hand, examination of the reasons why some people do not make much use of them, or use them only very infrequently, can provide a valuable insight into the types of improvements that need to be made to maximise their use and to ensure that their use is as socially inclusive as possible. The focus has particularly been on trying to discover the views of the under represented groups, of women, young people, people from an ethnic minority background, the elderly, and disabled people. Information about barriers to use comes from the literature review and, to some extent, individual local authority surveys, although these are generally too specific to local circumstances to allow comparisons or generalisations. The main sources, however, are the telephone survey and the focus groups.

Definitions of non-users and infrequent users

3.2   The main source of information on non-users and infrequent users in this study is the telephone survey of people in the areas covered by the case study local authorities. In this survey a total of 1588 people were contacted, among whom 1073 (68%) used their local parks, play areas and green spaces at least once per month, or more frequently, and were classified as frequent users. The remaining 515 people (32%) used these spaces less frequently or not at all and have been classified as 'infrequent users' and 'non-users'. People who said that they used urban parks, play areas and green spaces less than once a month, 2-3 times a year or once in the last six months have been classified as infrequent users while those who said that they had used these spaces once in the last year, less than that or never have been defined as non-users. The resulting definition of non- and infrequent users is in the box below. These 515 people provided the core sample for the remainder of the telephone survey, which provides quantitative information about reasons for non-use.

> **Non-users and infrequent users**
>
> Non-users are people who have used urban parks, play areas and green spaces only once in the last year, or less or never. Infrequent users are those who have used these spaces less than once a month or only once in the last six months.

3.3 Of the 515 respondents to the telephone survey 39% revealed themselves to be non-users and 61% to be infrequent users according to these definitions. This is equivalent to 12% and 20% respectively of the total number of 1588 telephone contacts, suggesting that overall 12% of people are non-users and 20% are infrequent users of urban green spaces. **Table 3.1** shows the proportion of non-users and infrequent users among these under-represented groups. Looking at the respective proportions of the non-user and infrequent users, the highest percentage of non-users was in the elderly age group (people over 65 years old). People with disabilities showed the second highest frequency of non-users, followed by women, ethnic minorities, excluding people of European origin and young people aged 12 to 19.

Table 3.1: Non-users and infrequent users, by under-represented groups (Source: telephone survey)

Group of people*	Non users (%)	Infrequent users (%)
65+ year olds	48	52
Disabled people	43	57
Women	39	61
All respondents	**39**	**61**
Ethnic minority (not European)	33	67
12-19 year olds	26	74

1 These groups are not mutually exclusive – for example some of those who are disabled may also be elderly.
2 In order to ensure adequate representation of young people who were initially under represented in the sample, a quota was set for each area to make sure that a small number of those under 19 were included.

3.4 The *'Park Life'* (1995) report clearly identified that the elderly and disabled people were under represented as users of parks and green spaces compared with their representation within the population at large. The above figures for levels of non-use, as opposed to infrequent use, in these two groups are therefore not surprising.

Previous research

3.5 There has been relatively little previous research in the UK about the reasons for non-use or infrequent use of parks and green spaces. *'Park Life'* did not specifically investigate this issue with non-users but contact with users of the spaces did identify several concerns including 'public drinking and policies of care in the community' as well as vandalism, dog mess, fear, the predominance of playing fields in some locations, and concern about the lack of character of many parks. These might well be reasons why users could become non-users over time.

3.6   Other studies have revealed some information about barriers to use. A survey undertaken in Islington suggested that the main reasons for people not using parks are:

- failure to provide activities or types of experiences that people require;

- lack of interest within parks;

- concerns about personal safety.

3.7   Further afield, a report on personal safety in parks in Toronto indicated the following barriers to people's use and enjoyment of public spaces, which, not surprisingly given the emphasis of the report, focus on safety concerns:

- fear of violence;

- perception of an unsafe environment;

- psychological barriers such as women's concerns about poorly lit paths, dark passages where attackers can hide and lack of information about where to find emergency telephones or assistance.

3.8   Other research (see references and bibliography) suggests the following range of reasons or possible reasons why certain groups may be under represented as users of urban green spaces:

- young Pakistani people are deterred by bullying: (Woolley and Amin, 1995);

- the elderly are particularly affected by fears for their personal safety (Toronto Parks and Recreation, 2001);

- ethnic minority groups are particularly deterred by barriers due to ethnicity, including fear of racist attacks, unfamiliarity with green space landscapes and open space cultures, a lack of attractive facilities or activities, an uncomfortable feeling of 'otherness' (DETR, 1996, MacFarlane et al, 2000, Thomas,1999, and McAllister, 2000).

What are the barriers to use?

3.9   The telephone survey asked the 515 people defined as non- or infrequent users of urban green spaces what puts them off using these areas. **Table 3.2** shows the main reasons mentioned by all those who responded, with the reasons ranked according to the percentage of people mentioning them. Across all groups, when analysed by age, ethnicity, able bodied or not, housing type, health, geographic location and whether working or not, dog mess emerged as the most mentioned issue in all but two groups: the most frequent response from people in **Oldham** and from the group of 56-65 year olds was vandalism/graffiti.

1   Centre for Leisure and Tourism Studies, University of North London, 1997. Survey of Islington Parks.
2   Toronto Parks and Recreation, 2001. Understanding Personal Safety.

Table 3.2: Main barriers to use for all non-users and infrequent users (Source: telephone survey)	
Reason	Percentage
Dog mess	68
Vandalism/graffiti	57
Poor maintenance	44
Safety fears	44
Lack of/poor facilities	40
Other preferences	30
Poor health	24
Unsocial hours	24
Not enough to do	24
Poor access	24
Disability	21
Too far away	20

3.10   All these potential barriers to use of urban green spaces were based on prompted questions in the telephone survey. It is also worth noting that respondents were also able to list unprompted additional factors which might put them off. Those that were mentioned, which overlap to some extent with the main categories in the table, included: gangs/tramps/drug addicts, behaviour of younger/older children, security/staff/lighting, lack of toilets, don't have enough time, nowhere to park, and traffic and inappropriate vehicles including bicycles and skateboards.

3.11   The telephone survey also asked the 515 respondents what would encourage them to use urban green spaces more, distinguishing between things that would encourage them 'a lot' compared with those that would encourage them less or not at all. The most mentioned factors across all respondents are listed in **Table 3.3**. Not surprisingly the most mentioned factors are broadly a mirror image of the main barriers to use, that is less dog mess, improved safety, better maintenance and better facilities. Other factors include more events and activities, more staff and easier access to sites.

Table 3.3: What would encourage you 'a lot' to use urban parks, play areas and green spaces more? (Source: telephone survey)	
Reason	Percentage
Less dog mess	70
Improved safety	62
Better maintenance	55
Better facilities	53
More events/activities	49
More staff	41
Easier to get to	39
Space that is nearer	39
More varied vegetation	32

3.12   The focus groups gave a range of different reasons for not using some urban green spaces. An adequate range of facilities or their poor quality was the issue mentioned most, followed by a number of 'psychological' issues. These included fear, not wanting to go alone, and a lack of confidence for some people. Concerns about other users were the third most frequently mentioned factor followed by issues relating to access. Compared with the telephone survey of non-users the issue of dogs came quite well down the list and related not only to dog mess, but also to the control of dogs in urban green spaces. Environmental issues such as litter and vandalism were also mentioned less frequently as were personal issues such as health and mobility problems.

Barriers for under represented groups

3.13   Information from the telephone survey, about both the barriers to use of green spaces and the changes that would make non-or infrequent users use them more, has also been analysed to explore differences between the groups of people who are known to be under represented among users. **Table 3.4** shows the rank order, and the frequency of mentions of the main factors that the different groups chose as putting them off 'a lot' from using urban green spaces. **Table 3.5** similarly ranks, and gives the frequency of mentions, for the factors that would most encourage them to use these spaces more. In each case it can be seen that the range of concerns mentioned is similar, although there are some differences between the groups in the order in which the issues are mentioned.

3.14   The importance of the main deterrents and barriers for different under represented groups can best be demonstrated by comparing the frequency of mentions by each particular group with the average frequency of mentions across the sample as a whole (which is shown in **Tables 3.2** and **3.3**). This shows that all of the groups are deterred by dog mess, but that it is of particular concern to women and the elderly. Everyone would be encouraged to make more use of urban green spaces if this problem was tackled. Vandalism and graffiti are also frequently mentioned as barriers to use, but particularly by disabled people and those aged between 56 and 65 years. Better maintenance and facilities, on the other hand, would particularly encourage greater use by young people who also want to see green spaces that are nearer and easier to get to.

3.15   Further analysis of the survey findings examined whether differences based on gender, age (both younger and older groups), ethnic minority background and disability were significant or not. This revealed that, in terms of the main deterrents that put people off using urban green spaces, the following statistically significant differences are apparent:

- women are put off more than men by dog mess, vandalism and safety fears;

- disabled people are put off more than able bodied people by poor facilities;

- 12-15 year olds are put off more than other age groups by poor maintenance, not enough things to do and safety fears;

- 16-19 year-olds are put off more than other ages because they work unsociable hours. More of this age group, than any other, are also put off a lot by their perception that there is not enough to do in these spaces;

- elderly people are put off more than all other age groups from using these spaces by vandalism and graffiti, with the 56-65 age group being particularly concerned about this factor;

- people from a non-European background are put off significantly more than Europeans due to working unsociable hours and by perceptions of there not being enough to do in urban green spaces.

Table 3.4: Top ten reasons that put people off a lot from using urban green spaces, in rank order by percent mentioning) across different types of groups of non-users and infrequent users (Source: telephone survey)

Rank Order	Women	12-15 year olds	16-19 year olds	Non European[1]	56-65 year olds	76 years and over	Disabled People
1	Dog mess (72%)	Dog mess (67%)	Dog mess (63%)	Dog mess (69%)	Vandalism/ graffiti (76%)	Dog mess (70%)	Dog mess (71%) =1
2	Vandalism/ graffiti (58%)	Poor maintenance (60%)	Work unsocial hours (50%) =2	Poor maintenance (47%)	Dog mess (69%)	Vandalism/ graffiti (60%)	Vandalism/ graffiti (71%) =1
3	Safety fears (49%)	Not enough to do (50%) =3	Poor facilities (50%) =2	Lack of facilities (46%)	Safety fears (50%)	Disability (43%) =3	Lack of facilities (56%)
4	Poor maintenance (45%)	Safety fears (50%) =3	Poor maintenance (44%)	Vandalism/ graffiti (45%)	Poor maintenance (48%)	Safety fears (43%) =3	Safety fears (54%)
5	Lack of facilities (42%)	Lack of facilities (47%) =5	Not enough to do (31%) =5	Safety fears (43%)	Lack of facilities (38%)	Too far away (33%) =5	Disability (52%)
6	Other preferences (29%)	Vandalism/ graffiti (47%) =5	Safety fears (31%) =5	Work unsocial hours (32%)	Other preferences (35%)	Other Preferences (33%) =5	Poor health (45%)
7	Poor access (27%)	Poor health (37%)	Vandalism (31%) =5	Not enough things to do (31%)	Disability (28%) =7	Poor health (30%) =7	Poor maintenance (42%)
8	Poor health (26%) =8	Disability (27%)	Too far away (25%) =8	Poor health (24%) =8	Poor access (28%) =7	Poor access (30%) =7	Too far away (36%)
9	Not enough to do (26%) =8	Poor access (20%)	Other preferences (25%) =8	Poor access (24%) =8	Poor health (26%)	Lack of facilities (27%)	Other preferences (33%) =9
10	Too far away (23%)	Too far away (17%)	Poor health (19%)	Too far away (18%)	Work unsocial hours (19%)	Poor maintenance (17%)	Not enough to do (33%) =9

Note 1: Includes all those who were of Black African, Black Caribbean, other Black, Chinese, Indian, Bangladeshi, Pakistani, other Asian, mixed race and other non-European origin (see **A1.4 in Appendix 1**)

Table 3.5: Factors that would most encourage more frequent use of urban green spaces, in rank order, across different types of groups of non-users and infrequent users (Source: telephone survey)

Rank Order	Women	12-15 year olds	16-19 year olds	Non European[1]	56-65 year olds	76 years and over	Disabled People
1	Less dog mess (72%)	Better maintenance (77%)	Better maintenance (81%) =1	Less dog mess (80%)	Less dog mess (76%)	Less dog mess (67%) =1	Improved safety (72%)
2	Improved safety (69%)	Better facilities (73%)	Less dog mess (81%) =1	Better facilities (66%)	Improved safety (70%)	Improved safety (67%) =1	Less dog mess (67%)
3	Better maintenance (56%) =3	Less dog mess (70%)	Better facilities (63%)	More events (65%) =3	Better maintenance (57%)	Better maintenance (43%) =3	Better maintenance (65%)
4	Better facilities (56%) =3	Improved safety (63%) =4	More events/ activities (56%)	Better maintenance (65%) =3	More staff (54%)	Better facilities (43%) =3	More events/ activities (59%)
5	More events/ activities (50%)	More events/ activities (63%) =4	Nearer (50%)	Improved safety (61%)	Better facilities (53%)	Easier to get to (37%) =5	More staff (57%) =5
6	More staff (45%)	Easier to get to (53%)	Improved safety (44%)	Easier to get to (50%)	More events/ activities (50%)	More staff (37%) =5	Better facilities (57%) =5
7	Easier to get to (42%)	Nearer (50%)	Easier to get to (38%)	Nearer (47%)	Easier to get to (40%)	Nearer (33%) =7	Easier to get to (41%)
8	Nearer (40%)	More staff (33%) =8	More staff (25%) =8	More staff (46%)	More varied vegetation (36%)	More varied vegetation (33%) =7	Nearer (30%) =8
9	More varied vegetation (33%)	More varied vegetation (33%) =8	More varied vegetation (25%) =8	More varied vegetation (41%)	Nearer (30%)	More events/ activities (17%)	More varied vegetation (39%) =8

Note 1: Includes all those who were of Black African, Black Caribbean, other Black, Chinese, Indian, Bangladeshi, Pakistani, other Asian, mixed race and other non-European origin (see A1.4 in Appendix 1)

3.16 In terms of changes that would encourage more frequent use of urban green spaces this analysis suggests that:

- women would be encouraged significantly more than men if safety was improved;

- disabled people would be encouraged significantly more than able bodied people if staffing levels were increased;

- 12-15 year olds would be encouraged significantly more than other age groups if there was better maintenance, better facilities, more events and a space that is easier to get to;

- 16-19 year olds would be encouraged significantly more than other age groups if there was better maintenance, provision of sports areas and events such as fairs. In addition all of this age group said that a café would make them more likely to use an urban park, play area or green space;

- 56-65 year olds would be significantly more encouraged than any other age group if there were more staff and also by provision of more seats.

3.17   Lower down the list, dogs being on a lead was the third most mentioned issue that would make people feel safer, for women, 16-19 year olds, 56-65 year olds and disabled people. Having more things for young people to do was acknowledged as desirable, not just by young people themselves, but also by all the other groups, who generally mentioned this as at least the fourth or fifth factor. No motor vehicles in urban parks, play areas and green spaces was a key issue for young people but appears much less of an issue for the other groups, except the older elderly for whom it was the third most mentioned factor. Dog free areas were mentioned fifth or sixth most frequently as being desirable by most groups. Lower planting near paths came well down the list and, no cycling, roller skating or roller blading was, perhaps not surprisingly, mentioned by very small percentages of young people, but considerably more frequently by the elderly and disabled people.

Tackling the main barriers

3.18   An overview of what the different sources of information show about factors that deter people from using urban green spaces is helpful in establishing common ground between them. It is clear that many of the issues came up in the focus groups as well as the telephone survey, and that the local authority surveys that were available and the previous research tend to support the conclusions about the nature of barriers. The importance attached to the different issues seems to vary widely. It is, however, very important to recognise the differences between the sources. The telephone survey is the only one that deals specifically with those who do not use green spaces at all or who only use them infrequently. For them the deterrent factor is clearly very significant, but on the other hand they also have less actual experience of recent use of these spaces and so may have limited knowledge of how real, or otherwise, the perceived barriers may be. Their perceptions may therefore be quite different and the barriers that they identify could be imagined as much as they are real.

3.19   The focus groups, by contrast, included both users and non-users who were specifically drawn from the under represented groups of women, young people, disabled people, the elderly and people from an ethnic minority background. The mix of users and non-users allowed discussion about possible barriers from both points of view and also allowed for exploration of the issues. The information from the case study local authorities comes from a mix of Best Value User Satisfaction Surveys, questionnaires conducted at particular events, or with community groups and surveys of residents living near to green spaces. They too combine both users and non-users but, unlike the focus groups, they also cover all groups in society rather than only the under represented groups.

3.20   The differences between the sources may explain differences in the ranking of perceived barriers or deterrents to use. The focus groups identified the poor condition or lack of facilities as the main factor putting them off using some urban green spaces, with the influence of other people also being very significant. For the non- and infrequent users these were both much less significant factors and other people were rarely mentioned. Lack of recent experience of using these spaces could explain why these are not perceived to be issues and would also explain why matters such as poor access and lack of things to do in green spaces come very low down the list of concerns for non-users. This appears to confirm that they are more concerned with the image that they have of urban green spaces, rather than with the realities of use.

TYPES OF BARRIER

3.21   The concerns that deter people from using urban green spaces fall into two broad groups. Firstly there are personal issues which relate to the personal circumstances of the individual and cannot be influenced by those responsible for urban green spaces. They include factors such as not having enough time, poor health or mobility, working unsocial hours and having a personal preference for visiting other places, although this last could of course be influenced to some extent by making urban green spaces more attractive to visit. Secondly there are issues relating to the urban green space resource which relate to the location, accessibility, environmental quality or user experience of urban green spaces and are therefore issues which could be overcome if the planners, designers and managers of these spaces could address them satisfactorily.

3.22   Looking at all the available sources of information, but particularly the focus groups and the telephone surveys, five main barriers emerge that deter people from using urban green spaces. They are all resource issues rather than personal concerns, and so could all be addressed by planning, design or management action. They are: lack of facilities, including play opportunities for children; the influence of other green space users; dog mess; safety and other psychological concerns; and concerns about environmental quality including litter, vandalism and graffiti. Other issues such as poor maintenance and not enough to do are linked to these main resource issues. Access issues, including poor public transport, spaces being too far away, and other aspects of accessibility seem to be of lesser importance overall, but were a particular source of concern in focus groups involving the elderly and disabled people and so also need to be considered. The five main barriers are explored further in the following sections together with suggestions as to how they might be overcome, drawing particularly on the rich information from the focus group discussions to throw light on the nature of the concerns.

LACK OF FACILITIES

3.23   A lack of, or the poor condition of facilities was the most mentioned concern in the local authority surveys and in the focus groups. It was only the fifth most mentioned deterrent for the non-users in the telephone survey, but this might be explained by the fact that these respondents do not make great use of these areas and so are less aware of the facilities. The focus group discussions throw more light on the nature of the concerns. Members of the groups expressed concern at the neglect of urban green spaces and their facilities, particularly areas for children's play. Concerns were expressed about the state of play areas, the lack of play equipment or its deterioration and poor condition, and the lack of interesting or adventurous play opportunities. A general concern, expressed in all the groups, that there is "nothing of interest" in these areas in itself keeps people away from them. Similarly a general concern was expressed about the lack of staff on the sites, whether they be wardens, park keepers, or play leaders. Only the young people's groups failed to expressed concern about this.

3.24   Many of the discussions focused on specific facilities that were considered to be lacking or in poor condition. Toilets were mentioned most frequently particularly in groups involving disabled people, the elderly and lesbian women. Seating was the next most frequently mentioned facility followed by poor lighting, given as a reason for not visiting some spaces by disabled people, by women, including lesbian women, and by young people. There was also a clear feeling that there is not enough provision for children and particularly for older children in some spaces, a view expressed by young people themselves, but also by some groups of elderly people and women. The quotes in the box below show the types of comments made about lack of or poor facilities.

3.25   The telephone survey asked the 515 non-users and infrequent users whether the provision of certain facilities would encourage them to use urban green spaces more frequently. **Table 3.5** indicates the reactions to a range of suggested facilities by each group. In summary it appears that for women, disabled people and the elderly the provision of a café, toilets, dog litter bins and seating would all be important in encouraging them to use urban green spaces more frequently. For disabled people provision of information centres or boards would also be an encouragement, while for young people cafes and toilets are most important but provision of sports areas and dog litter bins would also encourage them to use urban green spaces more.

3.26   The respondents were also given the opportunity to mention any other facilities whose provision would encourage them to use urban green spaces more frequently. Additional aspects of provision mentioned included: general facilities such as toilets/café/parking; additional staff, including park wardens/keepers/attendants; water features/water plants/boating; first aid facilities and sporting events.

What the focus groups said about facilities in green spaces

'(you want)..a toilet that doesn't knock you
out as you walk through the door'
Woman, Ipswich

'there's more stuff for younger kids
– there's not much for us'
Teenager, Sheffield

'(about tennis courts) It's no good
being free if you can't get in'
Elderly woman, Ipswich

'(about dilapidated playgrounds) it's the message
that young people and children receive – you're
only good enough for rubbish'
Woman, Sheffield

'I don't see the point in having a
tennis court with no nets there'
Young person from ethnic minority background, Newcastle Upon Tyne

'used to go to a park, but someone took
the bench, so I don't go any more'
Person from ethnic minority background, Sheffield

'people need light in parks, it is
not a fear thing, you just can't see'
Woman, Sheffield

'seating is too low and there are no
arms and backs on most seating – this
prevents you from sitting on them as you simply
cannot get up or down low enough'
Disabled person, Ipswich

'poor upkeep puts people off'
Young person, Newcastle Upon Tyne

OTHER USERS

3.27   In local authority surveys most comments about the deterrent effect of certain groups of 'other people' relate to concerns about young people in urban green spaces. Such young people were referred to as 'yobs' in some surveys. Conflict between adults and children were also mentioned in one location. Those in the telephone survey did not mention the issue of other people. This may largely be due to the fact that it was not listed among the choices available in answering the closed question 'to what extent do these factors put you off using urban parks, play areas and green spaces' because it did not emerge as an issue in the early pilot study. On the other hand it was mentioned only very infrequently (7%) by people answering the open question about other factors that put them off, which suggests that it is not perceived to be a particular problem by those who do not use urban green spaces frequently

Table 3.6: Facilities that would encourage people 'a lot' to use urban green spaces more frequently, across different types of non-users and infrequent users (Source: telephone survey)

	Women (%)	12-15 year olds (%)	16-19 year olds (%)	Non European[1]	56-65 year olds (%)	76 years and over (%)	Disabled People (%)
Café	80	83	100	80	80	70	83
Toilets	78	77	94	78	81	70	87
Dog litter bins	76	53	94	77	78	60	75
Seating	67	40	88	62	72	67	83
Litter bins	61	67	56	61	68	50	65
Information centre/boards	55	43	44	66	51	47	52
Children's play area	47	63	56	51	53	30	43
Sports areas	30	67	75	58	19	13	20

Note 1: Includes all those who were of Black African, Black Caribbean, other Black, Chinese, Indian, Bangladeshi, Pakistani, other Asian, mixed race and other non-European origin (see A1.4 in Appendix 1)

3.28   The data from the focus groups reveals more of the complexities about people's experiences and feelings about other users of urban green spaces:

●   the presence of drug users (and drugs and needles) was the category of users mentioned by most focus groups as being a reason for non- or infrequent use. All types of focus groups mentioned these concerns;

●   'undesirable characters' or the bad reputation of a park, play area or green space was mentioned by several groups of young people as well as some groups of the elderly and one group of disabled people;

●   disabled people, the elderly and women particularly mentioned concerns about teenagers or youths as a reason for not using some spaces but this is also an issue for some young people themselves. Several of the groups of young people mentioned that either older or younger children were a reason that they did not use some spaces;

- other people drinking (alcohol) was of concern to people with disabilities, some elderly people and some young people.

3.29   On more specific issues, verbal abuse had been experienced by some disabled people and lesbian women, while some people with disabilities and some women felt that in their area *"Asians have taken over the park"*. Bikes and skateboards, gay men, Asian men gambling, mobile phones, and a space being either too noisy or too crowded were other concerns relating to other people that were mentioned as possible reasons for not using urban green spaces across the whole range of focus groups.

What the focus groups said about the effects of other users of green spaces

'they (young people) don't value things today'
Elderly person, Plymouth

'cyclists and skateboarders are a complete hazard –
you cannot get up after you have been knocked down'
Disabled person, Sheffield

'you can get a problem with the older kids'
Young person, Bexley

'...it's not safe enough – I'm not talking about nasty men but other kids'
Young person, Stockport

'skateboarders put people off but that is because
they have nowhere to skate'
Woman, Ipswich

'adults make you feel uncomfortable'
Young person, Milton Keynes

DEALING WITH DOG ISSUES

3.30   Concern about dog mess featured prominently in all three sources of information and was repeatedly mentioned across all types of focus groups and in all but one of the urban locations where focus groups were undertaken. In addition the discussions raised concerns (sometimes by dog owners themselves) about dog areas being provided and not used, the lack of or poor position of 'dog bins' and worries about dogs not being controlled. As one elderly woman in **Ipswich** said *"a lot of children are afraid of dogs"*, a concern mirrored in the similar comments by someone from an ethnic minority background in **Lewisham** who said that *"even playful dogs can be frightening and knock over small children or the elderly"*. The importance of this issue is of course already widely recognised and the need to tackle the practical problems well established. This research simply confirms the great significance of the problem. As one woman in **Stockport** commented wistfully *"I wish that dog owners would clean up after their dogs. Dogs spoil parks – especially for children – there should be dog free areas"*.

3.31   The need to find ways of dealing with concerns about dogs and dog mess is all too apparent. Across all types of focus groups a range of views on possible solutions were expressed including the need for dog toilets, provision of plenty of dog bins in suitable locations, and proper use of fines for people not using such facilities. Ensuring that dogs are on a lead and provision of dog free areas would also aid the sense of safety, particularly for people from an ethnic minority background. Members of two ethnic minority focus groups thought that dogs should be completely banned from parks, reflecting previous research that has indicated that people from an ethnic minority background fear dogs for cultural and religious reasons.

SAFETY AND OTHER PSYCHOLOGICAL ISSUES

3.32   Fears about safety also featured prominently in all the different surveys. Such fears were expressed in the focus groups in many different ways, some being best described as a sense of apprehension. Such feelings were based on stories of real events – tales of muggings, stabbings and murder certainly abound – and sometimes on personal experience. On the other hand some in the focus groups, especially disabled people, the elderly, women and young people, commented that such fears could be overcome and that it was largely an issue of mind over matter.

3.33   Related psychological issues include not wanting to go alone to urban green spaces. This is not just a matter of fear, but of vulnerability, especially amongst elderly people, the sense of loneliness experienced particularly by those who are widows or widowers and the lack of confidence of some disabled people and their desire to be accompanied on visits. Other unrelated factors referred to in the discussions included laziness and inertia – some people, and particularly the elderly, admitted that they simply could not be bothered to go.

3.34   It is clear from discussion of barriers that safety concerns are an important issue. The 515 non- and infrequent users were also asked what would make them feel safer in urban green spaces. More lighting, more staff or rangers and more things for young people to do emerge at the top of the list as things that would make people feel safer, closely followed by dogs being on leads, no motor vehicles and dog free areas. The answer to this question has also been analysed to explore differences between groups of people and in particular to identify whether safety issues may be influencing the under represented groups. **Table 3.7** shows these reasons ranked by the frequency of mention by the different groups.

3.35   Measures to improve safety was the second most frequently mentioned change that would encourage more use of urban green spaces. This is particularly important for disabled people, for women and for the elderly and less of an issue for young people and people from an ethnic minority background. Staff and more things for young people to do would undoubtedly increase the sense of safety but in addition more lighting was the most mentioned improvement for non- and infrequent users being especially important for women, and also for disabled people, the elderly and people from an ethnic minority background. For some, especially the elderly and disabled people, removal of cars and restriction of cycling and roller-skating or roller-blading would make them feel safer. In all types of focus groups, the use of fencing for safety, either around a playground or to prevent balls going on to roads, was mentioned as a good thing and the introduction of CCTV as a safety measure was mentioned in four locations by three different types of groups.

What the focus groups said about safety and other psychological issues

'when you're older people are frightened
to go out….anywhere'
Elderly person, Plymouth

'scared of jewellery being snatched,
rape, muggings etc'
Women from an ethnic minority background, Leicester

'when parks had keepers you felt a lot safer'
Elderly people, Ipswich

'people should not feel locked up in their homes,
everything is fine if you show confidence and walk briskly'
Elderly woman, Ipswich

'some old people have no one to go with
and some are just afraid to go out'
Woman, Lewisham

'I don't go because I'm a widow and on my
own, I'm not scared, just lonely,
I don't like doing things by myself'
Elderly lady, Ipswich

'I feel unsafe in green spaces when it's getting dark –
not afraid but it is sensible not to go into green spaces after dark.
I feel safe in the town after dark, as there are more people about and it is well lit'
Lesbian women, Sheffield

CONCERNS ABOUT ENVIRONMENTAL QUALITY

3.36   Non- and infrequent users of urban green spaces are particularly concerned about issues such as litter, graffiti and vandalism which, together with their concern about dog mess, suggests that for these people there is an image problem. The concerns are, however, shared by both users and non-users suggesting that in some places at least, these are real issues. All of the under represented groups referred in at least some of the focus group discussions to issues such as litter and vandalism as things that would put them off visiting. Specific mentions were made of: lack of rubbish bins; rubbish and items like condoms, and food put out for birds, left lying around; and problems of broken glass, particularly as a hazard in or near play areas. Again these problems are not new but they are keenly felt, particularly by those with children. As one woman in **Bexley** said *"kids go to some places at night, smash bottles, spit on the slide and wind the swings up so they cannot be used"*.

> **What the focus groups said about measures to improve safety**
>
> 'Fences are good around parks but they have to
> be opened early to allow walking in the morning'
> *Person from ethnic minority background, Leicester*
>
> 'Older people worry – they must feel safe'
> *Woman, Lewisham*
>
> 'It would be well lit so that people can go for night time walks'
> *Young female from ethnic minority background, Oldham*
>
> 'The more well used the park is the safer you feel'
> *Lesbian woman, Lewisham*

3.37   The local authority surveys have similarly identified litter, vandalism and graffiti as issues that need to be tackled in urban green spaces. Litter is mentioned most and is linked with recognition of the need for plenty of litter bins as long as they are regularly emptied. This concern was endorsed as something that, if successfully tackled, would encourage more non-users and infrequent users to use urban green spaces, across all types of under represented groups.

ACCESS ISSUES

3.38   Although not among these top five concerns, the other main issues relating to the nature of the urban green space resource are to do with access. This emerged particularly in the focus group discussions with disabled people and also, to some extent, the elderly. The concerns are in four areas. Firstly there are concerns about ease of access to the urban green spaces, both in terms of proximity but also whether it can be easily reached without difficult physical barriers. Transport to sites can be difficult for those without a car and some perceive there to be a lack of decent and reliable public transport and, sometimes, difficulties in obtaining a taxi as an alternative. As one disabled couple in **Stockport** said *"we can't get to the more interesting local parks, as we don't have our own transport and there are no lower floor buses serving us. Many of the interesting parks are to the east of the main trunk road"*.

Table 3.7: Changes that would make people feel safer, in rank order, across different types of groups of non-users and infrequent users of urban green space (Source: telephone survey)

Rank Order	Women	12-15 year olds	16-19 year olds	Non European[1]	56-65 year olds	76 years and over	Disabled People
1	More lighting (73%)	More for young people (87%)	No motor vehicles (81%)	Dogs on leads (72%)	More staff (79%)	More staff (63%)	More staff (77%) =1
2	More staff (67%)	No motor vehicles (70%)	More for young people (75%)	More lighting (69%) =2	More lighting (75%)	Dog on leads (60%)	More lighting (77%) =1
3	More for young people (66%) =3	More staff (57%)	Dogs on leads (63%)	More staff (69%) =2	Dogs on leads (68%)	More lighting (57%) =3	Dogs on leads (71%)
4	Dogs on leads (66%) =3	Dogs on leads (53%)	More lighting (56%)	More for young people (68%)	More for young people (65%)	No motor vehicles (57%) =3	More for young people (67%)
5	No motor vehicles (62%)	More lighting (50%) =5	More staff (50%) =5	No motor vehicles (62%)	No motor vehicles (64%)	More for young people (57%) =3	Dog free areas (64%) =5
6	Dog free areas (59%)	Dog free areas (50%) =5	Dog free areas (50%) =5	Dog free areas (61%)	Dog free areas (59%) =6	No cycling or rolling (50%)	No cycling or rolling (64%) =5
7	Lower planting near paths (57%)	Lower planting near paths (40%)	Lower planting near paths (44%)	Lower planting near paths (57%)	No cycling or rolling (59%) =6	Dog free areas (43%) =7	Lower planting near paths (61%)
8	No cycling or rolling (39%)	No cycling or rolling (10%)	No cycling or rolling (6%)	No cycling or rolling (35%)	Lower planting near paths (56%)	Lower planting near paths (43%) =7	No motor vehicles (57%)

Note 1: Includes all those who were of Black African, Black Caribbean, other Black, Chinese, Indian, Bangladeshi, Pakistani, other Asian, mixed race and other non-European origin (see A1.4 in Appendix 1)

3.39　Access to and within urban green spaces can be a major concern to people with disabilities. Slopes and cambers and inappropriate surfacing on paths create difficulties for people in wheelchairs, others who do have full mobility and people who are visually impaired. Group members reported falling out of wheelchairs due to the camber of foot paths while others had experienced difficulties due to regular punctures in wheelchair wheels – one woman reported that only the best quality and more expensive tyres can avoid this problem. Other obstacles can also prove difficult for disabled people. There may be inadequate parking and gravel car park surfaces can mean that someone in a wheelchair cannot get to a play area from the car park. There can be particular problems with gates – as someone in **Milton Keynes** mentioned *"gate catches are difficult to operate from a wheelchair and gates are sometimes too heavy to open on your own"* while a disabled woman in **Oldham** spoke of particular problems posed by barriers designed to keep cyclists out, but which also prevent wheelchairs from passing.

3.40   For those with visual impairment, unfamiliarity with a particular space, combined with lack of cues and way-finding features can be a major deterrent. A visually impaired person in Sheffield summed up the problem, saying *"I don't like not being able to locate facilities like toilets and dog bins, path junctions, entrances and maps, or knowing about the condition of facilities like toilets, about rubbish on paths, removal of play facilities or the distance of entrances from bus stops"*.

3.41   These concerns take on added significance in the light of the 1995 Disability Discrimination Act because from 2004 service providers, in this case the local authorities who provide urban green spaces, will have to make 'reasonable adjustments' to overcome physical barriers to access. It will be unlawful for service providers to discriminate against people with disabilities by making it impossible or unreasonably difficult for them to make use of the services they offer to the public, including access to parks, play areas and other green spaces. This may require review of the design of the infrastructure of some green spaces and also some reconsideration of management issues. Sometimes the problems may be overcome simply by providing a helping hand. As a disabled person in **Ipswich** said *"disabled people need the option of having a ranger taking them round the park, they don't want to be told what to do but want the option of help for the first few times if they need it"*. Similarly a visually impaired person in **Sheffield** said *"I need a guide to show and tell me what's there"*.

PERSONAL ISSUES

3.42   All of the resource issues could potentially be addressed by those responsible for urban green spaces. This is not the case for the personal issues which deter people. In the focus groups, not having enough time to visit these areas was mentioned across all types of group but particularly by the groups of women. Preferences for going to other places were also mentioned in the focus groups with some saying that they preferred to go to the countryside, others preferring visits to the cinema or community centre. Young people, particularly young girls, commented that they preferred to visit the town centre and others suggested that having a garden removed the need to visit the park. Some groups of elderly people, and one women's group, commented that for children the park has now been replaced by the television and by computer games. Personal health problems, and changing personal circumstances, for example children and grandchildren having grown up or young people feeling that they had simply grown out of parks, play areas and green spaces, were also factors. Some of the groups of people from an ethnic minority background also mentioned the effects of parental restrictions on children's movements.

Revitalising urban green spaces

3.43   All of this information shows that there are many and varied reasons why people may be deterred from using urban green spaces, concentrating on the views of those who do not use them or who use them only infrequently. The main factors deterring use are the same ones that have been identified in previous research and relate mainly to issues concerning the location and the physical and environmental quality of these spaces. Despite the best efforts of many local authorities there is still a deep concern among many people that parks and green spaces are simply not what they used to be. One of the focus group participants in Lewisham summed up the feelings of many by saying *"there used to be a whole host of summer activities for kids in the parks. It was very safe and mums could sit and chat. Then the junkies took over and there were needles everywhere, the park keepers were removed and the cafe was closed".*

3.44   So clearly there is much still to be done if the barriers that deter non-users and infrequent users are to be overcome. But this is only part of the story because even those who do use urban green spaces regularly have views on their shortcomings and on the problems they face. **Chapter 4** considers steps that need to be taken, not only to overcome some of these barriers to use, but also to improve the image that people have of these places and to create the sort of 'ideal' vital green space that people of all types will want to visit on a regular basis.

CHAPTER 4
The Ideal Urban Green Space

SUMMARY OF KEY POINTS

- The perception that someone has of an urban green space can significantly affect whether they use that space, contribute to the collective opinion that a community has of such a space and shape the wider community's image of urban green spaces. This image can be as important as the reality in deciding whether people will make use of these areas.

- An overview of several different sources of information suggests that people's aspirations for their ideal, improved green space can be grouped into three broad themes – the overall design of urban green spaces, meeting people's needs and the nature of management.

- In terms of design the most frequently mentioned desire was for variety, of both spaces and of activities; then for vegetation, followed by water, the presence of birds and animals and sensory stimulation.

- To meet people's needs, improvements in the nature and condition of facilities were stressed and especially better provision of opportunities for play, more provision for young people, provision of comforts such as seating, toilets, shelters and refreshments, improved access and provision for a wide range of activities and events.

- Concerns about better management are mainly focused on the presence of staff and on a desire for quality rather than quantity in urban green space.

- Overall it is clear that the improvements that people want to see in urban green spaces are related to good design and management, focused on meeting people's needs, overcoming barriers to use and providing a high quality and varied experience for the whole range of different groups in the community as a whole. People showed considerable awareness of the needs of others and wanted the ideal green space to be inclusive – a space for all.

Introduction

4.1 **Chapter 3** reviewed the barriers that deter some people from making more use of urban green spaces and the types of actions that would help to overcome these problems. This chapter is concerned more with people who do use these spaces, their perceptions of them and their aspirations for what they could be. The perception that someone has of an individual urban green space can significantly affect whether they use that space and can also contribute to the collective value that a community attaches to such areas. Such views also shape the wider community's image of urban green spaces which can be as important as the reality of an experience when people decide whether to use a space or not.

Previous research

4.2 Much of the work on the attitudes and perceptions of users is focused on levels of satisfaction with current provision and with identifying the things that people value in the parks and other green spaces that they use. For example, the 'People's Panel' Wave 5 research undertaken by MORI in 2000, for the 'Modernising Public Services Group' in the Cabinet Office, showed that 25 per cent of the respondents were very satisfied with their parks and open spaces while 53 per cent were only fairly satisfied. Key expectations of park users were that they should be safe and clean, with cleanliness, tidiness, safety for young children and visitors and the provision of separate dog areas all identified as being important.

4.3 Previous studies of the Royal Parks in London[1] have also indicated a long list of elements in, and characteristics of, these prestigious parks that are considered to be particularly important. They include the presence of trees and greenery, flowers and gardens, appearing clean and well kept, fresh air, open spaces, peace and quiet, lakes and ponds, feeling safe, being away from noise and dirt, wildlife, good toilets, somewhere to watch the world go by, being well signposted, the historic setting and pageantry and good catering facilities. In the same survey responses to several proposed changes were well received, including: suggestions for more children's playgrounds; signposting and route marking; improved habitats for wildlife; provision of a visitor centre; the reduction of traffic on main roads adjoining the parks and more public toilets. Additional suggestions for improvements made by those interviewed included more litter bins, more and better catering and seating, more vegetation, drinking fountains, more wildlife and bar facilities.

4.4 Outside the Royal Parks, visitors to Islington's Parks[2], expressed general satisfaction with the environment and maintenance of the parks, but were concerned about safety and about facilities such as toilets, shelter, lighting and information and signing. The main suggested improvements included more shelter, more staff in uniform, more staff/wardens, more lighting, more toilets and solutions to problems relating to dogs.

---

1   Survey of People using *St James's Park, Green Park and Regent's Park*. Centre for Leisure and Tourism Studies, University of North London (1992).

2   *Survey of Islington Parks: Report for Islington Council Leisure and Libraries Service*. Centre for Leisure and Tourism Studies, University of North London (1992).

4.5   In this research surveys of user satisfaction carried out by the case study local authorities provide further insight into how those who use urban green spaces feel about them. Nine out of the fifteen authorities had carried out surveys of user satisfaction of some sort, involving either users or non- users or a combination of both. Levels of satisfaction with urban green spaces vary widely across the case study authority areas although the nature of the surveys makes comparisons difficult. In Cheltenham for example, 99% of those surveyed felt that the provision and maintenance of parks and gardens was good or very good; while in Doncaster management of urban green space was considered good or very good by only 10%. It is impossible to draw conclusions from such surveys without knowing more about the local circumstances and about the design of the surveys itself

The ideal urban green space

4.6   Satisfaction with current provision is only part of the story and can simply reflect relatively low expectations. It does not deal with how much more satisfied, or even delighted, people would be if their aspirations were raised and if these raised aspirations could be met. Each of the 43 focus groups of under represented users of urban green spaces was asked to think about what their ideal park, play area or green space would be like, initially without any prompting and then with the help of photographs of a wide range of different types of urban green space. From these discussions, but also drawing on other research and on local authority satisfaction surveys, it seems that people's aspirations for their ideal, improved green space fall into three broad themes – the overall design of urban green spaces, *meeting people's needs and the nature of management.*

DESIGN OF URBAN GREEN SPACES

4.7   The importance of the overall design of urban green spaces and the content of those spaces was referred to indirectly in the data from local authority surveys. However the depth of the discussion in the focus groups enabled people from the different under represented groups to make many unprompted mentions of design – either directly or indirectly. An acknowledgement that good quality urban green spaces do not just happen but need to be designed was well put by a woman in **Ipswich** who said that it is all about *"design, design, design, someone needs to sit down and create it – it cannot just be thrown together"*.

4.8   People were particularly keen to have **variety** of spaces within their ideal urban green space. Some, particularly young people, also mentioned that they would like a variety of activities – perhaps a management issue as much as a design one. All groups wanted to have open areas, open trees and spaces where you could see everything – this primarily relates to people's concern about safety and the desire to be able to see exit points from within a space. Disabled people particularly wanted to have quiet areas.

4.9   A disabled person in **Stockport** particularly explained this desire for variety, saying *"it's good to have many different experiences – meadows, formal areas, water"*. There was also a desire for a good network of paths – again for some this related to safety and being able to get to an exit if they felt the need so to do – and pounds that were of the right width and in good condition. Views were very much appreciated across all groups, whether they are views of the city, of the countryside or of the sea – the ability to see beyond the space adding to people's concept of an ideal space. Other references to variety in design in one or two groups, related to the desire for a 'spacious' feel, a big area and a modern approach to design, together with a few 'votes' for specific design elements including meeting places, a maze, monuments, hills and interesting walks.

4.10   **Vegetation** is clearly vitally important to people, being repeatedly discussed across all types of focus groups and in all ten locations. Discussions embraced the all-encompassing term of 'greenery' as well as trees, flowers (in a variety of forms) and grass. A wild area or trail and 'natural' or 'wild' plantings were mentioned by a few groups. Diversity of types of vegetation within a location was also expressed as an ideal. Individual mentions were made of an arboretum with labelled plants, a tropical plant house and interpretation of plant names with Braille. The value of such vegetation for aesthetic appreciation, especially of colour, and for education were acknowledged. One or two people showed quite sophisticated understanding of a link between design and management. A disabled person in **Sheffield** for example commented that *"if more of our parks had meadowland, you'd solve the problem of maintenance…as long as it's accessible"*.

4.11   **Water** was the second most frequently mentioned element after vegetation that people wanted in their 'ideal' space. Water for children's play was mentioned the most often across all the types of focus groups, with the added proviso that it must be safe. Fountains were the second most mentioned form of water that people, again across all the groups, would like to see. For disabled people the sound of fountains was something that they wanted while for some people from an ethnic minority background lights and sounds with fountains were felt to be a good thing. Water was considered as relaxing by most people with the disabled particularly wanting to have safe access to be able to enjoy the sounds of water. Ponds, especially with wildlife and ducks, streams, rivers and waterfalls were all mentioned and boating and model boating lakes were also mentioned by a few. The presence of **animals** within an urban green space was considered by many to be important for children. Disabled people, women and people from an ethnic minority background particularly mentioned this. Birds in general were often mentioned with ducks and ponds for ducks being particularly popular with women and disabled people.

What the focus groups said about the design and content of urban green spaces

'as you get older you need something
more interesting,not just acres of grass'
Elderly person, Bexley

'Some of the wild flowers are prettier than the real thing'
Elderly person, Plymouth

'Need to have trees with berries and crickets and bats,
so that you can teach children about them'
Woman from ethnic minority background, Lewisham

'Parks are too green,
quite bland – need more flowering plants'
Young person, Newcastle Upon Tyne

'a calm flowery area
where you can sit and talk'
Young person, Newcastle Upon Tyne

'Water, but not just something for the children,
maybe a lake with an island you could row out to'
Elderly person, Ipswich

'Different coloured lights shining on the water at night'
Person from ethnic minority background, Leicester

'you have to be able to hear water;
it is very relaxing'
Elderly person, Ipswich

4.12   **Sensory stimulation** through the presence of things to touch, listen to or see, were mentioned across most types of groups but especially by disabled people. Some of these sensory experiences were desired for their own sake – such as statues to touch and gardens with special planting to smell and touch – while others were more to aid in practical matters such as warning sounds near swings and brightly coloured litter bins.

4.13   One of the groups of disabled people wanted recognition that there are different types of disabilities, physical and sensory, and thus different people might benefit from different sensory experiences and have different requirements within a space. Another member of the same group was keen to point out that 85 per cent of stimulation to the brain is through sight. People with a visual impairment therefore miss out on most of the qualities of urban green spaces because so much of the design relates to visual aspects. Someone from the **Sheffield** group expressed this in a practical way, saying that there should be *"features that stimulate senses other than sight: running water, quacking ducks, scented planting, different senses of enclosure"*. For those who are sighted, young people particularly mentioned **colour** as something that they would like in their ideal park with some mentioning that coloured seats would be good.

MEETING PEOPLE'S NEEDS

4.14   Improvement in the nature and condition of facilities and the provision for activities were mentioned across all the various sets of information as things that would encourage non- and infrequent users to use urban green spaces more frequently and as elements within an ideal space. The local authority data particularly revealed concerns about the poor condition of a range of facilities in many areas. Even in some locations where the overall urban green space service was considered to be satisfactory or good the provision and/or condition of facilities was often considered to be poor.

Play and other provision for young people

4.15   Play is widely accepted as helping children to develop social skills, creativity, and confidence and is therefore an important part of early life. **Provision of opportunities for play**, and not just the issue of provision of playgrounds, was mentioned across all the sets of information. The local authority data did not reveal much information about the quality of current play provision though its importance was acknowledged in many locations. The Leicester survey of 1000 children throws light on the views of children themselves as users of urban green spaces. The telephone questionnaire shows that if a children's play area, presumably of a good quality, was provided then it would encourage all the groups of non- and infrequent users to use urban green spaces more frequently. Although this applied less to the older elderly play facilities of one kind or another were mentioned across all types of focus groups as being something that people would like to see in their ideal urban green space.

4.16   The adequacy, or otherwise, of provision for children's play and more generally for young people, is another issue addressed in several of the Local Authority satisfaction surveys. It is though notable that with one or two exceptions there is generally little feedback from the children and young people who actually use play facilities. Concern about play provision appears to be widespread, demonstrated by the fact that in:

- Cheltenham: just over half of respondents felt that play areas were good or very good but over three-quarters of people said that they wanted to see more local play areas that children and their parents can get to easily;

- Bexley: the provision of play equipment is considered to be good or very good by less than one-third of survey respondents;

- Wolverhampton: those surveyed consider that there is a problem with play areas;

- Sheffield: less than one-third of the respondents to the Talkback 2000 survey were satisfied with children's play areas;

- Doncaster: a survey of nearly 700 children revealed that nearly all of them would like to see 'better things to play on';

- Lewisham: young people attending the 2000 Junior Citizen event said, when asked what they would like to see in their local park, that a youth zone with shelter and basketball post was their top priority, with drinking fountain, toilets and a kiosk also mentioned as good things to have;

- Newcastle: a survey of residents around a specific site showed that 89% thought that a purpose-built centre for young people within the park was a good idea;

- Leicester: a 1998 survey showed that people wanted to see better facilities for children. An earlier (1993) survey of 1000 children provided a wealth of information about play in parks and in particular showed that:

    - Children use small, local parks more than large central parks, yet have more negative comments about the design, maintenance and equipment of small parks and their accessibility for children with disabilities;

    - Parks, especially local parks, are seen to be arenas for bullying and vandalism;

    - Many children are concerned, or distressed, by dogs and dog mess in public places;

    - The younger you are the more you like parks; interest peaks at 8-9 years of age;

    - Children are aware – and adults are not – of the differences between older and younger children's use of parks;

    - Asian children liked parks most of any ethnic group;

    - 94% of children wanted to spend more time out of the house;

    - In terms of desirable features in parks 'grass, trees and flowers' got an even higher rating than 'swings etc'. Nearly half of the children thought they were 'brilliant'.

4.17   Many in the focus groups expressed concern at the removal of play areas. Both adults and young people commented widely on the nature of play. Some of the young people, for example admitted that they like to sit on the swings, but that adults do not approve of this, while some of the boys said that they like to climb – either on a big climbing frame or on a tree. Some thought that more interesting and adventurous play areas were desirable but safety was also a concern, although as a person from an ethnic minority background in **Leicester** said 'children want a mix of safety and danger'. Safety concerns relate both to the provision of 'safer surfacing' and the general condition of the play area or equipment. One woman in **Sheffield** thought that 'a more natural style of play is missing'. Some people also mentioned other specific types of play provision – a kick about area, something for older kids, wooden play equipment, and a sandpit. This concern about good quality play opportunities reflects the views expressed in the survey of young people in **Doncaster** who wanted to see 'better things to play on'.

4.18   There is also a widely held view that urban green spaces would benefit from better **provision for young people**. This reflects the findings of other research like 'Park Life' which recognised the need to provide for teenagers in parks and also that the presence of teenagers is often a reason for others to avoid urban green spaces. In **Newcastle upon Tyne** residents around one site stressed the need for 'something to do' for both the under 13 year olds and over 13 year olds. This recognition of the need to provide something for younger and older children reflects the understanding that **Leicester** children showed of the differences between younger and older children's use of parks. More things for young people to do was also the third most frequently mentioned issue that would improve a sense of safety in urban green spaces for the non-users and infrequent users of the telephone survey and mirrors the mentions of teenagers or youths as deterrents to use for some people. This view was also held, to some degree, across all the different types of focus groups. Young people themselves can sometimes offer a solution, with one group member in **Plymouth** suggesting that ideally *'part of the park for older youths would have provision for different activities including baseball, hockey, basketball, skateboarding, roller blading and bicycle riding'*.

Comforts such as seats, toilets and shelters

4.19 People want to feel that their basic need for comfort will be met in urban green spaces and provision of suitable seating comes high up a list of things that people want to see provided. Inadequate provision of **seating** was briefly mentioned in some of the local authority surveys and when the non- and infrequent users were asked if the provision of particular facilities would encourage them to use urban parks more frequently the provision of seating was endorsed by all groups with most, except younger children, mentioning seating as the third or fourth most significant facility. Provision of seating, in a variety of forms and arrangements, was the most frequently mentioned 'comfort' wanted in the ideal urban green space across the focus groups. Not surprisingly it was particularly important for disabled people and for the elderly, while teenage girls wanted seats to chat on and watch the boys from! Some wanted seats to be by themselves while others wanted them to be arranged in groups where they could easily chat with friends. The lack of seats to watch football from was of concern in one focus group. Design of seating is important but preferences vary – according to one disabled person in **Sheffield** *'you need a variety of types of seating and chairs need to be high enough and with arms'* while young girls in **Bexley** and **Sheffield** said *'(we'd like) arm chairs –we don't like wooden seats'*

4.20 There is little in the way of positive comment about the state of **toilets** in urban green spaces. In the local authority surveys toilets are only mentioned when people are concerned about their absence and/or poor condition. This was particularly an issue for the elderly and disabled people. Many insisted that toilets should be more accessible, perhaps located inside a café, easily accessible for disabled people and should have baby changing facilities. The cleanliness and maintenance of toilets was also important to everyone. As one person from an ethnic minority background in **Newcastle upon Tyne** pointed out *'The toilet is very important. I use the park with my children and sometimes it is not clean....there should be better toilets'*

4.21 The provision of **shelters** only came up in the focus group discussions of the ideal urban green space and was particularly mentioned by disabled people and by young people. Shelters were considered important because they can provide opportunities for meeting and for sheltering from the heat or the rain. A disabled person in **Bexley** suggested that shelters could be time-shared – used by elderly people during the day and teenagers in the evening – *"An area should be provided for teenagers – somewhere to sit and hangout, a sheltered area and somewhere for them to play football etc. When teenagers are not using the sheltered areas during the day old people could use them"*

4.22 The provision of **refreshments** was not particularly mentioned in the survey information from local authorities and yet when non-users and infrequent users were asked which facilities would encourage them to use urban green spaces more frequently the provision of a café was at or near the top of the list for all groups. Every one of the 16-19 year olds said that the provision of this facility would encourage them. The availability of refreshments was mentioned across all types of focus groups and again by far the most frequently mentioned desire was for a café or restaurant, and especially for one that was affordable. Young people and disabled people mentioned the desire for a barbecue area while a picnic area, with tables that can be used by disabled people were repeatedly mentioned across the discussion groups with disabled people and also briefly in some of the other groups. A woman from **Lewisham** emphasised the social value of such provision, referring to a vision of *"a sheltered square with a cafe, where people could meet from every generation – it would help old people back into the community and create an environment of culture"*.

Sports facilities

4.23   When sports facilities were mentioned in the local authority surveys there was often a reference to the fact that there were no changing facilities or that they were in a poor condition. The provision of sports areas was endorsed by the telephone survey as something that would encourage greater use of urban green spaces although the level of enthusiasm was quite variable with young people and people from an ethnic minority background being most influenced.

4.24   Across the focus groups the provision of sports facilities was mentioned, particularly by young people, who stressed that the quality of provision was also very important. Women and disabled people acknowledged that the provision of football pitches is important; elderly people mentioned the desirability of bowling greens; tennis and basketball courts were mentioned both by women and young people accompanied by concern about a perceived need to dress correctly and the importance of easy access to such facilities. The focus groups revealed that in some locations there seems to be a move towards organised clubs having sole use of facilities causing problems for those who want a game on a casual basis. For some the frustration was that despite a park being open the tennis courts were locked or there was no net available. For some young people the lack of goal posts hindered their enjoyment of a casual, as opposed to pre-booked, game of football. A disabled person in **Newcastle upon Tyne** expressed some frustration, wanting *"the option to join in activities without becoming a member (re bowling club)"*.

Access, signing and information

4.25   Two aspects of access – having a space nearer and being easier to get to – were clearly identified as issues that would encourage greater use of urban green spaces more, although they were not generally very high up the list of factors. For some the desire to have spaces close to home was a reflection of a cultural tradition as a lady from an ethnic minority background in **Oldham** stated *"we need small spaces near to your house where you can nip out for a bit"*. For disabled people good access was an important dimension of an ideal urban green space. Good public transport and parking facilities were also mentioned particularly by groups of women. For one woman in **Stockport** this was the most important concern *"Above all it would have good accessibility with adequate parking and public transport links"*.

4.26   Good signing was mentioned in some of the local authority surveys with **Bexley** rating well in this area and **Doncaster** rating poorly. An information centre or information boards were identified as something that would encourage non-users and infrequent users to use urban green spaces more frequently, particularly in the case of people from an ethnic minority background. With the exception of one group of young people in **Lewisham**, the only other focus groups to mention provision of information or interpretation as an important factor in urban green spaces, were groups of disabled people. Display boards, interpretation, Braille signs and maps and audio tapes were mentioned as features of an ideal urban park, play area or green space – as someone from the lively discussion group in **Bexley** said, there is a need for *"Braille signs, things with texture on that can be used to move people in directions and a textured braille or push button map of the park at the entrance"*.

Events

4.27   All the different surveys and sources of information suggest, to varying degrees, that an active events programme is important in an ideal urban green space. In the focus groups many people mentioned music events and some, though far fewer, mentioned the desirability of theatre. Some tempered their desire for events with comments that these should not be going on all the time. Young people were the only group to mention the desire for a fair while women, disabled people and the elderly wanted to see a bandstand with a band playing. A young person in **Leicester** took a comprehensive view of events: *"Events attracting more people would make urban green spaces more interesting to be in"*.

Other activities

4.28   The focus groups revealed a desire to accommodate **wheeled activities** within an ideal green space from both women and young people. Local authority surveys reveal that in some locations bicycles are considered to be a problem and the exclusion of cycling and roller-skating or roller-blading would improve the sense of safety for some non- and infrequent users, particularly disabled people. The provision of a skate park was mentioned in focus groups in eight of the ten locations particularly by young people but also by women. Facilities for cycling, for leisure use by young people, and as a means of transport by women, were mentioned together with the desirability of a cycle track or routes. Provision for bicycles was also mentioned by two groups of disabled people. A limited number of other specific activities were mentioned in one focus group or another, including: provision for activities in a wheelchair; outdoor chess and draughts; a graffiti wall; and, a community fishing area

MANAGEMENT

4.29   The influence of concerns about poor management, or a need for improved maintenance, emerge from all the different sources of information. Good maintenance was mentioned across all types of focus groups as a key part of the ideal urban green space, which according to one lesbian woman in **Lewisham** *" would have to be well maintained – if an area looks good it has more value and gets less abuse"*. In addition the importance of the quality rather than quantity of space was also mentioned in the same focus group. *"I would rather have a small number of really good parks than twenty mediocre parks"*.

Staff

4.30   The presence of staff in urban green spaces is a regular focus of comments in a number of the local authorities. For example, in **Cheltenham** two-thirds of respondents said that they wanted to see gardeners based at the main parks in the town. Many detailed comments have been made about the parks ranger service, which is generally considered to be good, with an overwhelming view that their role is about deterring crime and vandalism and nearly all respondents agreeing that making parks safe and making them feel safe must be a priority for local authorities. In a similar vein the lack of a ranger presence on-site was a main reason for people feeling unsafe in urban green spaces in **Doncaster**. Surveys in **Bexley, Sheffield,** and **Leicester** also indicate concerns about staffing and a need for improved supervision

4.31   The presence of appropriate staff in urban green spaces emerged as a key issue in several of the local authority case study areas often linked with a view that such staff aid the perception of feeling safe. More staff was the sixth most mentioned issue that would encourage non- and infrequent users to use urban green spaces more, and was particularly important for the younger elderly, disabled people and women. Park keepers, rangers or wardens were thought to be features of the ideal urban green space across all types of focus groups, but were especially mentioned by disabled people who would like to see them provide the help that is sometimes needed. Some of the elderly people and disabled people suggested that walks organised by rangers would encourage them to use urban green spaces more, giving them confidence, providing company and introducing them to or guiding them through new locations. Many of the groups that raised this issue said that it was important that such staff should be identifiable and approachable.

What the focus groups said about the need for staff

'Just their presence helps'
Elderly woman, Ipswich

'I'd like to see more rangers
and them doing more'
Disabled person, Sheffield

'(it needs) a warden who cleans up the site
but is also on hand to give first aid'
Woman, Bexley

'It would have park keepers
who you could see walking around
but people would take notice of what they said'
Elderly person, Bexley

'A park keeper
to make you feel safe and secure'
Person from ethnic minority background, Lewisham

'Rangers to ask things
or get different directions from
and information points within parks.
Group activities to introduce
visually impaired people to new parks'
Person with visual impairment, Sheffield

Spaces for all

4.32   Overall it is clear that the improvements that people want to see in urban green spaces are related to good design and management, focused on meeting people's needs, overcoming barriers to use and providing a high quality and varied experience for the whole range of different groups in the community as a whole. Participants in the focus groups showed considerable awareness of the needs of others and wanted the ideal green space to be inclusive – a space for all. As a woman in Lewisham said *"you need a mixed environment with different generations; parks are a place where the family and the community can come together – life and death, it's a natural process"*. This social vision is often matched by a physical vision of the type of space that is needed. One woman from an ethnic minority background in Oldham described her own vision of an urban green space, saying *"an ideal space has to be local with lots of trees, flowers and grass. It has to be safe without spaces that are too enclosed and have interesting play equipment and accessible water"*.

What the focus groups said about 'spaces for all'

'Every activity that is going on
is important for somebody'
Disabled man, Newcastle upon Tyne

'..lots of facilities,
something for everyone..'
Elderly people, Oldham

'A park should have something for everyone,
not just our age group or younger children'
Young people, Stockport

'..activities for all ages, less crime, less glass'
Young person, Milton Keynes

CHAPTER 5
Adding up the Benefits

SUMMARY OF KEY POINTS

- The many important benefits of urban green space can be categorised as social (including health and education benefits), environmental, and economic, however a key feature of successful green spaces is their capacity to provide multiple benefits to urban communities.

- Many studies refer to the social benefits of urban green space. It has both an existence value, because people know it is there, and a use value for a wide range of different activities. It contributes significantly to social inclusion because it is free and access is available to all; it provides neutral ground available to all sectors of society and can become the focus of community spirit through the many and varied opportunities provided for social interaction; it contributes to child development through scope for outdoor, energetic and imaginative play and also has considerable educational value.

- The health benefits of urban green space are also extremely important and stem both from the opportunity to engage in healthy outdoor exercise and from the psychological effects arising from the way that they allow escape to a less stressful, more relaxing environment.

- The environmental benefits of urban green space include: contributions to maintaining biodiversity through the conservation and enhancement of the distinctive range of urban habitats; contributions to landscape and cultural heritage; amelioration of the physical urban environment by reducing pollution, moderating the extremes of the urban climate, contributions to cost-effective sustainable urban drainage systems and some influence as sinks for carbon dioxide; and provision of opportunities to demonstrate sustainable management practices.

- Economic benefits include both on-site benefits, such as direct employment and revenue generation, and less tangible off-site benefits, including effects on nearby property prices, contributions to attracting and retaining businesses in an area and an important role in attracting tourists. Further effort needs to go into promoting understanding of the role that urban green space plays in sustaining vibrant urban economies.

- There may be merit in local authorities using an adapted version of the Quality of Life Capital approach to provide a framework for presenting consistent arguments about the important multiple benefits offered by urban green spaces and also for evaluating individual sites and features.

Introduction

5.1   The vital part that green spaces play in urban living cannot be overstated. The wide range of benefits that they offer to urban dwellers has been extensively rehearsed and few would dispute the case that has been developed. And yet the detailed evidence in support of this case is rarely presented and it is also acknowledged that there are still notable gaps in the evidence base. In this research three sources of information provide insights into the benefits of urban green space. First there has been a wide ranging review of literature on the subject, mainly produced in the last five years[1]. This has identified a wide range of research showing the benefits of urban green space. It is, however, notable that much of the hard evidence comes from work carried out in North America and, to a lesser extent in Europe, and that there has been relatively little British research on this topic. It is also apparent that much of the information available, especially on social and health benefits, is linked to contact with nature, or often more specifically with trees, rather than with parks and green spaces. In addition to the literature, the interviews with case study local authorities and review of their documents, and discussions in the focus groups with under-represented users have also provided useful material on the question of benefits.

5.2   Both the 'Park Life' and 'People, Parks and Cities' reports placed emphasis on the value of green spaces to society. 'Park Life' in particular wrote eloquently of the challenge that now faces green space providers and managers in seeking to provide a legacy of rich, diverse and sustainable places where "people will find a sense of continuity, of relief from the pressure of urban living, places to be in touch with the natural cycle of the seasons and of wildlife and also places to meet and celebrate with others". Many of those who gave evidence to the inquiry into Town and Country Parks by the House of Commons Environment, Transport and Regional Affairs Committee similarly emphasised the benefits of green spaces, and the Council of Europe has also attempted to sum up the range of benefits of green space in towns throughout Europe.

5.3   A number of the case study local authorities who contributed to this research have given a prominent place to these matters in their green space strategies. Stockport MBC for example, has titled its service development plan for its new Land Services organisation 'Valuing Green Space", and among its overall statements of intent stresses that it will seek to "make people aware of the value of green space and its contribution to a balanced lifestyle and to develop the use of green space to encourage mental and physical fitness". In a similar spirit Oldham MBC opens its draft green space strategy by saying that "the green spaces around us are vital to our quality of life. They give us aesthetic pleasure, they mark the changing of the seasons, they relieve the harshness of the urban environment, and they provide habitats for wildlife and places for recreation". The council's future vision for green space sets out the benefits that can be gained from a quality green space network, under the headings of: benefits to individuals; parks as centres of community life; improving the landscape; and contributing to a sustainable future. There are also other noteworthy examples of such recognition, for example in **Sheffield** and **Leicester**. All these examples confirm the multiple benefits that urban green space offers.

---

1   Full details and references can be found in the separate report 'Improving Parks, Play Areas and Green Spaces – Interim Report on the Literature Review'. Department of Landscape. University of Sheffield, July 2001.

The range of benefits

5.4 There are various ways of classifying the benefits of urban green spaces but three broad categories – social, environmental, and economic – are the most commonly adopted. Within the social category it is clear that personal health and psychological benefits are extremely important and almost merit a separate category rather than simply being incorporated within the list of social benefits. Similarly educational benefits also deserve a separate mention. The main types of benefit covered in this chapter are therefore:

- **Social Benefits:** green spaces offer important opportunities for people to make contact with nature, to take exercise by involvement in both passive and active recreation, and to be involved in many kinds of social, cultural and community activities. The following two aspects merit particular attention:

  - **Health benefits:** the environmental and social benefits that green spaces bring in themselves create further physical and mental health benefits for individuals and communities;

  - **Educational benefits:** green spaces offer a wide range of both formal and informal educational opportunities to all age groups;

- **Environmental Benefits:** green spaces can be shown to play an important part in wildlife and habitat conservation, so helping to meet biodiversity objectives, as well as contributing to landscape and cultural heritage, improving urban air quality and ameliorating the urban climate, and reducing noise levels;

- **Economic Benefits:** green spaces can help to attract inward investment, to retain businesses, to create employment opportunities, to support tourism and to increase the value and marketability of nearby property.

5.5 The remainder of this chapter examines this full range of benefits in greater detail drawing on all three sources of evidence mentioned above.

Social benefits

5.6 Many people have recognised that urban green spaces can provide a range of positive social benefits. The Council for Europe, for example, wrote in 1986 that *"Open space is… important for social interaction and in fostering community development… In particular it helps reduce the inherent tension and conflict in deprived urban areas"*. Urban green spaces undoubtedly contribute positively to urban dwellers lives in ways that are often un-quantified but are nevertheless quite widely recognised. The research literature does contain a wide range of evidence about these social benefits and the focus group discussions particularly acknowledged the social importance of green spaces to people and communities.

5.7   Clearly some of the greatest benefits arise simply by virtue of the opportunities that green
       spaces offer for a wide range of both informal and formal recreation activities, of the type
       discussed in **Chapter 2**. The benefits do not, however, come simply from use of green space
       and many people value these areas simply because, to quote one of the focus groups, *"it's
       nice to know it's there"*. The participants often also recognised that if such green spaces did
       not exist in cities they would have to travel further afield, to the countryside, to find the
       experiences that they can offer. Green space therefore has a simple existence value as well
       as a use value. But they are easily taken for granted so that often people do not
       automatically think of the part they play in urban life – as a woman in Sheffield said
       "parks are part of your normal routine, you do not necessarily even realise you're using them".

5.8   There is also widespread recognition, demonstrated for example in Leicester City Council's
       'Parks, Open Spaces and Countryside Strategy', that urban green spaces contribute
       significantly to social inclusion. They encourage high levels of social and cultural
       interaction including both informal social contact and participation in community events.
       Free access is an important part of this and the inclusiveness of green spaces hinges on the
       fact that they are open and available to all. It has been argued by researchers that they are
       areas of neutral ground, where a wide range of users and uses are mutually tolerated – to
       paraphrase what our focus groups said – parks, play areas and green spaces are there for
       everybody not just for one particular group or another; for example they provide
       opportunities for different cultures to meet, places where business people can take a break
       at lunchtime and they are important for courting couples. Leicester City Council, with its
       high proportion of ethnic minority groups, believes that use of public parks is a tradition in
       cities throughout the world and that ethnic minorities therefore share similar cultural
       traditions of park use, which encourages them to use these spaces in the city.

5.9   Many in the focus groups identified green spaces as the hub or the spirit of their community.
       Focus groups of women, people from an ethnic background and disabled people particularly
       suggested that these areas are important for whole families, gathering together for events
       such as picnics. Groups of young people thought that parks and green spaces were
       important for the elderly, while several groups of elderly people thought that the spaces are
       important for teenagers, helping to keep them off the streets. Even dog walking, widely
       recognised as one of the most common uses of green spaces, is considered to be a social
       activity, with owners, as well as their dogs, meeting each other on a regular basis. All types
       of focus groups recognise the social benefits simply of meeting people and 'hanging out', an
       activity that does not appear to be confined to teenagers!

5.10   The social role of urban green space can extend beyond the provision of opportunities for
       gathering or meeting. **Case Studies 9.2 (Grove Park Gardens, Doncaster), 9.3 (Manvers
       Park, Doncaster) and 9.4 (Heeley Millenium Park, Sheffield)** indicate that parks and
       other green spaces can act as a basis for wider community strengthening and capacity
       building. Because such spaces can offer free, non-discriminatory and unlimited access, and
       because they can be very visible indicators of neighbourhood quality, parks appear to have a
       special value in galvanising community activity, often resulting in wider and unforeseen
       community benefit. These points are expanded further in **Chapter 9**.

5.11   The opportunity for outdoor, energetic and imaginative play is a vital benefit of urban green
       space. Taking children was one of the most frequently mentioned reasons for a visit to one
       of these areas among the focus groups – one person with a disability in **Stockport**
       emphasised that *"families need to get small children out of the house"* and another in **Sheffield**

expressed the widely held view that *"children need somewhere to play, to explore and to let off steam in a green environment"*. The contact with nature that green spaces offer is especially valuable, as is the socialising effect of meeting with others, both children and adults. There is also evidence that attractive or successful green spaces can positively influence the behaviour both of individuals and wider society, for example helping to reduce crime rates by providing alternative activities for the young.

HEALTH BENEFITS

5.12 According to the focus groups some of the major reasons for people visiting urban green spaces relates to what might be described as their 'psychological' benefits. These were consistently mentioned across all types of group. People spoke of the value of these places as somewhere to "get away from it all", "be quiet", "unwind" and "relax". An elderly person in **Bexley** reminded everyone that *"it's the convenience and they are free of pollution and houses and they are free to get into"*. Individually people also spoke of going to parks or other spaces to remember someone who is now dead, to cry after a family argument, and to relieve boredom. Elderly people and those from ethnic backgrounds spoke of the importance of views from green spaces while those with disabilities spoke both of the benefits of sounds such as birds singing and children playing to those who are visually impaired, and of the role that such spaces play in 'teaching independence'.

5.13 The groups also clearly indicated that green spaces are valued as peaceful areas where it is possible to escape from the surrounding buildings of the town or city, as well as from traffic fumes and smells, from the television, the telephone, and other people, (especially parents and siblings) and so to seek calm, tranquillity and relaxation and to reduce stress by allowing people to unwind. Despite being able to list these psychological benefits, only passing reference was made in the groups to the effects that these stress relieving properties of green space might have on health, and then only by disabled people, the elderly and people from ethnic backgrounds.

5.14 There is however a wealth of literature about the health benefits of contact with nature, of proximity to or views of greenery and of the presence of trees and woodlands. Much of this research supports the view that the presence and use of green space can have marked benefits for the health of urban dwellers. This observation is by no means new and in 1995 the *'Park Life'* report included a lengthy review of the links between urban parks and health, noting the convergence between leisure, health and urban policy. More recently a study in the Netherlands[2], exploring the relationship between health and green space in the living environment, concluded that people in a greener environment report fewer health complaints and have a better perceived general health and mental health. It is quite clear that investment in accessible high quality green space could have significant benefits in reducing health care costs, a link which has already been made by several local authorities who have set out to become actively involved in promoting the health benefits of parks, play areas and green spaces.

2   'Nature and health: an exploratory investigation of the relationship between health and green space in the living environment' ('Natuur en gezondheid een verkennend onderzoek naar de relatie tussen volksgezondheid en groen in de leefomgeving'). DeVries S., Verheij, R. A. and Groenewegen, P. P. Mens en maatschappij, **75**(4): 320-339, (2000).

5.15 The provision of clean, expansive outdoor space to promote the health and well-being of urban populations was, of course, the main reason for the original development of urban parks in Britain. Parks still have a large, and to some extent unexploited, role in encouraging physical exercise, beyond the obvious use of weekend pitch sports. The use of linear parks and greenways for cycling, running and walking is well established, as is the use of parks for personal exercise, whether this be through facilties such as outdoor trim trails, or simple jogging or walking. There is now great interest in linking urban green spaces to provide pedestrian and cycle routes between residential areas and community facilities such as shops and schools. In particular, many authorities are highlighting 'safe routes to school' that enable children to make off-road journeys between home and school.

5.16 Urban parks and other green spaces are being used by some towns and cities to promote healthy living. This may, for example, be tied to encouraging more healthy lifestyles through growing local food in community green spaces or allotments. Health walks in parks, either self-guided or lead by rangers or other officers, are increasing in popularity. In some places these are voluntary, but in others 'health walks on prescription' can be provided by GPs.

EDUCATIONAL BENEFITS

5.17 The educational role of urban green spaces should not be understated. School grounds can be used to support many aspects of the National Curriculum beyond the obvious areas related to nature studies. It still remains the case that in this respect the majority of school grounds in England are woefully inadequate. The work of Learning Through Landscapes and similar organisations can be inspirational in showing what can be achieved in educational, environmental and social terms through exploitation of the school grounds resource.

5.18 Educational opportunities abound in urban parks and green spaces. In more formal terms, urban nature parks have wide-ranging educational programmes attached to them and can be heavily used by educational groups throughout the week. Environmental education activities are often run by parks rangers in parks across a town or city. WATCH groups (children's environmental clubs affiliated to Wildlife Trusts) can be based around urban parks. For example, **Iris Brickfield, Newcastle**, which is managed by the urban ranger service, has its own WATCH group that has been instrumental in planning and implementing this relatively new inner city park.

5.19 Sites such as 'nature parks' or urban nature reserves, as well as many other urban green spaces are used frequently by school groups and others because of their high educational benefit. Inner city nature parks, particularly if they contain open recreational space, can provide a richness of experience often lacking in traditionally managed parks. A good example of such a site is **Benwell Nature Park in Newcastle (Case Study 5.1)**, that because of a permanent park ranger presence and a varied educational, arts and events programme is very popular with local children.

5.20 Since its formation, Benwell Nature Park has relied upon volunteers who provide most of the physical labour, volunteers have been at the heart of the park's success. Many local people have been involved in the development, and this involvement contributes towards the feeling of ownership in the area. The park serves the local community by providing:

- an area for informal recreation;

- a supervised area for children to play;

- an educational resource for the region – many visits are from outside the City;

- employment on a voluntary basis for local unemployed – learning new skills;

- conservation tasks for a Probation Service Team;

- a focus for a local recycling scheme;

- a resource for the community – minibus hire, tool lending and practical advice;

- a wildlife reserve;

- a venue for adult further education courses;

- organised community events;

- a community building to be used for events and meetings.

Many of these functions are of particular relevance in an area of high unemployment. The park's role in providing structured, easily accessible activities to children outside school hours also fulfils a real need. In an area with lower than average access to car travel, the Nature Park provides 'countryside' activities on people's doorstep.

5.21 Educational opportunities are also available formally for adults through training schemes attached to urban green space – such schemes are a common part of many current urban regeneration initiatives. Parks friends groups and urban parks rangers may host events and workshops that range from maintenance and horticultural skills to art activities and lecture series based around green space issues.

Case Study 5.1: Community Nature Park: Benwell Nature Park, Newcastle

Benwell Nature Park was built in 1982. Its role has grown to provide a facility of regional importance whilst maintaining its essentially local character. The park provides a community countryside facility in inner city Newcastle. The site is 1.7ha and is situated in Benwell, in the West End of Newcastle upon Tyne and is staffed by rangers. The park is open 365 days of the year and is one the best examples of a community-led urban countryside site in the country. The project is funded by Newcastle City Council with assistance from City Challenge, Single Regeneration Budget (SRB) and industrial partners. The park hosts a wide range of activities providing a year round calendar of events from school education visits to play schemes and from volunteer tasks to large public events attracting hundreds of visitors. Events are organised in response to local community need/demand so giving them relevance and greater popularity.

The Nature Park was created on a site of terraced housing that was cleared in the 1970's. Building work started in Spring 1982 by local people. The site was fenced and planted and different habitat

areas were created representing those seen locally in the region: these would later form the basis for the environmental education programme. Most of the features have been created by the Nature Park staff and volunteers, with help from local people and school groups. There has also been assistance from bodies such as the Probation Service and British Trust for Conservation Volunteers (BTCV).

During its early days it provided the local population, and a wider national audience, with a pioneering project. National companies and organisations such as Vickers, British Airways, The Tree Council, Trustee Savings Bank, N.E.I. Parsons and the National Trust all lent their support. These organisations, and a host of new companies such as Mark's and Spencer and Northern Electric have a continuing involvement with the park. It is these partnerships with industry that have been a vital part of the project's success.

As well as involving local people the park also maintains important links with other community organisations in the West End of Newcastle. These include: the City Council's Children and Young People's Section, The Riverside Health Project, Neighbourhood Housing Associations, Resident's Associations, Scouts and Guides. It provides training and other activities for Community Environmental Education Developments (CEED), the University Green Society, work experience placements, Community Service Volunteers (CSV), the School Attendance Projects, local children's clubs and the Probation Service.

Environmental benefits

5.22   Most people who live in a town or city intuitively understand the important contribution that green spaces make to their urban environment. In the focus groups some people alluded to the importance of parks and green spaces in a sustainable urban future by speaking of their importance for "the city and every generation" and of their role as landmarks within the urban fabric. It is, however, much harder to articulate the detailed nature of this contribution and harder still to marshal the evidence to support the arguments. Environmental benefits fall into four broad categories, namely biodiversity, landscape and cultural heritage, the physical environment and sustainable practices.

BENEFITS TO BIODIVERSITY

5.23   Urban areas have a distinctive range of wildlife and habitats that can be as important for biodiversity as those in rural areas. They occur in many types of urban green space, particularly the semi-natural areas and areas of what are often referred to as 'encapsulated countryside', but also in areas that are heavily influenced by people, such as parks and gardens. The level of importance of these areas for wildlife depends upon the way in which they are managed and the growing number of urban wildlife groups devoted to promoting urban wildlife and nature conservation management has led to increasing use of techniques designed to encourage ecological diversification.

5.24   It is also increasingly recognised that spontaneous urban vegetation, which colonises disturbed ground and is often characteristic of so-called 'brownfield sites' in urban areas, may often have greater species diversity than the majority of rural habitats. It may also be composed of particularly distinctive mixes of native species and introduced species that have 'escaped' from parks and gardens. The integration of these sites with other urban habitats, including more formal parks and green spaces, to form urban green space networks connected by linear green ways and corridors, now lies at the heart of much current thinking on urban nature conservation. This emphasises the importance of viewing green spaces as a whole.

5.25   Many of these urban habitats have recognised nature conservation value. Some are recognised as being of national importance by notification as Sites of Special Scientific Interest while others have been identified as locally important Sites of Importance for Nature Conservation, or similar. Stockport MBC, for example, notes in its strategy that it has 56 sites of biological importance in the Borough, covering an area of some 600 hectares. The importance of sensitive and intelligent stewardship of these sites is stressed and identified priorities for action include development of a nature conservation strategy, phased implementation of woodland management plans, work towards designation of some areas as Local Nature Reserves, and collection of appropriate ecological data from designated sites. Other authorities, such as Ipswich to name but one, can similarly demonstrate the nature conservation value of their green spaces.

5.26   Many local authorities have recognised the importance of urban green spaces for biodiversity and built this into their strategies and management plans. **Oldham**, for example refers specifically to the 21 steps to a more sustainable future set out in its Agenda 21 Plan, noting that better green space can make a significant contribution to at least 16 of these, and in particular to:

- biodiversity – improving the range and quantity of wild plants and animals;

- wildlife habitats – finding places where plants and animals can live alongside the rest of us.

5.27 Nature is not, of course, valued only for itself but also for the effects it has on people. In many of the focus group discussions, right across the spectrum of different types of under-represented users, people spoke of the opportunities that their local green spaces offered for contact with nature. An elderly person in **Ipswich** summed this up, saying *"there is something about trees and birds and animals…… it's about peace of mind"*. Several people also mentioned the special problems for people who do not have a garden and therefore do not have any other opportunities for contact of this type. One or two groups made more specific mention of the value of experiencing wildlife, nature, the changing scenery, flowers and indeed the environment in general.

5.28 While many urban green spaces can be enhanced to improve their wildlife value by habitat creation techniques and relaxed maintenance regimes, most of the larger metropolitan areas also have 'nature parks' or urban nature reserves managed specifically for their nature conservation value.

BENEFITS FOR LANDSCAPE AND CULTURAL HERITAGE

5.29 Urban green spaces provide the green fabric of the urban landscape, complementing the built environment that often dominates the scene. Both parts of the urban landscape have value in their own right, but it is often when high-quality buildings and green spaces occur together that special 'gems' of townscape are created. Urban conservation areas are often notable for this particular mix of historic buildings in a setting of green space. Many urban green spaces have considerable intrinsic landscape value. Some are important examples of designed landscape and have historic and cultural value as examples of the work of particular designers, or may represent a particular period of design history. Others may be valued simply because of the character and quality of the landscape itself and because of the enjoyment that they give to people, whether they are landscapes designed for amenity, or the by product of a functional green space.

5.30 Many parks and gardens are included on the English Heritage Register of Parks and Gardens of Historic Interest because of their historical and cultural value. They may also include individual features or buildings that may be of particular value even though the site as a whole is not recognised as having outstanding value. There may be important archaeological remains and important plant collections, each of which can in itself bestow additional value on an individual green space.

THE PHYSICAL ENVIRONMENT

5.31 The vegetation, and particularly the trees that occur in urban green spaces play an important part in reducing air pollution by intercepting particulate matter and absorbing gaseous pollutants and heavy metals. The most effective control is achieved when trees are planted close to sources of pollution and form a buffer around them. There is evidence to suggest that nature like plantings and naturally occurring urban woodlands may be the most effective filters, because of their multi-layered vegetation structures. Some of the focus groups showed awareness of these benefits of green spaces, referring to their part in combating pollution and providing oxygen and clean air. These references came particularly from ethnic minority groups and were related to reminiscence about the environment of the 'home country'.

5.32   The concentration of buildings and paved surfaces in urban areas creates a specific urban climate with higher temperatures, particularly at night, plus restriction of wind, in turn restricting the dispersal of pollutants, and causing increased run-off of rainfall. The increased temperatures lead to the so-called 'heat island effect'. The oceanic climate of the UK means that the heat island effects are not as severe here as in the continental areas of the United States and Europe, but this could alter with future climate change. Urban green space is therefore very important because of its effects in ameliorating these climatic effects. It can create local microclimates that are more comfortable for people and it can help to reduce temperatures and promote airflow and movement. Cooling results from shade effects and from the extra humidity produced by vegetation, which together produce a more comfortable environment. These effects have led to use of the phrase 'park cool island' to contrast with the 'urban heat island'.

5.16   Urban green spaces can be very important elements of sustainable urban drainage systems. Ponds and water bodies can be used for water storage and for biological filtration of run-off from surrounding roads and hard surfaces. Dry ponds and grassed areas can receive water in exceptionally wet periods and during times of flood. These roles are becoming increasingly important as flooding emerges as a growing problem for society and as greater emphasis is placed on sustainable urban drainage systems as an alternative or a complement to expensive drainage infrastructure. Using urban green spaces to manage water is one of the most straight-forward means to increase the environmental performance of urban areas.

5.33   Examples are springing up of multi-functional green spaces where run-off from roofs and surfaces is fed through wetlands and waterbodies that have a purification function, but are also valuable to wildlife and are aesthetically pleasing. Such a water management is at the heart of **Scotswood Community Garden (Case Study 8.5)**. The benefit of using urban parks for this purpose is that long-term maintenance of the drainage features can be secured. One of the main elements of Sheffield's new district park, **Deep Pits** (part of Sheffield's Green Estate Programme, **Case Study 9.5**) and a national demonstration site for the Urban Green Spaces Taskforce) is a sustainable urban drainage scheme that takes water runoff from an adjacent new housing area.

5.34   Urban vegetation, and particularly trees, also potentially act as sinks for carbon dioxide, which is, of course, a major contributor to the greenhouse effect and global warming. Much has been written about the potential of trees to counteract the rise in emissions of greenhouse gases. In general terms this represents only a temporary 'carbon neutral', steady state solution as when the wood is burnt or rots down the carbon dioxide will be returned to the atmosphere. Large areas are also necessary to achieve any effect – in the UK a hectare of new planting each year may only counteract the annual carbon emissions of a few cars. In the light of this, large existing blocks of multi-aged urban woodland can be best thought of as long-term CO_2 stores. New woodland may be best thought of as offering benefits in carbon displacement rather than carbon sequestration, if the products are used to displace fossil fuels, for example by growing bio-fuel coppice crops. Urban woodland planting, however, has relatively low potential in this regard compared to large scale planting on surplus arable land.

SUSTAINABLE PRACTICES

5.35 The criteria for judging good practice in managing parks and green spaces place growing emphasis on sustainable management practices. For example the criteria listed in 'Raising the Standard – the Green Flag Awards'[3] lists the following important considerations:

- environmental policy in place, in use and regularly reviewed;

- pesticide use minimised;

- horticultural peat eliminated;

- waste plant material recycled;

- high horticultural and arboricultural standards;

- measures to reduce energy consumption, pollution, resource use and waste.

5.36 There is no consistent evidence about the extent to which local authorities are adopting such practices in managing their urban green spaces. It is, however, clear from some of the Case Study authorities that they do recognise the potential for these spaces to bring benefits for sustainability. Oldham MBC, for example, lists several ways in which better green space can contribute to its Agenda 21 plan, including: reducing car use by encouraging walking and cycling, reducing energy demand through measures such as encouraging alternative building technologies and biomass planting, recycling by the composting of green and woody waste, increased self-sufficiency through the use of gardens and allotments, and demonstration of better use of resources.

5.37 Similarly the primary focus of **Cheltenham's** 'Green Care Strategy' is *"to provide a sustainable framework for the balanced provision, use and management of the publicly controlled and accessible green environment"* and the policies indicate an intention that the emphasis of horticultural and landscape management will shift towards environmentally and economically sustainable systems. The recent review of the strategy indicates the progress that the Council has made, and its future intentions, in areas such as the recycling of organic waste, review of environmentally acceptable weed control practices, reduction in the use of peat, use of waste materials as growing mediums, horticultural management policy and training in new ways of working with sustainable development policies. The review indicates the problems as well as the opportunities in a number of these areas. Overall **Cheltenham** views the whole of its Green Care Strategy within the context of sustainability and as contributing to the Council's Local Agenda 21 and Environment Management Programmes.

3 *Raising the Standard – the Green Flag Awards Guidance Manual.* Greenhalgh and Newton. ILAM, (1999).

Economic benefits

5.38   Overall the economic benefits of urban green spaces were somewhat neglected in focus group discussions of the benefits that they might bring to urban areas. Only one group of young people, in Sheffield, mentioned the possible benefits of green spaces in attracting businesses to the city and two groups mentioned the role they might play in attracting visitors and tourists. In general there has also been less research into the economic benefits of urban green spaces compared with the perhaps more obvious environmental and social benefits. This is despite the well recognised fact that large public parks such as Birkenhead Park on Merseyside and Central Park in New York were designed in the 19th century with the intention of increasing the attractiveness of the areas and enhancing surrounding land values.

5.39   The research that has been carried out recognises on-site economic benefits, such as the direct employment that parks, play areas and other green spaces can provide for local people and the opportunities for commercial operations such as community orchards and city farms, which generate revenue through the sale of produce to local people and visitors. It also identifies a range of less tangible off-site or indirect benefits including effects on nearby property prices, contributions to attracting and retaining businesses in an area and an important role in attracting tourists to urban areas. There have, however, been few detailed studies in England of these wider economic benefits of green space and this is an area where additional research would be valuable in informing understanding of the role that green space plays in sustaining vibrant urban economies.

Quality of life capital

5.40   It is extremely important that the multiple benefits of urban green spaces are constantly repeated and consistently stated, so that political arguments for retaining and increasing resources are well supported. A number of our case study local authorities use these arguments in their strategies and other policy documents but there is a need for more consistent presentation of the benefits, both in general and as they relate to individual areas and individual sites. All of these benefits of urban green spaces are essentially about the quality of life in urban areas. There may therefore be merit in local authorities adopting the Quality of Life Capital approach that has been developed recently by the four environmental agencies (Countryside Agency, Environment Agency, English Heritage And English Nature) for other purposes, as a broad framework both for assessing and reporting on the benefits of urban green spaces. This approach could be applied to the whole resource of green spaces in a local authority area, as well as to individual sites and indeed to individual features within sites.

5.41   The Quality of Life Capital approach[4] offers an integrated and systematic way of recording what aspects of quality of life matter to people and why. The key concern is for the benefits or 'services' that areas or features of the environment provide, rather than with the individual features themselves. This approach is designed to aid understanding of why people value the environment, allowing stakeholder values to be set alongside professional concerns. Such services or benefits are normally grouped under the following headings:

- **Health/survival:** such as absorbing greenhouse gases, reducing pollution or controlling soil erosion;

- **Biodiversity:** by providing habitats for or supporting populations of rare species;

- **Appreciation of the environment:** including for example birdsong or habitat for urban wildlife;

- **Sense of place:** aspects that gives an area its particular character including perceptual qualities such as isolation, remoteness or wildness;

- **Historical character:** including archaeology, built heritage and associations with well-known people or events;

- **Education:** use for both formal teaching and informal study;

- **Recreation:** use for sports and for informal leisure;

- **Value to the local economy:** including revenue from tourism and direct or indirect employment from use or management of resources.

5.42   Although the framework and these headings may not be transferable to urban green spaces in precisely their current form, it might usefully be adapted as a practical tool for assessing and presenting the wide range of benefits of these areas. For example, an amended list of benefits could be generated that is specifically relevant to urban spaces, although it would probably have much in common with the list above. This is certainly an area that merits further consideration and practical guidance could be issued to local authorities on the approach that might be taken.

5.43   Not every green space will provide all of these benefits. However, a key feature of successful green spaces is their capacity to be multi-functional, catering for a wide range of users and uses and providing multiple benefits to urban communities. Realising the multifunctional aims of green space and showing the multiple benefits it can bring should certainly be the aim everywhere. **Heeley City Farm (Case Study 5.2)** illustrates how one individual green space can bring a surprisingly wide range of benefits. This site and the adjacent **Heeley Millennium Park** in Sheffield **(Case Study 9. 4)** have been created over the past 15 years with a high degree of local input and have transformed a featureless 'Green Desert' into a thriving local resource. The two sites together address all the benefits discussed in this chapter and listed in Paragraph 5.41 under the 'Quality of Life Capital' approach.

4   *Quality of Life Capital: Managing Environmental, Social and Economic Benefits. Overview Report.* CAG Consultants and Land Use Consultants for Countryside Agency, English Heritage, English Nature, Environment Agency (2001).

Case Study 5.2 Heeley City Farm and Heeley Millennium Park

Heeley City Farm was established in the mid 1980s with the following aim: *'Heeley City Farm identifies, confronts and addresses the problems of poverty, inequality and lack of opportunity in our inner city community by supporting and promoting community regeneration and self-help within environmentally friendly and self-sustaining systems, using the background of a mini-farm, community gardens and related resources'.*

The site was developed on a brick rubble covered site that had been cleared following housing demolition. Now the site comprises two hectares of open space in an area of mainly terraced housing and light industry, around one mile from Sheffield City Centre. Facilities include a training and education centre, garden centre and plant nursery, community café, vegetable and herb gardens, demonstration gardens, a children's play area and recycling and composting facilities, and animal grazing fields. The site is visited by around 100 000 people per year. There is free entry and the site is open all year. Funding comes from a variety of sources: regeneration monies, further education funding, Sheffield City Council and earned income from the farm's community enterprises.

The benefits of the site can be categorized as:

Environmental quality: Provision of green space as a contrast to the surrounding dense urban environment;

Education and training: The farm provides training schemes for long-term unemployed adults and young people, leading to vocational qualifications in horticulture and animal husbandry. Over 50 schools or 3000 children visit and use the farm each year. Every year around 50 people attend adult education classes in areas such as back yard gardening, fruit growing, composting and alternative technology. A work experience, training and day care programme for people with a range of special needs is provided. Up to 16 people per week participate at any one time. Most of those involved have learning difficulties, but some have additional disabilities including physical disabilities, deafness and mental health problems. Up to 30 young people come on the farm on any one day for a variety of reasons. Most have left school or are unemployed, or are on work experience from Sheffield schools;

Children and Play – fun and enjoyment: The farm organises a four week summer play scheme with around 50 children attending. Up to 60 children go to the farm at weekends or during the holidays and help out in the daily practical work of the farm. This provides valuable out of school activities for local children;

Community enterprise and job creation: In addition to the employees of the farm (15 to 20 people) the farm has established two community enterprises: a community café and garden centre;

Local sustainability: The farm is the centre for local community recycling and composting schemes.

The partnerships centred around the farm have given rise to other local initiatives, one of which is the adjacent **Heeley Millennium Park (Case Study 9.4)** The Millenium Park provides expansive good quality open recreational space and has been developed to particularly cater for the needs of local children and young people. The site has developed even promoted a stronger sense of place, with a large white horse cut into one of the visible slopes of the park creating a new and well known local landmark. One aspect of the planting of the park has been the setting aside of new woodland and meadow areas, thereby promoting local biodiversity. The site hosts the annual Heeley Festival – a music and events festival that draws people from across the city.

CHAPTER 6
Structures and Mechanisms

SUMMARY OF KEY POINTS

- Demonstrating how parks and other green spaces meet wider council policy objectives linked to education, diversity, health, safety, environment, jobs and regeneration can raise the political profile commitment of an authority to green space issues.

- There is some evidence that urban green space service delivery from within a local authority's Environmental Directorate rather than a Leisure and Education Directorate may have benefit in terms of budget protection and policy implementation and a holistic approach to urban green space.

- Fragmentation of responsibility for, and ownership of, urban green spaces across different departments or directorates within a local authority is a barrier to efficiency and innovation, but also to community involvement. Unified divisional structures, bringing all aspects of green space service delivery together, as well as clear "one-stop-shops" for public contact all appear effective approaches to overcoming the problems.

- Greater emphasis on community involvement and support requires a change in the skills base and the structures of parks and open spaces services.

- A community development approach is greatly aided by a departmental structure that is based upon geographical area, and is tied into other area-based service boundaries, as well as the hierarchy of area based community consultation.

- Re-instating site-based gardeners /wardens /park keepers is very well received by site users.

- Breaking down demarcated site based roles (rangers, gardeners, security staff inspections, cleansing) can promote ownership and initiative by site-based personnel and produce savings sufficient to introduce static personnel.

- Enabling a ranger service to be responsible for all aspects of the management of a mainstream urban park, with their people orientated skills, can bring in low cost, low maintenance non-urban or "countryside" management techniques into a mainstream urban inner city park, with full public acceptance.

- Producing green space audits that incorporate qualitative as well as quantitative information, formulating green space categorisation systems and typologies that drive policy; and producing holistic green space strategies and green structure plans that consider parks as just one element in a larger environmental network are examples of emerging strategic developments related to urban green space.

- Developing local standards for provision enables provision of all types of green space to be matched to local social, economic and environmental need.

Introduction

6.1   It is clear that a diversification of urban green spaces, in terms of their form, content, range of users, as well as who is involved in their management and who owns them, is taking place and that the main examples of innovation and creativity are associated with this diversification. Local authority parks and open spaces services can drive these changes, in partnership with local communities and others, or they can react to them. This chapter considers how local authorities can organise their services and operations relating to urban green space to meet these challenges.

Institutional frameworks

6.2   It was noted in *People, Parks and Cities* (1996) that the most important aspect of local authority parks service provision is not so much the institutional structure of the authority and the place of a parks service within it, but more that parks provision is close to the core concerns of the authority. One of the questions in the current detailed survey of fifteen local authorities asked the chief officers of parks and open spaces services whether they thought that urban parks and green space were a high political priority within the council. Nine authorities answered positively to the question. Four stated that the council did not match verbal and written commitment in strategy documents with appropriate budgets, while two felt a lack of commitment. It was perhaps no coincidence that these last two authorities both had long-term declining budgets, and also that no case studies of creativity or innovation are included in this report from those authorities. Perhaps the most noteworthy finding here is that of the nine parks services that were positive about the commitment of the council, over half felt that this was a result of their strong lobbying and promotion of the importance of urban green space to the core concerns of the council. As one officer stated *"Members vaguely understand the importance (of urban parks) but the real importance has not been articulated to them. Members can see recreational value but not the value in terms of regeneration, social cohesion and economic benefits"*. Another authority made a similar point saying *"Parks have to demonstrate their links with high priority service areas"*.

LOCATION WITHIN AN AUTHORITY MANAGEMENT STRUCTURE

6.3   **Table 6.1** shows the location of parks services within the fifteen authorities. There is a wide range of terminology used in the naming of parks services (some perhaps more user-friendly than others). There is a roughly equal split between those that fall within a Leisure Services Directorate (or community services) and an Environment Directorate, with two falling within a Development and Transport Directorate. In **Sheffield**, responsibility fell within a combined leisure and environment directorate, although parks, woodlands and countryside had recently moved from the leisure section to the environment section within this directorate.

6.4   There was no overall relationship detected between the location of a parks service and budgetary factors such as spend per head or whether budgets had declined, remained static or risen over the past decade. However, two departments had switched from leisure departments to environmental departments within the previous three years in reorganisations (none had moved in the other direction). In both cases this move produced significant changes. In the case of **Bexley**, the aligning of the parks policy, cemetery services and grounds maintenance functions alongside Local Agenda 21 resulted in a holistic approach to strategic green space issues, as evidenced in the Borough's Parks Strategy. In the case of **Sheffield**, a move from the leisure service to environment within the overall Directorate of Development, Environment and Leisure was planned on the basis that the transfer would relieve a long-term squeeze on budgets. As discussed in **Chapter 8**, parks spending in the City had suffered continual pressure because of protected budgets in other areas of leisure spending.

Table 6.1: The naming and location of parks services within the fifteen local authorities		
Authority	**Department**	**Directorate**
Basingstoke	Parks and Open Spaces	Community Services
Bexley	Parks Strategy and Local Agenda 21	Environment
Chelmsford	Leisure Services (no separate parks service)	Leisure Services
Cheltenham	Parks and Landscapes	Community services (Leisure)
Doncaster	Open Spaces Services (part of Infrastructure Services)	Development and Transport
Ipswich	Parks and Landscape Services	Environment
Leicester	Parks and Grounds Maintenance Services	Arts and Leisure
Lewisham	Parks and Community Services	Environment
Milton Keynes	Landscape and Countryside	Environment
Newcastle	Parks and Open Spaces	Cityworks (Leisure)
Oldham	Parks and Open Spaces	Leisure
Plymouth	Parks Services	Street Services
Sheffield	Parks, Woodland and Countryside	Development, Environment and Leisure
Stockport	Parks and Recreation	Community Services (contains leisure)
Wolverhampton	Parks and Open Spaces	Leisure

STRUCTURE OF PARKS AND OPEN SPACES DEPARTMENTS

6.5   One of the major structural changes that has occurred in the structure of parks and open spaces departments over the last few years is the end of the Compulsory Competitive Tendering (CCT) system. Under this regime "client" functions of management, policy and strategy were separated from "contractor" or "operational" functions of grounds maintenance and service delivery. Not only did this result in a conceptual separation of parks functions, but in most instances the client and contractor roles were physically separated in different divisions or directorates of the local authority.

6.6 Some authorities, but by no means all, have sought to reverse this division as a matter of priority. Of the fifteen authorities in the main survey, five had merged the client and contractor roles within a parks and open spaces department. This was seen as highly beneficial in all five authorities. The advantages were summed up by **Plymouth** as *"smoother operations, quicker reaction times, improved performance, higher morale amongst employees, more stability, better communication and understanding of other roles, sharing of experiences and ideas, no more personality clashes"*. Similarly **Bexley** felt that merger has *"established a holistic approach to the management of public open space by combining policy development and strategic management with day to day management, operation and service delivery"*. Merger had not occurred in the remaining ten authorities, although in five the contractor role sat within the same division or directorate as parks and open spaces and there was said to be good communication between the two. However, in five authorities the CCT structure remained (mainly where the "client" role was based in a leisure services directorate, and the operational functions were sited in a different directorate).

BREAKING DOWN BARRIERS

6.7 A small number of authorities had taken the process further by not only breaking down the barriers between policy and operations, but also moving to combine responsibility for all aspects of urban green spaces within the same department. Fragmentation of ownership of different areas of green space, either across an authority but often with a single site, accompanied by fragmentation of responsibility for green space issues was seen as a major barrier to efficiency but also contributed significantly to public dissatisfaction.

6.8 A not untypical example indicates the problem. At one case study site, a meeting with the local authority ranger responsible for the park, a local authority parks officer and a member of the park's user group identified fragmentation of responsibility for the park as one of the biggest problems in achieving change. One section of the council was responsible for repairs to infrastructure such as paths and fencing; another for buildings and facilities, another for grass cutting and maintenance, another for litter collection and another for environmental health issues. The local authority personnel were frustrated at the complexity, while the park user said that local residents had given up trying to get anything done. This fragmentation went to the heart of the council's structure, with parks functions spread across three directorates: the "client" function rested in Arts and Leisure; Environment and Development were responsible for linear parks and riverside sites as well as biodiversity, planning and sustainability issues, while Commercial Services held the traditional grounds maintenance responsibility.

6.9 An example of a different approach was found at **Oldham** where restructuring had aimed where possible to bring all those responsible for green space management into the same department. The restructuring was partly influenced by local politics and a change of governing party, but had mainly come about because of a *"grassroots initiative"* from local authority officers from different departments who made a strong collective case for a unified approach. A distinctive feature of Oldham's Parks and Open Spaces section is that landscape architects have been incorporated into the service at managerial level and bring an added dimension so often missing from parks departments – design awareness, strategic planning and critical review of landscape management practices (**Case Study 6.1**). As a result, the relationship with planning has shifted, with the parks service driving green space planning in the borough. Similarly, **Stockport's** Parks and Recreation Services comprises

Service Development (policy and strategy), Arboriculture and Horticulture (grounds maintenance), Landscape and Development (parks, biodiversity and conservation) and Estates Management (infrastructure, rangers, allotments, cemeteries). **Newcastle's** Enviro-call has also, in a quite different way, effectively tackled the problem of providing a single point of contact for all aspects of urban parks and green spaces (**Case Study 6.2**).

Case Study 6.1: Central role of landscape architects in green space planning, Oldham

Oldham's landscape architects were formerly based in the planning department. At this time landscape architects were brought in by parks to design specific schemes, but this was very much a client and designer role. Otherwise the landscape architects were mainly involved in urban programme-type schemes – land reclamation, road enhancement schemes, community gardens. According to the senior landscape architect *"there was too much going on outside parks – there was more interesting planting on the roundabouts than in the parks"*.

The parks service realised that they needed to get landscape architects involved in the parks refurbishment programme (**Case Study 7.6**) in order to get high quality coordinated schemes. They therefore developed a working relationship with the landscape architects despite being in separate departments. This in turn resulted in the landscape architects moving to the parks and open spaces section.

The role of landscape architects is now far more than just scheme design – they are directly involved in discussion about how parks and landscapes should be managed and the strategic planning of open spaces. In planning terms, Oldham's UDP only looks at criteria for the provision of open space and has a solely quantitative outlook. Having landscape architects involved in green space planning is enabling, for the first time, a strategic view to be taken of all land being managed by the council, and how these form a network. This network or "green estate" is being considered as if it were a single park (**Case Study 6.10**). The position of landscape architects at the interface of management and design means that a more holistic view of the functioning of green spaces can be taken. For example, *"a review of grass cutting is now about much more than which machines to buy"*.

Case Study 6.2: One Stop Shop for parks, green space and environmental matters: Enviro-call, Newcastle

Enviro-call was set up in 1999 as a one-stop shop for all environmental issues. 20 operatives take 300,000 calls a year. The system is linked to a GIS system that can identify the relevant area through post code. The information is downloaded to the appropriate council department to be dealt with and tasks are relayed to the nearest operational depot, to be dealt with within 24 hours.

INNOVATION IN INSTITUTIONAL FRAMEWORKS AND SERVICE DELIVERY

6.10 While the statement at the start of this chapter indicated that it was the overall attitude of the council that had greatest influence on parks service delivery rather than the institutional structure, in a number of instances the structure of a parks service did appear to be in itself an influential factor. The majority of parks and open space departments where "merger" had occurred retained a traditional policy and operations split, with area-based operational staff, and officers taking responsibility for specialist areas, whether this be arboriculture, play, community issues, contract management, allotments and so on. This is an efficient, logical and well-tried arrangement. Some of the authorities had tried alternative managerial and departmental structures. These included contracting out the parks service; linking with Local Agenda 21 and environmental policy; adopting a community development focus; and moving to an area-based management structure.

Contracting out the parks service

6.11 The most radical departure from the norm, in terms of the relationship of a parks service with the local authority (although not necessarily in terms of the officer structure of the service), occurred in **Lewisham** where a private finance initiative arrangement had resulted in a large part of the parks service being transferred to a private contractor. This involved not only grounds maintenance functions but also managerial roles. The council itself retained a policy, strategy, and contract and quality-monitoring role. The initiative is discussed in detail in **Chapter 8 (Case Study 8.1)** and appears, in its early stages, to be highly successful.

Local Agenda 21 and Environmental Policy

6.12 **Table 6.1** lists the main strategic groupings within which parks services sit. There has already been a hint that sitting within a leisure directorate may, depending on the political prioritizing of parks within the council, result in budgetary squeeze from high priority areas such as education, libraries, arts and sport. One way in which parks had received greater recognition was in the small number of authorities where Local Agenda 21 and environmental policies were well developed and the parks service sat within an Environment Directorate. In these instances, urban parks and green spaces were seen as one of the main avenues for delivering environmental policy. The prime example of this was in **Bexley** where parks policy and Local Agenda 21 were brought together in a Parks Strategy and LA21 department. Landscape design, arboriculture and grounds maintenance and the operations teams were held in separate departments within the same directorate. The inclusive development of Local Agenda 21 within the parks section has resulted in a progressive parks and community engagement strategy. The department has responsibility for the development of biodiversity action plans: these are seen as key operational and policy documents with a direct link to the management and development of parks and other green spaces. Responsibility for events, sports and recreational activities in parks was retained in the Leisure Department.

6.13 In *People, Parks and Cities* (1996) the question was asked: Is Local Agenda 21 the key to a revitalization of the role of parks in urban areas? **Bexley** was the only authority that made such an explicit link (and this partly stemmed from the influence of this publication), although in **Lewisham** the Environmental Sustainability section is within the same division. While all authorities had some form of Local Agenda 21 Strategy, Local Agenda 21 (LA21) as a concept received very little mention in the interviews for this study with local authority parks and open spaces officers, apart from where the link of parks with environment was close. While the term LA21 has perhaps not caught on, one of its main characteristics, community engagement, had become a central way of working for some parks services.

Community Development

6.14   The change of focus of some parks services into a community engagement role is discussed in full in **Chapter 7**. A small number of authorities in the survey had transformed their operations to become community focused. **Leicester**, for example, had *"moved from a policy role to a community role"*; in **Newcastle**, the parks and countryside service aims to *"engage the public, find out what they want and channel this information to the grounds maintenance service"*; in **Stockport** the emphasis had changed to *"supporting and developing community groups as opposed to direct delivery. It is now more reflective of what the community wants and can turn out projects a lot faster"*. In **Stockport** and **Sheffield** this resulted in community development teams forming a significant component of the parks and open spaces service: the shape and structure of these services was rather different from that of a traditional service. As discussed in **Chapter 7**, and later in this chapter, this can be a challenging transformation because it requires a different skills set within a service than the more common emphasis on horticultural skills. It is also time consuming to involve groups that generally do not participate (for example ethnic minority groups) and a great deal of capacity building can be required in terms of training and development.

Area-based Responsibility

6.15   It was perhaps in **Newcastle** more than anywhere that community engagement had infiltrated the service at all levels. Rather than have a community development team, community engagement was a responsibility for all under the area-based and site specific Recreational Development Officer Structure (**Case Study 7.5**). The structure of Newcastle's countryside and parks service does not resemble that of a standard service. Gone are the specialist roles of officers, to be replaced by area or site based responsibilities, focusing on links with community groups, environmental organizations, sports clubs, schools and childrens and youth groups. The areas of the city that parks officers have responsibility for have been worked out to tie into other related area boundaries: grounds maintenance depot areas; community sub committees; children and young people's section boundaries; planning department areas; Single Regeneration Budget (SRB) and other regeneration areas; housing management areas and Leisure Newcastle areas.

6.16   The structure matches the services' Ward Stewardship Scheme for community consultation (**Case Study 7.1**) and relates to Enviro-call (**Case Study 6.2**) and other IT based methods of customer contact. The structure makes for efficient links with grounds maintenance, and in particular enables direct input from site-based park keepers (**Case Study 6.3**) into the managerial and community consultation structure of the service. As discussed in **Chapter 7**, the infusion of rangers, with their expertise in community engagement, environmental education, and environmental works, into urban park officer roles makes this structure work. A similar, although less developed structure, with some specialist officer roles remaining, had also been established in **Doncaster**.

Action on the ground

6.17 Discussions with parks friends groups and user groups as part of the follow up case studies for this report indicated that re-establishing a visual presence in a park was the main thing that would make an appreciable difference to their perception and use of the site. Research carried out by local authorities with their user groups confirmed this. One of the main casualties of budget decline and the CCT regime had been the removal of "static" gardeners to be replaced by private contractors or roving maintenance gangs. Front-line staff attached to particular sites were thought to be important for several reasons:

- Improvement in maintenance standards as a result of ownership and familiarity with a site, and through being able to work on their own initiative rather than to a contract specification;

- Increase in safety and security;

- A first point of contact for communication of problems or reporting of damage.

6.18 There are three main roles that can provide a direct and regular interface between a parks service and the public: gardeners (park keepers), rangers and security staff. Strict demarcation of duties can result in what seem to be anomalies to the public. In one case study site without a static gardener, it was remarked by a friends group that, even though rangers were based in a building on a site full time, a flower bed just outside the building received no maintenance because it wasn't in the job description of the rangers to undertake gardening tasks.

STATIC GARDENERS AND PARK KEEPERS

6.19 Several of the authorities in the study had re-instated a role for static, site based gardeners. **Wolverhampton** had retained such gardeners through the CCT regime, with the aim of both getting responsibility for maintaining a site to rest with one person and to create a stable work force that the public could associate with. In total 14 posts were created in 8 parks. The authority has two contractors working in parks – the Direct Service Organisation (DSO) and a private contractor – success is not linked to the nature of the contractor but is really down to the individual gardener and whether they see the benefits of working with the public. Some gardeners have developed good relationships with regular park users. The borough wishes to extend this service, but expansion has to be economically viable and at present funding does not allow further site-based gardeners. **Oldham** had a number of dedicated gardeners for some of its parks but found it difficult to recruit new young staff with the appropriate horticultural skills for this to be widely applied. In **Bexley**, a working arrangement with existing grounds maintenance contractors has resulted in a visible and approachable park presence during the undertaking of grounds maintenance, providing added value to maintenance contracts. In terms of innovation and creativity, however, it was again **Newcastle** that had taken a more radical approach and re-thought the role of "park keeper" (**Case Study 6.3**)

1. Formal planting schemes inject colour into urban green spaces.

2. A traditional playground offers limited opportunities for play.

3. Taking children to play in an urban green space is one of the main reasons for visiting them.

4. A more modern design of play area provides opportunities for developing an increased number of skills.

5. Multiple passive activities can take place simultaneously in an urban green space.

6. Good and well-maintained facilities such as cafés are desired by many users and non-users.

7. Events attract thousands of people a year across the country.

8. Schools can make use of urban green spaces for educational and sporting activities.

9. Drama is an increasingly popular activity in many locations.

10. Playing bowls is an important part of the weekly routine for many elderly people.

11. Football is an important part of the weekly routine for many young men yet the cost of maintenance is disproportionate to the level of use while the ecological value of the pitches is low.

12. Some dog walkers use urban open spaces 2, 3 or 4 times a day, yet there are issues of dog mess and uncontrolled dogs which deter others from using these spaces.

13. Children love to play in water.

14. Incidental spaces provide the opportunity for a range of passive activities such as listening to the local band.

15. Feeding birds can be an interest of some groups

Case Study 6.3: A new type of Park Keeper, Newcastle

In 2000 a process of change was initiated to rationalize the roles of park based staff. It had been noted that many different staff could at one time be in a park doing different things, with little cross-over in responsibilities.

A new park keeper role was created with horticultural quality at its core but with a people-centred emphasis (reflecting the whole culture of the service (see **Case Study 7.2**)). Under CCT the council had managed to ensure that gardening staff remained static in key parks. These staff were turned into park keepers, given a uniform and the remit to talk to people. This change in culture was accompanied by all park keeper staff being given the top gardener wage. An attempt was made to give security staff the same uniform and additional tasks such as litter picking and graffiti removal, again to extend the area of responsibility. This was not successful, mainly because it was poorly received by the security staff management. As a result in 2001 the parks service terminated its service level agreement with the security service and used the money saved to employ more park keepers. The person specification for the park keeper was changed so that good security staff could be employed as park keepers. All park keepers are provided with mobile phones and those without a horticultural background receive training at the city's horticultural training centre. For most parks there is now a minimum of two park keepers, with a rota system at weekends, and more hours worked in summer than winter. Currently, therefore, park keepers have the following responsibilities:

- Horticultural maintenance

- Security

- Inspection of play equipment

- Community liaison

- Cleaning of toilets

The next phase is to rationalize roles further and transform other grounds maintenance operatives e.g tree care workers into park keepers. It is planned to create a head park keeper role and also to "*introduce a competitive element*" by having a city park of the year award, using agreed performance indicators.

The overall aim of the initiative is to create a great sense of ownership for staff for the park in which they are based and to encourage as many things to be done on the initiative of staff as possible.

Currently over two thirds of the city's parks have full time permanent park keepers. They are supplemented by gardeners and in some parks by horticultural trainees.

Park keepers attend the regular user groups and friends groups meetings for each park. The feedback from the user groups is that they are delighted with the park keepers, and the feedback from the staff is that they are highly motivated, because of that sense of ownership.

It would appear, from an outside viewpoint, that the final stage of this process would be to merge the client and contractor roles into the same section so that everything is under the direct control of the parks service.

6.20   The key points about the Newcastle example is the link of the site-based park keepers with the pervading community focus of the service at all levels, and the breaking down of demarcated roles to promote ownership and initiative. Barriers were also being broken down in a pioneering pilot in **Stockport** to remove the barriers between gardeners and rangers. In an attempt to provide two static staff per park, a trial has been set up that enables grounds maintenance staff to support rangers. Gardeners, although working fixed hours, have been given the initial remit of interacting with the public and being a point of contact for help, as well as assisting in events if required. Rangers work at weekends and in the evenings when the parks are at their busiest, organize events and interact with the public, but will also carry out small-scale horticultural tasks if necessary.

RANGERS

6.21   Urban parks ranger services are now part of the mainstream activity of many parks and open spaces services. Of the 50 authorities in the profiling survey for this report, 32 had a ranger service that worked in urban parks. As such there is little to report here in terms of innovation. **Table 6.2** shows the range of duties and the size of ranger services across the fifteen surveyed authorities. Two authorities, **Chelmsford** and **Milton Keynes** had no parks ranger service, although for both it was an aspiration prevented by lack of funding. **Oldham** had a countryside ranger service that did not operate in its urban parks. The main role across the board for ranger services was to run events and to interact with the public (in some, but not all cases, this involved setting up and running user groups). Site management (predominantly conservation tasks) and security tasks were common duties.

6.22   Noteworthy aspects of some ranger services merit comment here. In **Newcastle**, the countryside ranger team had been integrated with the parks and open space service. The influx of ranger skills at officer and policy level had a stimulating effect on the service and was one factor in the success of the community orientated approach. Rangers had full responsibility for four of the city's urban parks (**Case Study 6.4**) and it was notable that countryside management practices had been successfully adopted in these mainstream urban sites. In **Sheffield** the urban ranger service was partly funded through a training partnership between the City Council and Sheffield Wildlife Trust. In **Bexley** the ranger service works with the probationary service. 'Volunteers' come in two days a week and carry out environmental improvements, cleaning graffiti and some grounds maintenance tasks. In **Newcastle**, two rangers for Jesmond Dene were funded through the lease of a conference room and café in the park.

Table 6.2: The range of duties and the size of ranger services across the 15 surveyed authorities							
	Number *	Events	Community liaison	Education	Site Management	Gardening tasks	Security	Inspection
Basingstoke	2	•	•	•	•			•
Bexley	8	•	•		•		•	
Chelmsford	0							
Cheltenham	2	•	•				•	•
Doncaster	3	•	•				•	
Ipswich	12	•	•	•	•		•	
Leicester	14	•	•	•	•			
Lewisham	23	•	•		•	•		•
Milton Keynes	0							
Newcastle	N/A	•	•	•	•			
Oldham	0							
Plymouth	13				•	•	•	•
Sheffield	28	•	•	•	•			
Stockport	35	•	•					
Wolverhampton	8	•	•				•	•

*Numbers refer to peak summer numbers, not winter numbers. N/A indicates that figures were not available

111

Case Study 6.4: Low cost, low maintenance management in a mainstream inner city park: Iris Brickfield, Heaton, Newcastle

This neighbourhood park in inner city Newcastle is managed by the urban ranger service and is an example of the integration of the ranger service within the management structure of the city's parks service. The site has been developed since 1997, with the aims of improving community involvement and use of the park, consulting with the wider community over the future of the park, and managing the site to increase its value to wildlife. Prior to this the site was a featureless large area of regularly mown grass.

An initial on-site public meeting to set out the way forward for the site was held and decisions were made about how the both the city council and local people could make improvements to the park. The meeting attracted 60 people. From this meeting a Friends Group was formed and a series of community festivals organized and run every summer. A management plan has been developed with the friends group and is being implemented with the involvement of schools, volunteers and the very active children's nature club which does practical work on site, craft activities and wildlife recording. The site is managed in a non-horticultural manner, with large areas of wildflower meadow, an extensive pond and wetland, unmown grass, willow, gorse and broom plantations, as well as a new 5-a-side pitch.

Two things stand out about this site:

● Public acceptance of a low cost, low-maintenance, ecological approach. Because of the extensive consultation and community-based work that the ranger service has carried out, there is a high degree of public acceptance of the extensive meadow and unmown areas (covering around 50% of the site);

● Active community involvement in maintaining and planting the site.

Both are a direct result of the ranger service bringing in non-urban or "countryside" management techniques and people orientated skills into a mainstream urban inner city park, with full public acceptance.

SECURITY

6.23   While a number of authorities maintained some form of park security service, often under private contract, several felt that this didn't represent good value for money, because security personnel, although a presence in a park, did not get involved in any other park based operations or activities. Two authorities had terminated security contracts and used the money to create site based park keepers (**Newcastle**) or re-instate a park ranger service (**Wolverhampton**). **Chelmsford**, under an initiative termed "Parkwatch" had entered into an innovative arrangement with a private security contractor. Council officers operate a 24 hour telephone service that the public can ring to report any problems or incidents in parks. The mobile security firm responds immediately. The scheme is popular with the public and there has been a significant drop in parks vandalism, although it clearly places demands on officer time.

6.24   **Cheltenham** has established a partnership with the police known as "Inspector Neighbourhood". A park ranger attends monthly meetings along with the police, usually represented by an inspector or duty sergeant and a Community Neighbourhood Officer, together with council housing, environmental health, legal, and community safety staff. The advantage of the scheme to Cheltenham Borough Council parks is that it has formed a good working relationship with the police – *"they take us more seriously now"* and the council also feels that it gets a better response to crime / security issues. In **Leicester** a potentially ground-breaking partnership had been formed between the police and the parks service to build a new police station in a park (Spinney Hill Park). The development would serve several objectives – a permanent security presence would be put into the park, there would be a visible deterrent to vandalism and damage, and the new building would incorporate community meeting rooms. However, the proposal has not as yet been accepted partly because of the opposition of the park's user group who did not welcome the eating away of part of the park for a new building.

Tools for the task: strategic approaches to greenspace provision and planning

6.25   It was stressed in the introduction to this report that its main focus was on innovative and creative approaches to delivering services. In *'People, Parks and Cities'* [1] the importance of sound strategic thinking to guide urban green space policies was stressed. Emerging good practice at the time centred around mapping and inventorising an area's open space for management purposes, developing a hierarchical classification system for parks according to user needs, and producing parks and open spaces strategies. Such practice has now become widespread, but by no means universal. The profiling survey showed that three quarters of the 50 authorities contacted had a green space strategy of some sort, with half of these linking into other strategies. Two thirds said that their strategy was formally adopted and a further 68% said that they used a green space classification or typology of some sort.

6.26   From the results of the current research it is suggested that innovation in this field now lies in extending these principles forward to take a more holistic view of the place of parks in the wider network of urban green spaces, and investigating how this network as a whole can meet the needs and aspirations of urban populations. Producing *Green Space Audits* that incorporate qualitative as well as quantitative information, formulating green space *categorization systems and typologies* that drive policy; and producing holistic *green space strategies* and *green structure plans* that consider parks as just one element in a larger environmental network are examples of these developments.

6.27   These three areas all relate to a more considered approach to urban green spaces that moves beyond a focus on parks alone and also takes into account local and community need to a greater extent than has happened previously. In many ways the initiatives discussed below arise from the local authorities concerned finding that national standards for provision of green space are too prescriptive and do not deal in depth with issues beyond sports and play provision. Partly this concern arose from a perceived lack of guidance on non-sports-based

---

1   *People, Parks and Cities: A guide to current good practice in Urban Parks*. Department of the Environment, (1996).

green space issues from the most relevant Planning Policy Guidance note, PPG17. (At the time of writing this report, this guidance is under revision and comments on the consultation draft have been received), .

GREEN SPACE AUDITS AND MATCHING PROVISION TO NEEDS

6.28   The main benefit of CCT that all authorities identified was that it had resulted in a detailed inventory of the urban green spaces for which they were responsible. However, the inventories, by their very nature, concentrated on maintenance issues, whether this related to grounds maintenance or buildings and facilities, and also included only those areas that an authority maintains. A small number of authorities in the study had found that in order to develop worthwhile open space policies and strategies, it was necessary to build a much more detailed picture of their green space resource – one which dealt as much with quality as quantity, and one which had community as well as professional input.

Case Study 6.5: Basingstoke Open Space Audit

In Basingstoke, the open spaces audit was one of the recommendations of the parks strategy that was produced in 1996. The audit was undertaken over a period of two years by external consultants and completed in March 2001. The aim of the audit was to give a quantitative and qualitative assessment of the open space system of the town and five of the larger settlements in the borough. Green space under all types of ownership (local authority, county council and private) were included. Very small pieces of open space were grouped together. In all around 600 sites were included – each site could take 45-60 minutes to audit.

An important part of the work involved setting standards to assess quality against – a set of criteria were developed based upon a vision of developing "good quality landscape". The audit produced a set of recommendations that would largely be funding led. It also produced a great deal of baseline information to help inform issues around planning – for example protecting open space from inappropriate development and gaining Section 106 funds from developments. It was also used to feed into the local plan.

The audit was led by the parks strategy but went further. The strategy only looked at the major parks, centres for sport and neighbourhood parks whereas the audit looked at all open spaces. The audit also confirmed that the borough contained a lot of open space of a very similar nature and lacking in any local character. The audit itself didn't assess the quality of existing maintenance but it confirmed perceptions of how management practice needed to change. Maintenance is currently still locked into CCT procedures.

It was felt that the production of an open spaces strategy and an audit of open spaces was very closely linked. Ideally, a strategy should be based on a good knowledge of the extent and quality of the existing open space system, and there is therefore an argument for carrying out the audit first. On the other hand, if the authority was to repeat the audit they felt that it could be simplified (there was no need to collect so much information) and this would be aided by having a clear strategic vision at the outset.

6.29   One of the earliest comprehensive audits was that undertaken by **Basingstoke** in 1996 (**Case Study 6.5**). In this instance, the main benefit of the audit was to provide a sound basis for strategic planning of investment in green space, and to begin a process of matching provision of green space to local need. This enabled strong arguments to be made both for disposal in areas of over provision of low quality space, and also for protection from development of green space where this was an important local resource.

6.30   The most comprehensive and far-reaching audit was carried out by **Doncaster** as part of a long-term process to develop a rigorous community orientated green space strategy. As with all new approaches, there are learning points, but the basic aims and rationale behind Doncaster's approach are presented here as a model of good practice. The important points about the Doncaster audit is that it weighted judgements of quality against standards of quantity, and most importantly, based those judgements of quality on user opinion as well as professional expertise. Officers in Doncaster were adamant that it was the right policy to produce the audit before their green space strategy. However, the length of time involved in undertaking and producing the audit had caused problems – decision making was effectively halted until the strategy was produced. This resulted in massive accumulation of Section 106 funds awaiting allocation. Perhaps the main drawback to the Doncaster audit was the absence of consistent national guidelines for standards in non-recreational green space provision, so that the National Playing Fields Association (NPFA) standards were applied across the board for all types of green space.

Case Study 6.6: Comprehensive green space audit and strategy: Doncaster

The main objectives for the audit process were:

- to steer future open space development and provide a framework for decision-making

- to identify areas of deficiency and set out an action plan to remedy this, based upon a full assessment of quality, quantity and need

- to identify areas of surplus provision and develop policies which may involve disposal to re-invest funding to improve quality of provision

- to set borough-wide standards for recreational and environmental provision which meet community needs

The audit covered all green space types in the 'publicly accessible domain': allotments, play areas, incidental green space, sports provision, public parks, linear sites, routeways and transport corridors, woodlands, public parks, and nature conservation sites (but not school sites).

The audit assessed the following criteria:

- **Quantity** – the extent and area of all types, including on site facilities, and including data on the extent of their use

- **Quality** – a full and detailed assessment of the state of spaces and facilities, their character and aesthetic qualities

- **Need** – public requirements for green space services, including supply, quality and improvement priorities

The audit was carried out by external consultants and was achieved by carrying out a full land use survey of the borough using aerial photographs and site visits to assess quantity and quality of provision using a standard pro-forma, preloaded into electronic "palm pilots". Public consultation was carried out at three levels:

- Park user groups and community organizations

- Individual residents

- Primary school children

All the information is stored in a GIS system and the consultation identified for the borough as a whole:

- The types of green space that were used, and how often

- Whether provision of the different types was adequate

- The distance travelled to different types of green space

- Problems relating to green space and barriers to use

- Rating of the quality of green spaces

- Suggestions for improvements to green spaces

- Issues relating to security and safety

Interestingly, in terms of numbers of visits per year, the survey identified that after informal green spaces (28 million), it was woodlands that received the greatest number of visits per year in the borough (21 million). Formal green spaces and parks received around half this number of visits. The most frequent requests for improvement related to the need for better and more facilities, improved maintenance, and increase in supervision and on-site personnel.

The audit has formed the basis of the borough's draft green space strategy, that again considers policies for all types of space. The parks and open spaces service have invested a huge amount of time, effort and investment in the audit, in the belief (already proven) that the data included provides a basis for decision making and strategic thinking that will be extremely difficult to challenge. As with the **Basingstoke** example, however, if the audit was to be repeated it would be simplified to reduce the amount of data collected.

6.31   NPFA standards relate to the amount of different recreational space that should be provided for given sizes of population. These standards have been criticized for their emphasis on active sports-based recreational or formal play space provision, and the lack of consideration of local social conditions in their application. Two other authorities in the survey had developed their own standards because they found these national standards unsatisfactory. In particular they wished to develop standards that took into account local needs and conditions, and in particular reflected the social and economic make up of different communities. The **Chelmsford** Open Space policy (**Case Study 6.7**) can be regarded as a genuinely innovative attempt to overcome this problem. The policy has been accepted by the borough's planners because of its rigour. **Basingstoke's** locally developed formula for allocating play provision (**Case Study 6.8**) according to social need rather than on a purely quantitative basis, has again enabled a strategic approach to be taken to play allocation across the borough.

Case Study 6.7: Chelmsford open space policy

The development of the policy started in 1990. Prior to this the borough had a policy written in the 1970s known as "10% provision", requiring developers to provide 10% of land for public open space. The provision was largely focused on children's play and kick about areas. When this was reviewed in 1990 it was apparent that it wasn't delivering 10% – more like 8% because of the problem of interpreting what was the 100% – for example, did this include the roads on the site?

An important part of the policy was to move away from provision on a purely percentage basis to assessing whether communities had got the type of open space that they wanted and whether the spaces worked. Meetings were held with local people and parish councils to discuss this, and the council's complaints records were also checked to see where spaces weren't working. In some parts of the borough people were happy with provision, but in others there was more dissatisfaction.

In addition to the local review, national policy was also considered to see if this could be applied.

For example, the NPFA '6 Acre Standard' was felt to be flawed because it didn't deal with passive recreation but only active (usually sports) recreation. It was also felt it didn't really look at local park provision – only sports pitch provision. Various national standards for play space provision were at the time found to be lacking. As a result, the parks and open space service brainstormed their own open space categorisation:

- Children's play space

- Sports pitch provision

- Courts and greens

- Local parks

- Country parks

- Amenity open space, of which two types were distinguished:

- *Amenity space that was primarily recreational*

- *Amenity space that had planning importance i.e it contributed to visual setting*

- Linear spaces and riverside walks

From all of this a new Public Open Space policy was developed. The amount of each type of public space was assessed across the borough and equated with a requirement per dwelling. This was then defined in terms of local provision (i.e spaces that could be walked to and played an important role as a community resource) and strategic provision (i.e spaces that people would travel to and played an important role across a wider area). A total figure of 6.83 acres per 1000 people was arrived at.

On a new development this equates to 47 square metres of local provision and 25 square metres of strategic provision per dwelling. For the latter the Council would accept a commuted sum to provide equivalent levels elsewhere in the borough.

All existing provision was examined and areas of deficiency identified for all types of open space. The minimum size of Public Open Space to be provided in developments was described, and what was to be provided in terms of the type of facilities that were expected. These definitions and expectations were built into the local plan in 1994. However, for political reasons the local plan was not adopted until 1997.

The process was considered to be very time consuming but very valuable. The local plan went to public enquiry. It was anticipated by the council planners that the inspectors wouldn't approve the POS policy, but it was accepted. Developers made some objections, but the methodology was sound enough to allow the policy to be defended.

The policy identified the need for two new local parks in the borough – there had been new developments in the 1960/70s with no local parks having been provided. This requirement was built into the local plan and development briefs produced.

Case Study 6.8: Play area strategy, Basingstoke

Prior to 1994 the borough had 188 play areas. The aim of the strategy was to look at what was the appropriate level of provision; because of the massive expansion of the town in the 1960s there was thought to be an over provision – *"careless provision"*. Before 1994 the council experienced difficulties in allocating funding for childrens play – money was very limited.

External consultants were appointed and had to undertake a wide ranging consultation with specialist interest groups, the public, and members through discussion and focus groups. The key recommendations were that there was a need for a hierarchy of provision, there was a need to consider provision for particular age ranges and that there were far too many badly located, poor quality play areas with poor play value. A seven-year plan was produced to reduce the number of sites from 188 to 90. An executive version of the strategy was produced to show ward by ward the number of play areas needed to satisfy different age groups. This was approved by the council Leisure Services committee and officers were asked to dictate which wards to start on as a priority.

A detailed ward by ward appraisal was carried out to assess what would satisfy each ward in terms of play provision and then recommendations for spending in each ward were produced. Five relatively deprived wards were initially targeted. The consultant's strategy was reviewed – they had failed to take into account the distribution of the facilities: some wards had play areas clustered in only one part of the ward. The recommendations were adjusted so that a more even geographical spread within wards was achieved so that everyone had equal access to play. In 1995 a detailed consultation exercise was undertaken in each ward – a trailer was set up in each ward, discussion groups were held, fliers sent out, advertisements placed in local shops, and local press releases and questionnaires issued. Following discussion with councillors, agreement was reached as to which play areas would be improved as a priority with the limited money available.

In 1996/7 eight play areas were improved in the five wards. Politicians and the public were very keen to see improvements before any removal of provision. By 1998 a total of 13 wards out of 25 in the borough had been consulted. In some cases this has resulted in a completely new play area where there had not previously been a play area. The consultation process evolved over time, from the trailer in each ward in the first place, to an information leaflet and questionnaire being sent to each household along with a display in local supermarkets in year two. In year three very detailed consultation leaflets and questionnaires were sent out and public meetings were held.

Because of the prioritisation of some wards over others, members became concerned about how the wards were being allocated in terms of priorities for improvement. So in 1996 a formula was developed for allocating the funds using an external consultant. This not only considered needs and deficiency or surplus of provision but also included census information (social deprivation) data to give a priority ranking for each ward. In 1999 the formula was refined to take into account enumeration district level deprivation statistics (unemployment, children in low-earning households, no access to car, households lacking basic amenities, overcrowded households). The age-range covered was also increased, from 0-15 to 0-18.

The adoption of the formula-based approach has been the authorities "greatest tool" in achieving rationalization of provision – the formula is not often challenged. By overlaying NPFA recommendations for provision by catchment size with local population data, the formula has enabled reduction in the total number of play areas and improvement in quality of those remaining. However because of some public and political opposition, it is likely that the total number will be reduced to 124, rather than to the 90 originally planned.

SITE CATEGORIZATION

6.32   The majority of the fifteen case study local authorities in the survey used a classification system for their parks. Two authorities didn't use this sort of classification. In one of these authorities (**Milton Keynes**) this was a philosophical point partly because of the legacy of the New Town idea where green space was seen as a continuum with no fenced play areas and parks, with no concept of hierarchies, and everything maintained at the same level (this was seen now as an unsustainable approach, but lack of resources and officer time meant that an alternative strategy had not yet been adopted). **Oldham** had not developed a classification system because the parks service felt that, in a community orientated service, the concept of a hierarchy of parks with some being more important than others did not necessarily apply. Most authorities had used variations on the theme of City, District, and Neighbourhood Parks (see **Chapter 1**). **Basingstoke** had the most distinctive system, adopting a use-orientated approach that indicated a particular focus on activities on a site and enabled targeting of resources to boost those facilities. Like **Chelmsford, Sheffield** had also developed its own site categorization. This has again been used to introduce a qualitative element to what is usually a quantitative exercise. The Sheffield Site Categorisation Strategy (**Case Study 6.9**) is a good example of a practical application of a hierarchical classification.

Case Study 6.9: Site categorization strategy, Sheffield

Sheffield, like many other authorities, has adopted a quantitative hierarchical approach for the provision of public green space. The system is incorporated into the city's Unitary Development Plan but other than this there is no other definitive management categorisation system for all the parks, woodlands and other green space areas managed by the council. In 1993 the council produced its widely acclaimed "Sheffield Parks Regeneration Strategy" which has achieved many of its aims. However, mainly because of budgetary decline, many areas of the service have not been perceived by the public as being adequate. The city provides more public green space per head than most other comparable cities, while spending is less per head. Conservative estimates suggest that the budget available is just one third of what is required to provide the level of service aspired to. The site categorisation system was developed as a means to make efficient use of scarce resources, but also to provide a rational base for allocation of additional resources and bringing in of external funding. Sites were classified initially into one of three categories: City Sites, District Sites or Local Sites. Then, based upon predominant characteristics, the sites were classified by type, as either:

- Park

- Garden

- Sports Site

- Playing Field

- Playground

- Playground/Open Space

- Woodland

- Moorland/Heathland

- Allotment

- Closed Churchyard/Open Space

- **City sites** were defined as those which have potential as significant visitor attractions to people inside and outside of the city, with appropriate facilities, good accessibility, at least one dedicated member of staff and an aspiration for dedicated maintenance teams.

- **District Sites** play a major role in the economic, social, environmental and recreational regeneration of the city, consistent with meeting the needs of the surrounding district and local community and will have specific features or attractions. They serve a sector of approximately 1.2km radius.

- **Local Sites** serve a sector of approximately 0.4 km. They are generally accessible on foot and form part of the local landscape, and possibly heritage.

All sites in the city were considered "local" even if categorised as city or district parks.

The City's UDP identifies 31 sectors in the city. Each of these was taken as a catchment area for the Site Categorization Strategy. The aim of the strategy was to provide each of these 31 sectors with either a city or district site. In some sectors there was no such provision, but the need was identified. The strategy has enabled limited resources to be targeted. City Sites and District Sites are the first priority because this is where the greatest number of visitors and users are. Local sites are supported according to need and opportunity as part of the city's regeneration planning process. It has set standards of provision of facilities and maintenance quality for these categories. It has also driven a restructure of the organisation, and the transfer of permanent maintenance staff back into city and district sites (although at present there are not permanent staff in every district site).

One of the important aspects of the Sheffield Categorisation system is that it isn't just a parks categorisation, but a site categorisation system, making an assessment of levels of provision and quality standards for other types of green space. This more holistic view of green space as a whole forms the basis for the following consideration of open space strategies.

Green Space Strategies

6.33   Table 6.3 indicates whether the various authorities in the survey had developed a parks or open spaces strategy, and whether this had been formally adopted. Around half the authorities had a completed Park Strategy document, and the majority of these had been formally adopted by the council. Several of the strategies (for example **Lewisham**) had been developed as a direct result of the 'Park Life' and 'People, Parks and Cities' reports and had taken on board the main recommendations for good practice in the latter. However, in terms of innovation or creativity, most of the strategies were rather similar in content and intent. Certainly, innovation in the area of Parks Strategies had occurred a decade earlier with some of the pioneering examples. For example, **Sheffield's** Parks Regeneration Strategy (1993) yielded benefits that included the establishment of an urban ranger service, a large network of friends groups, consultative networks, substantial external funding, partnerships with the voluntary sector and business, an events programme, and a restructuring of the parks service: themes echoed in many more recent strategies. It would appear that where parks strategies are being developed, in most cases, previous examples of innovation have now become accepted good practice.

Table 6.3: Development of parks and open spaces strategies		
Authority	**Parks or Open Spaces Strategy?**	**Formally adopted?**
Basingstoke	Yes	Yes
Bexley	Yes	Yes
Chelmsford	No (existing open space policies to be collated into one document)	
Cheltenham	No	
Doncaster	Yes (draft)	No
Ipswich	No	
Leicester	Yes	No
Lewisham	Yes	Yes
Milton Keynes	No	
Newcastle	No (in development)	
Oldham	Yes (new version in draft)	Yes
Plymouth	No	
Sheffield	Yes	Yes
Stockport	Yes	Yes
Wolverhampton	Yes	Yes

6.34   **Leicester's** Park's Open Spaces and Countryside Strategy (draft in 2001) was in some ways a remarkable document, the bulk of which forms a coherently argued and detailed statement, drawing on a wide range of sources, of the key role of green spaces in meeting the council's wider policy objectives. Although the document contains a clear action plan for change, its main purpose is educational: to raise the political profile of green space in the authority. The strategy outlines how *"high quality parks and green spaces"* and *"low quality parks and green spaces"* contribute in a positive or negative way to the City Council's Corporate Priorities in Health and Social Care, Education, Diversity, Safety, Environment, and Jobs and Regeneration. The document also looks in detail at 22 external funding sources and illustrates how the authority can benefit from them.

6.35   In this survey, however, perhaps only **Oldham's** strategy took the most truly innovative approach in extending and developing the core concept of its highly successful Parks Strategy (a rolling, community focused programme of park investment and refurbishment) into all other types of green space (Case Study 6.10). This is one of the very few examples in the UK where a parks and open spaces department is in the driving seat in terms of strategic green space structure planning (and one of the few examples where the potential for such planning exists). This is largely due to the enhanced role of landscape architects in the division (Case Study 6.1).

Case Study 6.10: A unified green space strategy: Oldham

Oldham's Green Space Strategy, the draft of which was produced in August 2001, is a replacement for, and a development and extension of, the borough's Parks Strategy and Countryside Strategy, both produced in 1995. The former Parks Strategy itself was an innovative document, setting a course for the community-related rolling park refurbishment and investment programme discussed in detail in **Chapter 7** of this report. The aim of the new Green Space Strategy is to extend this process of rolling investment across the whole of the "green estate". The production of the strategy is a direct result of the forming of a single unit in the council, the "Operational Services Unit" which has responsibility for the development, improvement, management and maintenance of all open space under the authority's control. The Unit also controls a 'Green Budget' which brings together a range of previously separate sources of funding.

For the purposes of the strategy, green space covers the whole range of spaces included in the typology in **Chapter 1** of this report. The aim of the strategy is to develop and promote: *"comprehensive networks of accessible, high quality and sustainable greenspaces"* which:

- contribute positively to the image and overall strategic framework for development;

- promote economic development and social inclusion;

- have individual spaces planned, designed and managed to serve a clearly defined primary purpose;

- deliver important secondary benefits, where appropriate, for local people, bio-diversity and wildlife.

As with most park or open space strategies, the benefits to the borough are outlined under four headings:

- **Putting People First** – benefits to individuals of all sections of the community;

- **Creating Confident Communities.** The social benefits of green spaces that Oldham's Park Strategy has promoted are evident from the case studies from Oldham given in **Chapter 7**. The Greenspace Strategy acknowledges this success: *"the success of many of Oldham's "Friends of the Park" groups in not only regenerating their local park, but in going on to promote community action on crime and antisocial behaviour, to generate funding for new facilities, to organise activities for teenagers, and to provide networks of support for the elderly, confirms the value of this approach, and it is not surprising that parks with a strong "Friends Group" are becoming more heavily used, safer, more respected and better managed. Closer links between residents, ward councillors, police and council officers creates an ever-widening sphere of influence that contributes to related initiatives aimed at local regeneration"*;

- A quality environment: contributing to a sustainable future – a link is made here with Oldham's Agenda 21 plan.

Perhaps the most interesting idea in the strategy is the concept of bringing the attractions and experience associated with "countryside" into the urban centre: *"Countryside" landscapes can penetrate deep into the urban core.... An important issue for this strategy, then, is to review the contribution which "countryside" design and management makes to the value of the green estate and to distribute resources accordingly."*

The main conclusions of the strategy are that:

- *"The council will undertake a major review of all its open spaces and develop a Strategic Green Space Plan which identifies a connected parks and green spaces system as an integral part of the planned infrastructure of the borough;*

- *The council will prepare a rolling 5-year Green Space Investment Plan, integrated with the Strategy, to meet the requirements of external funding agencies, build confidence and enable the sustained targeting of matching resources;*

- *The Parks and Open Spaces Division will lead the development and implementation of the Green Space Strategy, working closely with other departments of the Council, Government Agencies and other partner organisations, community and special interest groups, local people and their councillors".*

The Parks and Open Spaces Division is an example of a unified co-located service, with responsibility for landscape design and development, the countryside service, construction and arboriculture, horticulture, cemeteries, grounds maintenance. It is therefore strongly placed to take responsibility for *"everything green across the public realm"*. It is also a very rare example of a parks service having a strategic planning role in an authority.

CHAPTER 7
Communities and Involvement

SUMMARY OF KEY POINTS

- Community involvement in urban parks and green spaces can lead to increased use, enhanced quality and richness of experience and, in particular, to facilities suited to local needs; but it requires support and investment to reap the benefits.

- Both local authority officers and communities were able to list many benefits of community involvement, including: encouraging local 'ownership; giving access to additional funding; increasing understanding of local problems and local authority constraints; providing expertise; responding to local need and contributing to long term sustainability.

- There are also costs. For local authorities they include: demands on officer time and other resources, lack of appropriate skills, conflicting demands and potential for diversion from normal activities and investment. For communities they include: undesirable levels of responsibility; over reliance on volunteers; shortage of volunteers and the need for long term commitment.

- There are two basic and different objectives for community engagement: one involves communication, information exchange and consultation, and the other takes the process forward into active collaboration in decision making, design, planning and management. The development of self-management activity on a site can be the ultimate expression of community involvement.

- A small number of parks services in this study have changed the way they operate, changing their focus from direct service delivery to supporting and developing community groups. Developing a community focus requires a new skills balance within parks services.

- It is possible to actively and strategically manage groups into the more advanced stages of partnership, and this can happen in the more deprived areas of a town or city as well as the more affluent. The importance of a group being representative of a local community varies according to the objectives of the group.

- Promoting networking and co-ordination of Friends Groups activities can help to promote good practice across a town or city.

- Increasing a local sense of ownership, accessing additional funding and promoting communication and understanding were seen as the main advantages of community involvement by both local authorities and community groups. Mechanisms may be needed to recognise (and reward) local voluntary input.

SUMMARY OF KEY POINTS

- The potential involvement of local communities in urban parks and green spaces is related to the culture of the local authority and parks service, the resources available, the type of site and local capacity.

Introduction

7.1 The process of reaching out to and engaging with local communities and relevant user groups is widely accepted as being one of the cornerstones of effective and sustainable management of urban green space. It is also a key point in the UK Government's Urban White Paper. This stresses the need to identify opportunities for both building and supporting partnerships for managing open space in and around towns, particularly where this involves businesses and local communities. *People, Parks and Cities* (1996) listed community involvement as one of the most fundamental aspects of successful urban parks. A number of what were then innovative, albeit at that time rather isolated, examples, were described, of how a community development officer within a local authority parks department had stimulated mechanisms by which local people and groups could have real input into decision-making. Now, five years further on, this principle has been taken up on a much wider basis and can be seen as a mainstream activity for many local authorities. This has partly been spurred by a duty to consult being part of the system of Best Value, partly because it is a funding requirement of many grant making bodies and award schemes, and partly because it is just plainly seen to be a good thing to do. However, the methods of community involvement that are used, their effectiveness and potential outcomes vary considerably between local authorities. This chapter discusses the different models for community engagement that are being employed and outlines the factors that appear to contribute to success.

The range of community involvement

7.2 The range of types of community involvement that are employed can be viewed in terms of the degree of active participation in decision making and management that they allow, or conversely, the degree to which power is devolved away from the local authority into the hands of local users. Within this continuum there are two basic and different objectives for community engagement: one involves communication, information exchange and consultation, and the other takes the process forward into active collaboration in decision making, planning and management (as in Arnstein's widely recognised 'ladder' of participation[1]).

1 A Ladder of Citizen Involvement. *Journal of the American Institute of Planners*. **35**, 216–224. Arnstein, S.R. (1969)

COMMUNICATION, INFORMATION EXCHANGE AND CONSULTATION

7.3   The most widespread purpose for increasing community involvement in urban green space is related to the gathering of information that will serve to improve strategic development and service delivery. This may be achieved by both indicating successful and failing aspects of current services, and by directing services more closely to the needs of current and potential site users. A distinction can be seen in terms of whether consultation is a one-way process of information gathering to inform remote decision making, or a genuine two-way dialogue that involves communities in decision making. The question must be addressed here of what 'community' actually is. It has been suggested[2] that it is possible to identify two main communities to be addressed in involvement processes:

- communities of common interest (perhaps of shared values or needs) that may or may not be geographically related to any particular site;

- communities of neighbourhood or geographical proximity to a particular site.

7.4   In either case, the more representative the consultative mechanism is of the community in question, the greater the chance of genuine benefit on both sides. Many of the 'market research' types of activity, such as focus groups, citizens panels and questionnaires (discussed in more detail in **Chapters 2 to 5**) occur at city or area-wide basis and most address parks and open spaces at some level to give limited base-line information. However, in terms of reaching 'communities of common interest' with direct relevance to urban green space, a few local authorities have established city-wide bodies that focus specifically on urban green space issues and include representatives of all relevant local and city groups as well as officers and members. If well managed they can be useful vehicles for two-way exchange of information and help to build trust and understanding between council and community: examples include **Stockport's** 'Green Space Forum', or **Sheffield's** 'Environment Forum', and 'Park-User Forum' (see **Paragraph 7.41**).

7.5   However, the central focus in this chapter is how information may be gathered that can be related directly to the wishes, aspirations and concerns of local communities. A distinction must be drawn between one-off consultation processes relating to a specific development in any one area, and interactions where there is a long-term commitment to communication. In reality, the former may lead on to the latter, but again this chapter is primarily concerned with community processes relating to green space that can be sustained beyond the short-term.

7.6   Engagement with geographically-based communities can occur at a number of scales, from regular area-based public meetings through to the development and support of park user groups and friends groups. Many local authorities have re-organized, partly as a result of Best Value to promote greater democratic accountability, setting up a system of area or ward-based panels of officers and members that meet regularly to address relevant issues at public meetings. However, the provision and quality of parks and open spaces may be just one of many conflicting demands and priorities for discussion at such meetings.

---

2   *Community Involvement in Parks*. ILAM Information Sheet. Fact Sheet 98/6. Richardson & Daggett (1998)

7.7   The most effective way that information from the different scales of consultation informs green space service delivery, is when responsible departments have taken on a community development focus (see below) and the various levels of democratic input are closely and coherently tied in with the structure of the department and the responsibilities of officers. Of the local authorities surveyed, the Parks and Countryside Service of **Newcastle City Council** embodied this ideal (see **Case Study 7.1**)

ACTIVE COLLABORATION IN SITE-BASED DECISION MAKING, PLANNING AND MANAGEMENT

7.8   It is at this level of engagement that a greater range of creativity and innovation was found, perhaps because, where it can be made to work, involvement of communities in the management of sites can bring greater potential rewards, both for the local authority and the individuals and groups involved, than pure information gathering and exchange. These rewards stem from the commitment promoted in users from the feeling of ownership and empowerment engendered in genuine collaboration with a council over the improvement of a site.

In this sense, the local authority forms a *partnership* with the users and potential users of a site to achieve fixed or on-going objectives. While partnerships with external groups or organisations are considered fully in the next chapter, the partnership of councils with local groups that are affiliated or attached to, or have concern over a particular green space, whether this be a friends group, user group, tenants or residents association or neighbourhood action group is a central concern here.

7.9   Active collaboration can involve real participation in decision making and planning for the future, fund-raising and income generation, organising of events and publicity, and practical maintenance. The ultimate manifestation of community involvement is self-management of all or part of a site by a community group.

CASE STUDY 7.1: Ward Stewardship, Newcastle City Council

The Parks and Countryside Service was reorganized in 2000 to reflect the community planning structure of the authority. Officers were titled 'Recreation Development Officers' and given responsibility for sites within one of three community planning areas, which themselves were based upon ward and police division boundaries. The primary responsibility for these officers is to ensure that the management and maintenance of green spaces is based upon user requirements, through the facilitation and support of site-based user groups, and they also sit on the regular public consultation area committees with other officers and members. Moreover, the structure enables cross-cutting integration of initiatives. For example, the recreation development officers work closely with ward-based community development officers in the housing department. However, there is another level of interaction. One officer is assigned to each ward to coordinate environmental activities and issues across the public realm, which are raised through public meetings, and is allocated a budget to achieve this. This is linked to ward-based 'ecopanels' that have responsibility for developing biodiversity action plans for each area. The ward stewardship structure links with the one-stop-shop 'Enviro-call' (see **Case Study 6.2**) to produce a network of different layers of central involvement in service delivery, and gives officers, groups and individuals clear points of contact for consultation and communication

Models for active community involvement

7.10   There is a range of mechanisms by which such participation can be achieved.

FRIENDS AND USER GROUPS

7.11   This is the perhaps the most direct mechanism by which local authorities can form direct partnerships with site users. It is also the most widespread approach. Because of this, the roles and characteristics of friends and user groups are dealt with in detail in **Paragraphs 7.28 –7.31.**

VOLUNTEERS

7.12   Volunteering in practical tasks (usually maintenance-related) takes many forms. While in many sites the main volunteers are those who may be the most active in a friends or user group, volunteering is also a way of bringing in a wider range of people on to a site. Although most community activities are essentially voluntary, the examples given here are where people give their time for the improvement of a park, play area or green space outside of meeting, committee or administration-orientated activities. Examples of voluntary activities are discussed below.

SITE MAINTENANCE

7.13   The degree of volunteer or non-local authority input into site maintenance varied between the councils included in the survey. By far the greatest application of volunteer labour was in conservation tasks on sites that were seen as having a wildlife focus. In general this was carried out by conservation groups such as the British Trust for Conservation Volunteers or student groups that tended not to be attached to any particular site. Where site-based conservation groups were active, they tended to be associated with non-urban or countryside sites within a local authority's boundaries.

7.14   It was a common characteristic of most of the non-metropolitan local authorities that friends or user groups that took an active role in site maintenance were associated with countryside sites (and strictly therefore outside the remit of the survey). For example, the **Basingstoke Community Forests** initiative is managed by a member of staff who plays a supporting role in enabling community groups to take responsibility for and managing certain woodlands within the Borough. For example, the **Oakley Woodlands Group** was set up in 1996 and has its own bank account and constitution. They sell 70% of the material produced from the woodland management work they undertake – mainly coppice products. They run an events programme and training courses.

7.15   This is not to say that voluntary maintenance does not and cannot occur in urban parks, but again this tends to be either conservation related, or to occur in parks with high horticultural or historic interest. In such cases enthusiasts are attracted, often keen gardeners who may have small plots of their own and relish the opportunity to work in larger or more beautiful surroundings, or feel they are contributing to the upkeep and maintenance of an important site. For example **The Friends of Sheffield Botanical Gardens** hold weekly garden work sessions at which 30 or more people regularly attend. Although the gardens now have received substantial Heritage Lottery Fund monies for their restoration, it was largely through the practical efforts of the friends group that the gardens were prevented from running down completely when severe budget cuts in the 1980s and 90s reduced the grounds maintenance staff to a basic grass cutting service. The friends group are a significant player in the partnership that is now raising the £1.5 million required in matched funding for the HLF sum.

7.16   A similar example of specialist input is **Down Grange Walled Garden, Basingstoke**, a former walled garden attached to a manor house (now a restaurant but owned by the local authority). There is a friends group who undertake 90% of the work on the site and in recognition of this effort have their own allotment plots which are set up as a demonstration project with Hampshire Gardens Trust. They also run a regular programme of events. However, all income and expenditure is controlled by the council: income from events is not put back directly into the site. As such this can not really be seen as a fully self-managed site.

7.17   One of the few examples of a friends group actively and regularly helping with routine maintenance of a more mainstream urban park was found in **Christchurch Park, Ipswich** (although this has an historic character) where the group help renovate shrub beds and carry out planting activity. The work is managed by park rangers who say that working with volunteers allows them to achieve far more than originally thought possible within the fixed budgets they had for park improvement. The volunteer group secured funding for their own garage in the park and a golf buggy to carry themselves and tools around the site.

7.18   There are several reasons why active involvement in maintenance in local authority-run urban parks is restricted in general to special interest sites. There is usually a strong social aspect to the activities that involves bringing like-minded people together to achieve tasks that reflect the skills, expertise and the enthusiasm of those involved. Volunteer maintenance was most often coordinated by rangers, and the concentration on non-urban sites reflects the non-urban bias of many ranger services. Several local authorities mentioned that their own grounds maintenance staff were wary of volunteers because they posed a threat to their own jobs, and were concerned about health and safety issues. But there is also the question of ownership, and a general feeling that the upkeep of a park is the responsibility of the local authority that is a major barrier to community maintenance initiatives.

TIDY-UPS AND LITTER PICKS

7.19   Such activities, although commonplace generally attract small numbers and are often restricted to those active already in friends groups. In **Bexley**, Keep Britain Tidy initiatives have been used to develop a Litter Picking Volunteer Group that has 80 members and works across the borough's urban green spaces.

CORPORATE TEAM BUILDING

7.20 A particular form of volunteering that is becoming more common is the use of business groups who undertake maintenance activities as a team building event or through staff initiatives to "put something back into the community". This was a particular feature of activity in **Newcastle** where voluntary groups can be contacted and sourced for projects through an environmental volunteer agency. At least one site, the **Benwell Nature Park (Case Study 5.1 , Chapter 5)**, a highly used neighbourhood public park, is maintained entirely by volunteer activity, including regular 'business in the community' groups. The reduced intensity maintenance of the ecologically orientated park helps greatly in achieving this: what is interesting about this site is that it is openly accessible, very popular and probably used with greater intensity by children in particular than other more traditional 'mown grass and trees' parks in the locality.

SCHOOLS

7.21 The logic of involving children in urban green spaces to encourage greater care is widely accepted. The majority of local authorities in the survey had some sort of initiative involving schools and bulb or tree planting in at least one public park. A variation on this theme was found at **Glass Park, Doncaster (Case Study 8.7, Chapter 8)**, whereby parents at the local primary school were asked to buy and plant at least one tree in the name of their child for a new community woodland on the site. A donation of £5.00 per tree was required. The resulting 'Mother's Wood' was planted in 2000, at a planting day by mothers of the children. This project means that a significant proportion of the local adults and children have a direct stake, not only in the future development of the woodland, but of the site as a whole. There were also sufficient funds left over from the exercise to cover future maintenance costs.

Self management

7.22 The development of self management activity on a site can be the ultimate expression of community involvement, so long as the site caters for the broad range of needs of the community it serves and that unrestricted access is maintained. Full self management requires a good degree of financial control and delegation of budgets as well as the running of activities and facilities.

SELF-MANAGEMENT OF INCIDENTAL GREEN SPACE

7.23 Incidental green space (for example small patches of mown grass in housing areas or roadside verges) are often unattractive and monotonous (and a maintenance liability to a local authority). Unfortunately, after the private garden, they can be the most visible and closest fragments of green space to residential areas. A number of initiatives were encountered in the study that enabled local residents to take control of and personalize such incidental areas. The most coordinated was the **Adopt-a-Plot Scheme** run by **Newcastle City Council (Case study 7.2)** that enables groups or individuals to enter design and maintenance agreements over suitable pieces of land with the city council.

A number of examples were also found of residents groups or tenants associations taking control from the council of small patches of green space within their estates (**Examples: Longley Greens, Sheffield, Paragraph 9.21 – other examples in Basingstoke and Oldham**)

CASE STUDY 7.2 Adopt-a-Plot, Newcastle City Council

The Adopt-a-Plot scheme was started in 1998 following constant complaints about the quality of maintenance of green space outside houses. The Parks and Countryside Section decided to take an innovative approach to tackling this problem by giving people the opportunity to care for and improve these areas themselves. The Adopt-a-Plot Scheme is publicised as part of a city-wide 'Greener, Cleaner City' Campaign. The scheme is seen as a key way in which individuals or groups can '*join the campaign to care for our environment*'. The plots concerned can be of any size, from an area only a metre or so across to a large area of open space. For example, residents may come together to look after their own street, looking after the verges, or take over bits of incidental green space. The scheme is managed straightforwardly because all green space plots in the city are numbered in a GIS system established under CCT.

Participants in the scheme have to present a proposal to an Adopt-a-Plot officer about their intentions for the plot. The only work that is specifically prohibited is tree surgery work and pruning, although the Local Authority can arrange to have this done if a case is made. Once the ideas for the plot have been finalised then the participant is free to go ahead and care for the plot. A photograph is taken of the site before work starts, and a second photograph within the year to indicate any changes or improvements. Each plot is reviewed annually.

Although the scheme works smoothly now, there were many problems in its initial stages, mainly revolving around multiple ownership of green space in the city between the parks service, housing and highways. Although the housing department was supportive of the scheme, the highways department objected on health and safety grounds. Eventually a formal license was drawn up by the council's legal department that satisfied highways and is signed and agreed by all participants. People find out about the scheme in several ways. Anyone who contacts the council with a complaint about a piece of land adjacent to housing is shown the Adopt-a-Plot agreement. The scheme is publicised in the council newsletter and also in the City Paper, which carries occasional 'Adopt-a-Plot' tips.

SELF-MANAGEMENT OF FACILITIES OR EVENTS

7.24   Examples of self-management of specific facilities within local authority-owned urban sites were encountered frequently during the survey. The distinction is drawn here between high involvement in maintenance of a particular site, such as the example of the **Down Grange Walled Garden** given above, and examples where community representatives or groups have a significant stake in financial or organizational decisions. In particular where revenue can be ploughed back into the facility and used at the discretion of the group involved, the sense of 'ownership', achievement and encouragement of entrepreneurial spirit can pay great dividends in the quality and range of activities. In most cases self-management was associated with building or sports-related activities. Examples include the café at **Coalshaw Green Park, Oldham (Case Study 7.6)**, the Pavilion and nursery at **Grove Park Gardens,**

Doncaster (**Case Study 9.2**) and the café and community tool hire enterprise at **Longley Greens, Sheffield (Paragraph 9.21)**. A number of examples of self-management of bowling greens and sports facilities were encountered. For example a community group at **Crossroads Playing Field, Stockport** has taken over a pavilion and junior football pitch and pay for grounds maintenance and a rent to the council.

SELF-MANAGEMENT OF SITES

7.25   **Community Gardens:** Complete sites with a high degree of self-management by local groups that were retained under full local authority ownership and control were encountered relatively rarely in the study. Apart from the allotment sites discussed above and residents group take-overs of incidental spaces in housing estates, the only other examples were **community gardens**. For example, **Handsworth Community Allotments, Sheffield (Case Study 7.3)** is a thriving community resource on a former derelict site, **Scotswood Community Garden, Newcastle** and **Walkley Millenium Green, Sheffield**. This garden was created in 1999 on a patch of land within high density housing as part of a coordinated resident's campaign against built development on a patch of 'incidental' open space. A small committee was formed and residents living within walking distance of the site were invited to pay an annual subscription for upkeep of the site. A plan for the site was drawn up by a local authority landscape architect. Funding was obtained under the Countryside Agency's Millenium Green initiative. Work parties of local residents cleared the site, but the bulk of the planting and land shaping was done by the council. The site is fenced and locked each night by a local resident, and all maintenance (apart from grass cutting) is done by residents. The site is regularly used for community events and contains planting of a quality absent from local parks in the area.

CASE STUDY 7.3 Handsworth Community Allotments, Sheffield.

The site in its present form was created in 1998 on a derelict 2-acre allotment site which the City Council was in the process of closing down. A residents group had been working in the area to clean up a recreation ground and decided also to take on the allotment site. The city council indicated that if enough local support could be generated then the site could be turned over to community use. Initially 8 families became involved and this was enough for the council to clear the site. The proposals for the site were widely advertised to local residents, and a committee formed, which is now a registered charity. Now, out of the original 29 plots, eight have been set aside for community green space, while 16 plots are tenanted for productive use. Of the eight community plots, three have been combined and turned over to grass and plant beds to create a community garden. One contains a community meeting room, with kitchen and disabled toilet. One is devoted to a children's play area and the others form a wildlife garden/nature area. All maintenance is carried out by volunteers. The main problem the group has is finding enough time to produce local publicity to increase support and involvement.

7.26   **Allotments:** Although allotments are not the main concern of this report, they were cited by a few authorities as good examples of self-management of urban green spaces. For example, **Wolverhampton** has ten fully self managing allotment sites. Each group collects rent from each plot and passes on £1 to the council. They pay water rates and some have built installed facilities such as toilets on site, and also provide tools. The benefits to the authority are reduced administration charges, while self management has improved the spirits of those on site and created a sense of community amongst plot holders through social meetings. Plot take up is also very high, partly as a result of an incentive for sites to maximise rental income. Some issues are not resolved, however, particularly relating to who is responsible for infrastructure and fencing repairs. The council is reluctant to do this (having had an income reduction from £23 per plot to £1) but the allotment holders do not see this as their responsibility. In addition, in **Stockport,** 22 of the council's 39 allotment sites are self-managed through the **Stockport** Metropolitan Allotment Gardeners Association.

7.27   **Trusts:** From the results of the survey undertaken from this report, trusts appear to be a viable means of enabling urban green spaces to be managed in a way that is in tune with local needs, of promoting a good degree of local involvement, and above all, ensuring a higher quality of green space than was available in sites under local authority management. In *Parks, People and Cities* (1996) it was stated that *'there are to date almost no examples of local authority parks being bequeathed into trust ownership'.* Those examples that were given were rather specialised: an urban National Trust site, and parks funded from endowment funds, either through ancient agreements or New Town Development Trusts. In the survey described in this report, trusts were encountered in a wider range of urban situations, including mainstream urban parks. Trust mechanisms are discussed more fully in **Chapter 8.** See also **Exhibition Park, Newcastle (Case study 8.6), Glass Park, Doncaster (Case Study 8.7), Heeley Development Trust, Sheffield (Case Study 9.4) and Scotswood Community Garden, Newcastle (Case Study 8.5, Chapter 8).**

The role of friends and user groups

7.28   The great majority of local authorities that were included in this study worked with park user or friends groups. Of the original 50 councils in the scoping study, all but six collaborated with friends groups, while only one selected for further study did not do so. However, the number of groups and the percentage of total sites to which they were attached varied enormously, as did the role and perceived function of the groups. In general, while all local authorities accepted in principle that working with user groups was worthwhile, the majority of the original 50 authorities studied in the profiling survey actually worked with relatively few such groups.

Table 7.2 The scale of involvement with friends or user groups among local authorities in the profiling survey

Number of friends or user groups that the local authority works with	Number of local authorities
0	6
1–2	11
3–5	13
6–10	6
11–20	7
*21+	7

*Sheffield (80), Stockport (49), Wolverhampton (40), Manchester (30), Liverpool (30) – (all local or conservation sites), Richmond (30) – (all conservation or heritage groups).

7.29   Out of the 50 authorities in the profiling survey, 30 worked with less than 5 groups, while 17 worked with less than 2. Of the 11 authorities that worked with only one or two groups, 5 only had friends groups that were associated with conservation sites or heritage sites. Closer examination of the 15 case study authorities in the study revealed three main approaches or routes to creating links with user groups:

- Working primarily with existing, well established friends or neighbourhood groups. Where this was the main mechanism by which an authority worked there tended to be relatively few friends groups, and these were associated with historic landscapes or parks, with semi-natural or conservation sites, or with more affluent areas of the town or city.

- Groups set up in response to funding or development initiatives. In many authorities where resources are or have been limited, user groups have been set up as a priority for parks where funding, or the strong possibility of funding, is available and consultation is required to provide local input into the development process. While again this route may result in relatively few groups being set up, those that are can be very successful if managed well because they are tied into a process that yields visible results. The parks development strategy in **Oldham** is an outstanding example of this approach (**Case study 7.6**).

- Where there has been a change in culture in a parks department from direct service delivery and contract management to a community development approach, friends and user groups assume a particular importance. In this instance, user groups may be set up for a large proportion of parks or green spaces where their size or importance to local populations makes this appropriate. Where this has occurred, very large numbers of friends groups may be in existence. Examples in this study (although many groups may fall into the above categories also) include **Sheffield, Stockport, Newcastle and Leicester**.

7.30   The terms Friends Group and Park User Group are to some extent interchangeable. However, User Groups tend to be set up and run by councils and generally (but not exclusively) are unconstituted, and have a relatively small membership. They usually exist for the consulting and communicating purposes described above. For example, **Wolverhampton** has 40 user groups, known as User Panels. These are linked to their park typology and are attached to all 'town' and 'neighbourhood' parks. Each of these parks also has their own management plan, based upon planning for real exercises at each site. The groups meet quarterly, or up to monthly if required. The panels are fed the results of user surveys which are carried out twice a year for each site by rangers, discuss what should go into site action plans as a result of these surveys and review progress on the management plans. The groups were all set up by the council: they are given a council designed constitution, but do not have their own bank accounts and do not raise money for the group. Officers call and chair the meetings and produce minutes. The benefit of this approach is that it does result in regular user consultation, it is also very much a top-down process, controlled by the council, without encouragement being given to become more involved in the running of the site, securing funding, or arranging events.

7.31   Friends Groups, on the other hand, while having communication and consultation functions, may also have larger membership, formal constitutions and bank accounts, with chair, secretary and treasurer positions. They also tend to be either involved in, or more open to, active collaboration in management. Some authorities have clear strategies to move their user groups on from being consultative bodies to active friends groups. For example **Leicester** have converted three user groups into friends groups, partly through the incentive of giving control over how a small part of the park's budget (£500) is spent to the group. However, the major developments and innovations in this area have come in large part from local authority park sections that have changed their philosophy completely to one of community engagement and development.

Community engagement and development

7.32   Previous studies have pointed to the central importance of a specific post, referred to as a 'community involvement post', as a facilitating and coordinating 'go-between' linking council and community. This has been considered as representing good practice in community involvement. While this is still the case, there have been more recent innovative developments that have pushed this principle forward. In particular, a small number of parks sections have changed the way they operate, moving from the idea of one officer having this responsibility to much larger development teams. Examples include **Sheffield** and **Stockport (Case Study 7.4)** Where this has happened the focus of the section begins to move from direct service delivery to supporting and developing groups. This is clearly a large shift in culture: moving from a policy and contract management role to a community based role.

7.33   Such a shift is by no means straight-forward because it either involves existing staff meeting different challenges and acquiring new skills, or building a new skills mix in a section. Certainly a certain tension was encountered in one or two of the local authorities, where a dynamic and creative development team, working with local groups, raised aspirations that were not matched by operations officers and personnel. One way of overcoming this, as suggested by **Sheffield City Council**, is to refocus the entire section so that all personnel are involved somehow in a community development role. The Parks and Countryside Service at **Newcastle City Council** has also taken on such a complete change of ethos **(Case study 7.5)**. This was aided enormously by the integration of the former countryside ranger service into the parks team and the associated infusion of skills in community engagement, management planning and environmental education at park development officer level.

7.34   It is clear from the research carried out for this study that many factors dictate the amount and type of activity that friends and user groups may get involved in. But it is equally clear that given appropriate support and commitment from the local authority, and equally importantly, a long-term vision and strategy for the development of groups, groups could indeed evolve from consultation bodies to very active partners. The Park Refurbishment Programme developed by **Oldham MBC** (see **Case Study 7.6**) exemplifies this. There were no friends groups in existence at the start of the programme in 1994 but the Borough now has friends groups for two thirds of its urban parks. Although the programme was the subject of a brief case study in '*Parks, People and Cities*', this was written at the outset of the process when few lessons could be learned from the experience of officers and groups involved.

MANAGING THE DEVELOPMENT OF FRIENDS AND USER GROUPS

7.35   Now, 14 active friends groups later, the Oldham officers feel they can point to certain principles behind the successful management of friends groups. First and foremost it requires continuous commitment from both sides, especially parks officers and active participants within the local community. For parks officers this usually requires out of hours working, and the acceptance that they will lose full power over what might happen on a site. Oldham's officers have had to learn community engagement skills 'on the job' and they realise that many traditional parks officers may have a temperamental unsuitability to this way of working. There is also a cultural viewpoint to overcome which may be held by officers as well as local communities that it is the council's duty to provide all services because that is what local people pay their council tax for. This is a valid point, but the question must be asked about how to proceed when the council patently is not providing an adequate service. This question is addressed further in **Paragraph 7.51**.

CASE STUDY 7.4 Stockport MBC Community Development Team

Stockport is one of the few authorities to have created a specific community development team within the parks service, as part of a move to becoming more pro-active, community led and externally funded. The team comprises a community development officer, two community support workers, an external funding officer and crime and green space officer. The team provide advice and support to local people who make contact and wish to improve a site. The team finds that groups come in at different levels – some want to raise funds, others to undertake site improvements, others practical conservation tasks. Some may just wish to promote dialogue with the council or be informed of any potential developments. The team supports groups to whatever stage they may wish to go. The team works with a wide range of groups, from friends of large Victorian Parks, to smaller sites and recreation grounds, community woodlands and small housing estates projects (CUPS – Clean Up Our Stream).

Support mechanisms:

The team has produced an *information pack* for new groups that deals with how to set up constitutions, bank accounts, recruiting members etc. A series of *networking events* and *workshops* is held that try to match groups and people with similar sites and issues to deal with. The *Green Space Forum* to which all groups are affiliated has open meetings four times a year and is intended to be a body that gives feedback on strategic issues. In addition, *training* may be provided at evening meetings in aspects of participatory work, consultation techniques and consensus building. *Grants* are available to all groups. Groups are given a start up grant of £95 and then £90 per year. There is a community project grant that has been given to many groups of up to £500 for production of newsletters, training courses or one-off events. Finally a *charter* has been produced that sets the basis for the relationship with the council. The charter is negotiated with each group and renewed each year. The aim is to achieve an equitable approach so that the less vocal groups get an equal service.

7.36   There is also a need to tap into the motivation of key individuals in local communities who may have a passion for their park or neighbourhood. All the successful friends groups encountered in this study had such individuals at their core. Part of the key to Oldham's success has been that such individuals have been actively courted and brought into friends groups. It is a common characteristic that many of the more dynamic groups and individuals involved in community activity are there initially for negative reasons: they are active because of a gap or shortfall in provision by the local authority. Oldham's officers have become skilled in *managing negativity* in the early stages of friends groups. Part of this process involves a certain degree of empathy with the concerns of the group and possibly meetings with key individuals outside of the friends meeting itself. But the most valuable weapon is a *task-orientated approach* whereby the friends groups are given responsibilities in the early stages, whether this be the drawing up of the blueprint for a refurbished park or the election of committee members. This is obviously helped by the rolling refurbishment budget for each park, but it must be stressed that this refurbishment funding did not result from any additional resource being put into the department, but rather from a creative redirection of existing resources.

7.37   The lesson of Oldham is that it is possible to actively manage groups into the more advanced stages of partnership, and that this can happen in the more deprived areas of a town or city as well as the more affluent. The Head of the Parks Service believes that people in more deprived areas are not necessarily as *'involvement ready'* as others, and therefore the educational role of officers in building capacity and acting as the catalyst for action is vital.

CASE STUDY 7.5 Community Engagement Focus, Newcastle City Council

The Parks and Countryside Service *'covers everything green across the public realm'*. The management of countryside sites was brought under the control of Parks in 2000. Structurally the priority of the service is to engage the public, find out what they want, and channel this information for grounds maintenance (managed within the service since 1998), and site development. The ethos of working with the public in the management of sites and moving towards a people motivated service as opposed to one primarily concerned with policy development and contract management, means that the department structure does not resemble that of a traditional parks department. Ward-based Recreation Development Officers (see **Case Study 7.1**) have Assistant Recreation Development Officers that are attached to each of the councils green spaces and *'act as the eyes and ears'* of the authority on the ground, working closely with community groups. The merger of the countryside service with Parks has been very important in helping shape the community orientated approach. The countryside ranger team has become fully integrated into the managerial structure of the service, with some former rangers taking up Recreation Development Officer posts, and rangers also taking complete responsibility for some urban parks. In so doing, the core skills of a good ranger service – community involvement and environmental education – have been brought into the heart of the parks service. Bringing ranger skills in at officer level is seen as *'a model to spread into all parks'*.

7.38   The integration of landscape architects as leaders in the formation of friends groups in Oldham is undoubtedly beneficial to this process. Similarly in **Sheffield**, a sizeable number of landscape architects have been recruited into the parks development team because of their all round expertise. However the focus has been on landscape architects with a strong community focus: not only do such landscape architects tend to have community engagement skills and experience developed as part of their normal involvement in consultations over design work, but also they have a strategic vision of the potential of a site that enables a co-ordinated refurbishment to be achieved rather than, as so often happens, a piecemeal and bitty approach to redevelopment.

7.39 The success of **Oldham's** refurbishment programme and the setting up of the friends groups can be attributed to several factors:

- An acknowledgement by the council that the standard of maintenance and facilities in the parks was not acceptable and a willingness to work in partnership with local communities to change the condition of parks;

- Setting aside a ring-fenced budget for improving the infrastructure and facilities in specific parks in an on-going programme of refurbishment;

- providing guaranteed goals and a fixed timetable of works so that local people have positive outcomes to work towards;

- A high commitment of parks division officers to seeing the process through and their skill in tapping into the energy of key individuals and groups in local communities.

7.40 The Oldham Green Space Strategy (2001) states that;

'the growth and success of the friends groups demonstrates that the council's aim of enabling communities to have some power and responsibility in raising standards of green space in their own neighbourhood is achievable in a relatively short time. In many cases it has provided a means for a community to gain experience, attract dedicated individuals and establish networks, thus developing the confidence to tackle wider social issues'.

This vision of parks and green spaces as centres for community spirit, with wider regeneration spin-offs is discussed in more detail (with further examples of dynamic friends groups), in **Chapter 9**.

CASE STUDY 7.6 Oldham Park Refurbishment Programme

In 1994, the Parks and Open Spaces Division of Oldham MBC produced an Urban Parks Strategy (approved in 1995) that acknowledged that the council would be unable to solve the problem of degraded urban parks without substantial community involvement. The strategy set out four main ways to address the revitalisation of the Borough's parks: review of existing budgets, engaging the community, events in parks, and seeking external funding.

In the new Borough *Green Space Strategy* (2001), (**Case Study 6.10**) it is stated that *'the most pleasing success of the* (Park) *strategy has been the establishment of a network of 'Friends of Parks' Groups'.* The establishment of these groups was integral to the Parks Refurbishment Programme that formed the basis of the Parks Strategy. This programme is a rolling process that targets a different park each year and works through a consultation process to regenerate the site. Funding for the programme was obtained following an internal budget review that redirected £400,000 to £500,000 per year that was previously used in an uncoordinated winter works programme. Rather than spread this money around a larger number of parks, it was decided to use it on a single park each year so that meaningful and long-lasting effects could be achieved.

CASE STUDY 7.6 Continued

For each park the refurbishment programme has the following components:

- Establishment of a Friends Group for the park

- Extensive consultation with the group, and others, over the content and character of the refurbished park

- A programme of works over the space of a year to achieve the agreed

- A grand opening at the end of the process. This takes the form of the annual Tulip Funday festival. This is a revival of a festival formerly held in Oldham, but now, rather than being attached to a single site, the festival is a roving, celebratory event held on the opening of a refurbished park. Not only does this symbolically mark a new beginning, but the event, fixed in the calender in advance, makes a clear deadline to focus minds and is a clear and high profile outcome of the whole process.

The first friends group was set up in 1995 in a small park (Lees Park), which had an array of problems that could be tackled in a simple way, and with visible results. This sparked great interest, because people were clearly able to see the difference the refurbishment programme made. In particular, council members saw how having a friends group could be potentially good for their area. In the following year 'everyone wanted one'. 14 groups have now been set up (the Borough has 23 parks in all). There is now a waiting list of groups wishing to work with the council. However, no more are planned in the immediate future because the division has reached saturation point in being able to support the groups, although the aim is to have a thriving friends group attached to each park when resources allow. The council organizes an annual programme of 3 meetings for each group (although some groups also organize their own meetings outside of these times).

Managing Friends Groups

As indicated above, the Parks and Open Spaces division undertakes a consultation exercise with a friends group as soon as it is set up before a refurbishment happens. The first such meeting is held with two senior officers of the division. The Head of Service makes a presentation about Oldham's parks and the various ways by which local people can get involved. The senior landscape architect puts forward some general ideas about how he sees the park and what is and isn't successful. A plan is never produced at this meeting, but the officers will take inspirational images and ideas of what might be considered successful parks elsewhere. They also, where possible, take along someone from another friends group – they see this as helping to build credibility and trust with local people.

At the second and subsequent meetings, the senior landscape architect takes along a proposed masterplan to discuss, and a senior development manager to explain the implementation process. Groups may also be taken to other refurbished parks to show what is possible (this is a positive aspect of having a rolling refurbishment programme).

It may take several years to get a scheme agreed. The order in which parks are refurbished is decided by council members. Initially refurbishment was aimed at the areas of greatest deprivation and need. However, groups often lobby members to get their park moved up the timetable and the original order has changed. Up until 2001, 12 parks in the Borough (50% of the total) have been through this process.

The 14 friends groups are all at different levels of involvement. Many can be initially adversarial (see main text) but others have moved onto and formed partnerships, running services in the park

Examples:

Coalshaw Green Park, Oldham

The Parks and Open Spaces division started work on this park following the burning down of an old pavilion in 1995. Consultation meetings were held in 1996. The council 'got a bashing' about the lack of progress on improving the park, but the consultations indicated a range of priority areas for action. A flier was sent door to door around the area to start the friends group off. A new pavilion was opened in 1998. The pavilion now houses a café run by the friends group. Initially it started in 2000, opening 7 days a week, selling hot drinks and snacks (summer 11–4 pm and winter 11-3 pm). Subsequently they became more ambitious, serving hot lunches through the week. The café is staffed by three volunteers, all food and hygeine trained. They lock and unlock the toilets on request. A Christmas party is run for pensioners and the money raised is used to take local children to the pantomime. Through the café, there is now a 'Junior Friends Group' that is working to get sponsorship for a skate park and will be involved in the design, with the council.

The Head of Service says that '*vandalism costs have been reduced massively in the park since the café was opened*'. There has been a small amount of damage done by youths, but this has been countered by a 'name and shame' notice board in the café of known offenders. The driving force behind the friends group has been a local resident who joined the group in 1999. She volunteers in the café and has been responsible for organising children's activities such as the pantomime visits and easter egg hunt, and manages the junior friends group. Working for the park has become a significant part of her life: '*I'm working harder now as a volunteer than when I was paid to work!*'

Stoneleigh Park, Oldham

Stoneleigh Park was refurbished in 1997, accompanied by the formation of a friends group and consultation. The group have gone on to fund raise for a further phase of works and are now looking at running events in the park. They have become involved in various partnerships to secure funding, including the Healthy Living Initiative, Neighbourhood Renewal Fund and Landfill Tax. Stoneleigh Park was also the Borough's first application for a Green Flag Park Award and won. This was a remarkable achievement, given that the park had formerly been used by the authority as an example of how bad a park could become through neglect.

CREATING LINKS, FORGING NETWORKS AND REWARDING EFFORT

7.41   A number of the local authorities included in the survey took active steps to facilitate and promote links between friends groups. This only occurred effectively in authorities that had developed a community engagement culture (see above). Bringing together friends groups as a way of sharing good practice furthered the aims of such authorities. It also provided another level of community engagement. However, such networking was only encountered in a small minority of authorities. Some of the surveyed authorities questioned the value of doing this, feeling that groups would not want to give up their spare time to attend additional meetings, or that they are only interested in their own space and would not be interested in those of others. On several occasions, the meetings associated with this survey provided the first opportunity for different groups in a city to get together and share experience. Examples of coordinating mechanisms included:

- **Park User Forum, Sheffield**. The idea for the Park User Forum originally came out of Sheffield's Park Regeneration Strategy who suggested an annual parks conference. However, the friends groups themselves were not keen on an annual event and thought it would be more useful to have more regular meetings. The forum now meets four to six times a year. The group is chaired and managed semi-independently of the council by Sheffield Wildlife Trust, which is a major partner with the council in the management and regeneration of the City's green spaces. A typical meeting may involve information-giving by the council on national policy and developmental issues of relevance to parks, relevant city-wide policies and development matters, raising of issues by those in attendance, and a general training session which may focus on such areas as applying for external funding, involving volunteers, or promoting wildlife. From the council's point of view, the forum has been very useful in that it has increased the understanding by local groups of the financial restrictions under which they operate and has resulted in a significant reduction in negative attitudes. The aim of the council is to turn the forum into a significant lobbying group to increase the profile of parks with council members.

- **Green Space Forum, Stockport**. This group has a wider remit, and is open to anyone involved in green space management, and not just friends groups. The council feel that it has made the approach of the authority to green space management more open, but that the meetings are prone to the same disadvantages of friends groups (see **Paragraph 7.45** below) of infighting between special interest groups, and battling with the council. Stockport also has a number of sports fora that bring together representatives of all the teams or groups to discuss common areas of interest. The **Soccer Forum** has been established for 13 years. As a result of the success of the Soccer Forum, a **Bowls Forum** has been established. Recently a bowls development sub group has been set up as part of this to investigate how to increase the number of people playing the sport, through initiatives such as junior bowls coaching and taking short mat bowling into schools.

- **Park Life Conference, Newcastle**. Newcastle's first Park Life Conference was held in April 2001, following attendance by two parks officers at Regeneration Exchange Conference in October 2000 (Regeneration Exchange is a networking group for regeneration partnerships in the North East). It was agreed to hold a follow-up conference in Newcastle, focusing specifically on parks and green space, but again bringing together groups from across the region. One aim of the conference was to allow groups to get together and share experience, but it was also intended to inspire newly formed groups, or those interested in forming a group, to get going. Apart from a keynote talk on Mile End Park, London, the bulk of the day consisted of case studies that went through the life of a friends group, from start-up through to partnership working. The highlight of the event was the marketplace whereby all groups had a stall and were able to communicate and make contacts to continue after the conference (some follow-up exchanges have happened). The conference will now become an annual event.

Encouraging involvement

7.42 Baggott and Richardson (see Footnote 26) make the point that while a number of local authorities have developed successful approaches to involving local people, whether this be through events, arts projects, discussion groups or planning for real exercises, sharing of good practice in this area is rare. Letter drops, questionnaires and working with school children were the most common methods encountered in the survey carried out for this report. For example, **Doncaster**, following the great success of two friends groups in revitalising their park (see **Chapter 9**) is forming 15 new friends groups in 2002. This is being done by a mail shot to all residents in a set radius around each park. This entails 30, 000 letters in total, and a series of awareness raising events. For example, in the summer of 2001, a four day event consultation event took place in one of the town's main parks, Elmfield Park, with over 400 questionnaires being filled in each day. The event cost £1300 per day but reached a large number of regular park users.

7.43 Some innovative approaches were also encountered that specifically targeted under or non user groups, as defined in **Chapter 3**:

- **Young people**. Many authorities were concerned with involving young people in park-based activities. Where an authority expressed success in working with a group of young people this, almost without exception, revolved around BMX tracks, or skate parks. In many instances the promise of such a facility encouraged high involvement by potential users in its planning, but it was generally considered difficult to maintain that interest once the feature had been built. In many ways, features such as skate parks and BMX tracks promote active male use and reinforce the issue of dominance in use of much green space by male adult dominated sports. A very successful project that had involved groups of young people in decision making and management over extended time periods, and specifically encouraged involvement by girls was linked to **Manvers Recreation Ground, Doncaster (Case Study 9.3)**;

- **Ethnic Minority Groups**. All local authorities in the survey stated that involving people from an ethnic minority background in green space management was a particular problem. No examples of ethnic minority-lead projects were encountered. In some areas, so-called 'bridging organisations' such as Groundwork, the Black Environment Network or the Sensory Trust can have a facilitating role in encouraging greater participation, although again, no such examples were encountered in the survey. However, a number of initiatives were identified that had been successful in increasing participation. The **Participation in Leisure Programme, Newcastle (Case Study 7.7)** is an innovative cross cutting and revenue generating initiative that aims to involve traditionally under-represented groups in environmental and horticultural activities. At the **Scotswood Community Garden, Newcastle (Case Study 8.5)**, a group of Asian women have been involved in an organic food growing project, organized by a Charity 'First Step' that provides informal learning and confidence building ventures for Asian women in the Benwell area of the city. Funding also came from Newcastle's Community Food Initiative that encourages healthy eating and encourages home food growing. The group meets weekly and the women go with their children who use the two acre site as a play space.

7.44   The desire to make community engagement inclusive and representative is also an important issue. An attempt is being made at **Exhibition Park, Newcastle (Case Study 8.6, Chapter 8)** to engage all sections of a local community on a long-term basis with regeneration of the park. The importance of a community group being totally representative of the local community does though vary according to the objectives of the group. If the purpose is primarily for consultation then clearly wide and inclusive representation is important. If however the aim is to achieve results on the ground through active participation in management, then it is perhaps more important and practical, at least initially, to involve people who will get things done as a priority. Certainly, the majority of friends and user groups included in the study were not representative of the breadth of their communities, but part of the role of local authority officers working with the groups was to ensure that any developments occurred were of benefit to all sections of the community.

CASE STUDY 7.7 Participation in Leisure Programme, Newcastle

The scheme was set up with City Challenge funding to encourage people to use leisure facilities in the five most deprived wards of the city. A team of four officers with different specialties from different departments of the council were involved, resulting in a mix of community outreach and arts development skills within the team. Although each member of the team has their own projects, they work together where possible. One member of the team has responsibility for involving people in environmental and horticultural activities. To stimulate projects, each worker has a small development budget. In operation the group exceeded expectations: the numbers of people involved in projects and the additional funding that was generated was much higher than forecast. As a result, at the end of City Challenge funding, the council continued the programme.

The success of the scheme is put down, by those involved to:

- The possession of delegated budgets that the officers are able to use as they see fit. This has enabled monies to be re-directed and used as matched funding to bring in additional resources.

- 'Partnership working' within the council. The cross-cutting team is able to overcome more traditional divisions between departments.

- 'Distance Management'. There is no overall manager for the project, although the objectives of the scheme are clear. The officers involved feel they have a strong incentive to continue the success of the scheme.

The officers identified the main problem with working closely with groups that are identified as under or non-users of green space as striking a balance between being accessible and accepted and developing good relationships with the groups involved, and being an official representative of the council.

CASE STUDY 7.7 Continued

Examples of projects include

as responsibility for involving people in environmental and horticultural activities. To stimulate projects, each worker has a small development budget. In operation the group exceeded expectations: the numbers of people involved in projects and the additional funding that was generated was much higher than forecast. As a result, at the end of City Challenge funding, the council continued the programme.

Hanging basket project: This project took place in North Benwell, a high density housing area of terraces with very small back yards, with a predominantly Asian population. The project involved community groups, tenants associations, an action group and was based around the Asian Community Centre. The aim of the project was to involve people in horticultural or gardening activities. Around 300 people took up the scheme, making up their own baskets over two activity days, organised to run from 12.00 – 7.30. Many people participated and the event was supported by horticultural trainees. Plants were provided by allotment holders and were also donated from the city. The project has subsequently been repeated.

Allotment clubs for children: This project involved joint working between the parks section and the childrens and young people's section. Again the intention is partly involvement in environmental activities, but also to encourage healthy eating. While ostensibly the activities are primarily environmental, the main focus is on youth and social work. In one example, again in Benwell, 6 children have been regularly involved. The children were selected originally via social services, from the local youth club and summer play schemes. The group meets every Saturday. Following the success of the initial project further clubs are to be set up in other areas.

Costs and benefits of community involvement

7.45 In principle, increasing the level of community involvement in decision making and management of green space can result in the enrichment of the space, in terms of use, quality of maintenance, range of facilities and visitor experience. However, there are clear costs as well as benefits in promoting greater community involvement. As part of the survey, local authority officers were asked to outline what they saw as the main benefits and costs to their service.

BENEFITS AS VIEWED BY LOCAL AUTHORITY OFFICERS

- **Local ownership** This was the most commonly stated benefit. Encouraging local ownership was seen as essential in empowering communities to become active in decision making and site management;

- **Funding** This was the second most common response. Community groups are able to access additional funding sources that local authorities cannot access on their own. These may range from small scale local fundraising to applying for grants from funding bodies. The sums involved can be substantial. For example, the Sheffield Botanical Gardens Trust evolved from **the Friends of Sheffield Botanical Gardens** and now both organizations support the gardens and are instrumental in raising £1.2 million required to match a Heritage Lottery Fund for the restoration of the gardens. There is a danger, however, that excessive reliance on community groups to raise funds can cause strains, both within the group, and with the local authority;

- **Communication and increasing understanding** was also frequently mentioned. This was seen very much as a two-way process. While a council may be better able to gain more direct knowledge of local problems, it was also felt that the council also benefits from people gaining a greater understanding of the constraints under which it operates;

- **Safety and security** Increasing user 'ownership' and involvement with a site, and trust with the local authority, can lead to increased 'eyes and ears' on and around the site, and rapid reporting of incidents;

- **Additional expertise** Community groups can bring specialist and additional expertise, as well as detailed local knowledge of a site and its history. While this can often be used to inform decision making, or achieve maintenance tasks through volunteers, it may save considerable officer time also. For example, **the Friends of Sheffield General Cemetery**, led a successful bid to the Heritage Lottery Fund, supported by Sheffield City Council council, using professional expertise that was within and available to the group.

- **Ability to respond to local need** This was seen as important, especially when a park or green space served diverse local communities. Being able to identify important local issues was also seen as important in efficient planning of the use of financial resources, and in policy formulation;

- **Increased use of a park or green space** through greater involvement of the local community;

- **Political profile** Some local authorities saw high community involvement as an important way of influencing politicians in an attempt to raise the political profile of parks, and therefore to secure funding;

- **Spreading the work load** Volunteers can supply significant additional labour, and sometimes skills, which supplements that available from rangers or grounds maintenance staff. In some cases this labour can be factored in to matched funding;

- **Sustainability and long-term viability** Community input and support was seen as vital to sustain the long-term viability of park or green space regeneration schemes;

- **Partners in regeneration** In some localities where resources were limited, developing partnerships with local communities was seen as one of the few viable options for regenerating green space;

- **Best Value** One authority felt that its community activity would produce a good impression for its Best Value review.

COSTS AS VIEWED BY LOCAL AUTHORITY OFFICERS

- **Officer Time** was stated by virtually all the authorities as the major cost of increased community involvement. Some authorities had seen a significant increase in workload related to dealing with community enquiries and supporting groups, without a complementary increase in resources. Supporting groups often entailed frequent 'out of hours' working for officers;

- **Demand on resources** In addition to officer time, there is also a requirement to adequately resource community groups. In terms of both time and resources, undertaking community involvement without full commitment is likely to end in disappointing results in the longer term;

- **Lack of appropriate skills in officers** to allow them to engage confidently in community involvement programmes, possibly bringing a need for retraining;

- **Raising expectations** was a commonly mentioned potential problem. If a council is unable to deliver what is promised then it can rapidly lose the support of a local community;

- **Managing conflicting demands** A common problem in managing groups was mediating between special interest groups and keeping an eye on a bigger picture rather than being deflected by other objectives of a group;

- **Identifying leaders** Some local authorities were keen to build relations with positive leaders, but often it may be difficult to find out who these may be in initial meetings;

- **Turning negativity into constructive engagement** Overcoming initial feelings of distrust was seen as one of the main hurdles to be overcome in forming a successful group;

- **Representativeness** The majority of community groups were not seen as being fully representative of their local communities. Many were seen as being dominated by older women. This was partly related to whether meetings were held during the day or in the evening;

- **Maintaining momentum** Groups can become stale and attended by a core of 'usual suspects'. There is also a resource and officer cost in maintaining capacity and supporting groups as they develop their skills;

- **Motivation** Getting local groups to become involved in things seen as the council's responsibility;

- **Time delay** Community involvement and consultation can result in extending the development process, and budget slippage;

- **Job Security** Grounds maintenance staff may feel threatened by volunteer activity;

- **Community development versus ongoing maintenance** One officer in an authority with a high community focus felt that this diverted attention from continuing good quality site maintenance;

- **Community involvement as a substitute for proper investment** Concerns were expressed that if community involvement was seen as being too successful then there may be pressure to reduce budgets in future.

7.46 To explore whether the same perceptions of costs and benefits were also shared by the community members actually involved, mainly through Friends groups, the same questions were also discussed with a variety of groups in different locations.

BENEFITS AS VIEWED BY MEMBERS OF FRIENDS GROUPS

7.47 Several of the benefits mentioned by members of friends groups were the same as those listed by local authority officers, although there were some differences in emphasis, particularly in regard to safety issues and young people. The first three points were commonly raised:

- **Communication** was the most commonly stated benefit and in fact for the majority of 'user groups' with little direct involvement in the management of the park, was the only stated benefit. Being informed about developments in and around the park and being able to give views back to the council officers was highly valued;

- **Getting people involved and increasing the use of a park** was seen as vital in creating a viable future for the park, and in promoting safety;

- **Achieving additional funding for the park** Again this was commonly stated as an important benefit.

7.48 Only those groups that were more actively involved in a particular park or green space raised the following points:

- **Bringing the community together** from different areas and different sections of the community;

- **Personal development** Learning of new skills for those involved. In some cases, people gain employment through the volunteer route;

- **Personal satisfaction** in achieving real results;

- **Reporting of crime** Having a Friends Group means there is a first point of contact for security issues – members of friends groups can act in a surveillance role if a good relationship has been developed with the police;

- **Putting something back into the community** This was expressed on several occasions by people who had fond memories of a park that had since deteriorated, and wished to do something to bring it back into a better condition.

- **Providing a safe and secure environment** for young people within the park;

- **'Community Care'** – In a number of cases (e.g **Grove Park and Manvers Park, Doncaster, Case Studies 9.2 and 9.3**) this had developed into a 'community care' approach, using the park as a base to develop activities and programmes – as was stated by some of those involved in Doncaster – *'we have the children in the park for more time than they are actually in school!'*

- **Reduction in vandalism** through provision of activities and forming an attachment to the park for young people.

COSTS/PROBLEMS AS VIEWED BY MEMBERS OF FRIENDS GROUPS

7.49   Participants were less forthcoming about the negative points, in terms of the costs or problems of this type of community involvement, perhaps because people had made the choice to become involved. Several points were, however, frequently made about the difficulty of the process:

- **A testing learning process** There can be a hard process of trial and error in learning the best ways to do things;

- **Long-term process** Long term vision is required to retain the enthusiasm to see a project through;

- **Over-reliance on volunteers** One group queried whether a local authority could give non-monetary benefit for the volunteer time put in – an equivalent of the American 'time dollars' or a Local Economic Trading Scheme (LETS) type bartering or exchange scheme for local authority services;

- **Responsibility** Those involved in park based youth projects felt that involvement resulted in the added responsibility of needing to live up to young peoples raised expectations;

- **Managing a project that becomes much bigger than originally thought** can be a daunting prospect for a group of volunteers;

- **Getting volunteers who are committed** enough to replace others who drop out of a group was a frequent problem;

- **Jealousy** from other areas or individuals about a particular park getting special treatment was regularly encountered by one group, even through the additional benefits to the park had only been brought about by committed voluntary activity.

Conclusions

7.50 The case studies presented in this chapter (and also in **Chapter 9**) show that community involvement in urban parks and green spaces can lead to increased use, enhanced quality and greater richness of experience, and in particular help to create facilities suited to local needs. In this chapter, two main aspects of community involvement have been discussed: communication and consultation, and active participation in decision making, planning and management. It is at the second stage that real 'value-added' benefits, such as increased funding, additional facilities, events programmes and so on, really arise. The evidence in this chapter contradicts the commonly held view that such benefits often come only with the involvement of more affluent and articulate communities in towns and cities. There are many examples to show how with strategic management and support, community and friends groups in all sectors of a city can achieve excellence. It must be emphasised that involving groups that often do not participate is time consuming and can require a lot of capacity building in terms of training and development.

7.51 From the evidence in this study, the potential involvement and role of local communities in urban parks and green spaces seems to be particularly related to:

- **The culture of the local authority and parks service.** Examples have been given of parks services that have embraced a community development ethos and moved from being contract managers to a philosophy of community engagement;

- **The resources available.** Supporting local groups is time and resource consuming. The example of Oldham demonstrates what can be achieved if resources can be dedicated to individual groups and if achievable goals are set;

- **The type of site.** Voluntary maintenance input was shown to be related to the nature of a particular site with the greatest use of volunteer labour being on sites with a wildlife focus;

- **Local capacity.** Social factors have an important influence, but the examples of **Oldham** and **Stockport** demonstrate the benefits of capacity building as a precursor to greater involvement;

- **Sense of ownership.** Greater ownership of a site, whether it be through empowerment and delegation of responsibility to local groups, self-management of facilities through lease arrangements, or full ownership through trust status encourages greater local commitment and input. This relates to the philosophy of the authority and its willingness to relinquish power and control over sites;

- **The quality of maintenance and service delivery.** The existing state of a site in terms of its maintenance quality and the extent to which its facilities meet local needs emerged as perhaps the main driving force behind community involvement.

7.52 The last two factors appear to be most crucial. A high degree of involvement or self-management is fairly common in situations where groups have a great sense of ownership, often in restricted access sites or sites where members have a financial stake, such as bowling greens or allotments, or in specialist locations such as walled gardens. However, in this research, several examples were also found of high levels of local management in mainstream urban parks. In these situations there is a paradox. Community involvement in site management often comes about initially because a local authority is failing to meet the aspirations and needs of local communities on its own. While it can be argued that community involvement is a method by which local authorities ensure that they do meet those needs, in the great majority of cases, the most dynamic and effective of groups were formed as a result of grass roots initiatives to tackle shortfalls in provision.

7.53   This raises a key question: ethically, to what extent should community and voluntary effort be used to provide services and quality standards that should, in theory, be provided by local authorities? There is a valid view, expressed by some local authority officers as well as by members of friends groups, that local community and voluntary management in parks is not acceptable and indeed is a form of exploitation because people pay their council taxes for the provision of basic services. Alternatively, and much more positively, it can be argued that community input can result in a much better and richer spaces and places than would be possible with local authority input alone, and that those individuals and communities concerned gain real and quantifiable benefits from their input. It is certainly true that at least one authority viewed community partnerships as the only viable option to make good a continued decline in quality of urban green space provision. Is that exploitation, or rather an enlightened attitude that seeks to harness the creativity and energy of local groups?

7.54   From the evidence of the local authorities included in this study, it is suggested that an ideal and equitable approach to working with community groups should involve an individually negotiated and renewable contract between the local authority and the community group. This should agree minimum standards for local authority provision and defines realistic targets for a community group, backed up by officer support, training and financial resources, and tied to achievable goals.

CHAPTER 8
Making Things Happen

SUMMARY OF KEY POINTS

- The parks and open spaces budgets of the great majority of authorities in the survey had been subject to budgetary decline in real terms over the past decade.

- Wide variations were observed in spend per head of population between the authorities in the survey (although the figures were not necessarily comparable). There does not seem to be any clear correlation between levels of spending and the extent of good or innovative practice.

- Lack of capital funding is a major problem and the long-term success of capital projects in urban green spaces can be jeopardised by a failure to provide associated revenue funding for maintenance.

- In terms of the importance of different external funding sources the Heritage Lottery Urban Parks Programme and Section 106 Agreements were consistently named as the most valuable.

- Effective partnerships between a local authority and community groups, funding agencies and business can result in significant added value, both in terms of finances and quality of green space. However, time and resources have to be put into forming and supporting partnerships.

- In most cases private sponsorship does not appear to make a significant contribution in terms of overall budgets, however, it does enable features or facilities to be created or operated that would otherwise not be viable.

- A range of approaches was encountered that either increased the financial resources available, or made better or more efficient use of existing resources. These included: private finance initiatives; partnership with grant-making organisations, business and community groups; creative re-direction of revenue spend; opportunistic use of targeted grant funding to achieve wider strategic aims; flexible use of Section 106 funds.

- There is potential for creation of city-wide partnerships for parks and green space to raise the level and quality of open space and parks in an entire city, through neighbourhood organisations and park partnerships.

- Self-management and trust status is becoming a means to create and manage mainstream urban parks. There is a reduced financial and administration cost to the local authority in the long-term involved in transfer of a park to a self-managing trust.

Introduction

8.1 Making things happen in relation to urban green spaces depends to a considerable degree on the resources that are available to local authorities and on how those resources are used. This chapter concentrates on these matters though the aim is not a comprehensive review of local authority funding, but rather to try to give a general picture of current levels and sources of funding and levels of spending. The main focus, however, is to investigate creativity and innovation in the way that resources are used, in developing funding partnerships, and in developing alternative models for the provision of urban green space.

Funding and budgets

8.2 It is widely accepted that local authority core budgets for parks and green spaces have declined over the last 10–15 years, and this was generally found to be true of the fifteen case study local authorities. When asked about trends in their budgets over the last decade, only two authorities reported a long-term increase in real terms. In one case this was partly explained by very active lobbying of councillors by the parks department, but also because they had taken over responsibility for green spaces formerly managed by other departments. Two authorities reported static budgets in real terms, while the remainder had been subject to a downward trend. The degree of decline varied, however. For example, in **Chelmsford** and **Sheffield** budget allocations had increased over the previous ten years, but by less than the rate of inflation (although both authorities had seen an increase with inflation in 2001). **Plymouth** had witnessed a budget cut of £1 million over 10 years, while **Wolverhampton** had been subjected to a series of cuts every two to three years (for example a 7.5% reduction in 2000). **Milton Keynes**, as an expanding town, had in the five years preceding 1999 witnessed a 29% increase in the area of green space it was responsible for but had been subject to a 26% cut in budget.

8.3 Nevertheless, the general impression was that in 2000 and 2001 there had been a slight improvement in financial allocations. For authorities such as **Doncaster** this was evidenced by a lack of cutbacks for the first time in a number of years, while other authorities, such as **Stockport, Sheffield** and **Bexley**, had for the first time received an increase in line with inflation for that year. In **Bexley** this was thought to be related partly to the authority's success in winning Green Flag awards.

8.4 The local authorities were asked whether parks and green space budgets had been subject to different treatment compared to other aspects of leisure or education spend. Only half the authorities were forthcoming with this information but among those that did address this, it was generally suggested that budget cuts fell across the board, with all departments expected to bear the brunt. Three authorities did, however, believe that parks had suffered disproportionately in comparison to sports and arts development, while two said that the only department that had been protected from cuts was libraries. In **Sheffield**, leisure spending as a whole was said to have suffered a disproportionate cut over the years, but parks were in a different position to other aspects of the service. Because the city's museums and art galleries were now operated by trusts they received a fixed grant each year. The parks budget, however, was still flexible and therefore tended to be squeezed if cuts were required.

8.5 As part of this study a comparison was made of the spend per head of population or per hectare of green space for each case study authority. It must be emphasised that these figures are notoriously difficult to compare. Local authorities have not adopted a consistent typology for green spaces and therefore one authority may calculate their amounts of green space in a different way to another. Different authorities may have a variety of different services related to urban green space in their budgets, and again this may influence their calculations of total spend. These figures give no indication of quality of green space: high total spend may mask inefficiencies in service delivery. Spend per head of population as a means of comparing authorities does not take into account the total area of green space that the authority is responsible for. There may be considerable differences in the cost of maintaining different types of green space, and the amount of these different types will vary between authorities. Figures of spend per hectare were only available from a proportion of the authorities in the survey and have therefore not been used as a basis for comparison here. It would be very desirable for standardised definitions of what constitutes urban green space to be adopted by local authorities to enable direct comparisons to be made which take account of population size, extent of green space and type of green space. The approximate range of spending per head of population across all 15 authorities is shown in **Table 8.1**.

Table 8.1 The range of core revenue spend per head of population per year (information from 15 case study local authorities)	
Spending per head of population	Number of authorities
£25.00 – £27.00	2
£20.00 – £24.00	1
£15.00 – £19.00	2
£10.00 – £14.00	6
£5.00 – £9.00	4

8.6 The highest spend was £27.36 per head, and the lowest was £6.58. In terms of spend per hectare there was a similar range, with the highest spend being £8,360.28 per hectare and the lowest being £1,740. There was, however, no relation between spend per head and spend per hectare (although spend per hectare figures were only available for a minority of the authorities). It is clear that there were striking variations between authorities in their levels of spending on urban green spaces but there does not seem to be any consistent correlation between levels of spending and the extent of good or innovative practice. There are certainly cases where higher spending authorities are performing at a high-level and appear to have a highly innovative culture but there are also good examples of innovation in less well funded authorities.

8.7 Striking differences between authorities were also found in relation to the amounts of external funding that had been accessed and in the availability of capital funding. In particular the lack of capital spending was identified as a major problem. In combination with continuous pressure on maintenance quality as a result of reduced revenue spending, the absence of capital funds has resulted in a serious decline in the infrastructure of parks and other green spaces in many areas. This was not only a frustration to officers but an issue of increasing importance and concern to park friends and user groups in many of the authorities included in the study. Of the 15 authorities in the study, only two (**Ipswich** and **Bexley**) had a parks capital budget, although **Plymouth** had allocated significant capital spend to one park and to its play areas. **Stockport** and **Leicester** had a general capital fund which was open to bids from the parks services, although in **Leicester** the parks department had received little from this because of the priorities of the council which favour spending in other departments. **Lewisham** had received £1.5 million to spend on capital works over three years as a result of a private finance initiative-style arrangement with a private contractor (see **Case Study 8.1**). Capital spending on green spaces did occur in these and in the other authorities, but this was generally tied to external funding sources, which usually had tight specifications on how the money should be spent and also on the type or location of urban green space that was eligible.

EXTERNAL FUNDING

8.8　Opportunities for external funding for urban green space differ in their reliability from year to year, in the amount of funding available, and in the type of situation in which funding may be forthcoming. For example national agencies may only have funding available for heritage or sports related projects, while business sponsorship will only be possible for highly visible initiatives where the business receives recognition. In 'People, Parks and Cities' it was stated that the range of external sources of finance and other forms of support given to local authority parks services are 'likely only to amount to a small proportion of the mainstream budget needed to maintain basic quality standards in green space management and maintenance across any one borough.'

8.9　This statement still remains largely true for many local authorities in relation to the whole spectrum of urban green spaces across an area, although for specific parks and green spaces external funding and partnerships can play a significant if not total role in their regeneration. It is also particularly true of revenue funding because it was apparent from a number of the case study authorities that external sources were absolutely crucial for capital works. This is, however, a double-edged sword, because in a context of reduced revenue budgets, local authorities are faced with the problem of having limited funds for subsequent maintenance of the assets that result from externally funded capital programmes.

8.10　Perhaps the main issue here is what is meant by 'basic quality standards in green space management and maintenance'. As discussed earlier in this chapter, and from the case studies quoted in **Chapters 7 and 9**, it is clear that parks service budget cuts in the 1990s, combined with the lack of capital spending, and the legacy of CCT have meant that in many instances these basic standards have become less than acceptable. What is apparent is that in most cases, partnership working to achieve additional funding, expertise and community involvement is becoming the only way to lift standards above this minimum and to provide facilities that may be desperately needed by local communities.

Sources of External Funding

8.11　The fifteen local authorities in the detailed survey were asked to indicate those sources of funding that were most significant to their operations. Again, there was a wide variation in the success of different authorities in attracting funding, in the amounts that had become available, and in the way the resources were used. To some extent the differences were tied to geographical location and the nature of the town or city – whether it was a large metropolitan authority or a smaller borough. But other factors that came into play appeared to be the political priority that the council gave to urban green space and also the culture of the service. For example, one of the larger metropolitan authorities, **Leicester**, reported little success in obtaining any external funding for parks, and this was attributed to a lack of political will in the council in contributing any matched funding to park or green space issues.

8.12 Other authorities had taken a more proactive approach to obtaining external funding in an entrepreneurial manner. **Wolverhampton** and **Stockport**, for example, had full-time external funding officers in the parks section whose role was to investigate and source funding and support resource generating partnerships. In the same way that some parks and open spaces sections had taken on a pervading community development ethos (as discussed in **Chapter 7**), it was apparent from the case study authorities that some departments, such as **Sheffield**, had embraced an entrepreneurial culture aimed at seeking and exploiting resource opportunities. It was also notable that in most cases, it was the same authorities that had embraced both of these approaches. This may well have been a necessity for survival in the face of dwindling core budgets, but never the less, it has apparently resulted in a greater degree of creativity than in other authorities. Concerns were, however, raised in discussions that an over-emphasis on such creative and innovative approaches, both to gaining external funding and pursuing community development could divert officer time away from more general aspects of service delivery and maintenance which are often key to public perceptions of urban green spaces.

Table 8.2 The main sources of external funding given by the 15 local authorities in the survey

	HLF	SRB	Landfill	S106	Business	City Challenge	ERDF
Basingstoke	●			●			
Bexley	●		●				
Chelmsford	●			●			
Cheltenham	●	●	●	●			
Doncaster	●	●			●	●	
Ipswich	●						
Leicester	●	●		●		●	
Lewisham	●	●	●	●			
Milton Keynes		●	●	●			
Newcastle		●	●	●		●	
Oldham	●	●	●	●	●		
Plymouth	●	●	●	●			
Sheffield	●	●	●	●		●	●
Stockport	●	●	●	●	●		●
Wolverhampton	●	●				●	

8.13 **Table 8.2** lists the main sources of external funding used by the local authorities in the survey. All these sources, apart from SRB and ERDF funding, were for urban green space initiatives alone. In the case of SRB and ERDF green space projects were funded as part of wider neighbourhood regeneration schemes. In terms of the importance of different external funding sources, two were consistently named as the most valuable: Heritage Lottery Funding and Section 106 agreements relating to development. The **Heritage Lottery Fund's**

Urban Parks Programme was particularly well regarded because it was seen as one of the few funding sources that is dedicated to parks alone, and because of the significant sums that were potentially available, at least in the early years of the scheme. **Sheffield**, for example, will have benefited, if matched funding is taken into account, by close to £10 million spread over three important urban green spaces: the **Sheffield Botanical Gardens, Norfolk Park** and the **General Cemetery**, with a number of other applications in the pipeline. The award of such significant sums has had a revitalizing effect on the parks section as this success changed the culture of the department and kick-started the process of seeking wider funding opportunities. While the funding is restricted to parks deemed to have historical value, it certainly does not need to be restricted only to historical restoration projects. Again in **Sheffield**, the Heritage Parks Programme has creatively used this funding to provide facilities for city-wide benefit, as well as catering for the specific contemporary needs of local populations. A proportion of authorities had not benefited from Heritage Lottery Funding, either through unwillingness or inability by the council to raise matched funding, or a perceived lack of what are regarded as historically important parks.

8.14   **Section 106** was the other source of external funding widely regarded as being significant. Different authorities had several methods of administering and allocating the funding so that the value to urban green spaces, and the way the money was used in parks, both differed. Section 106 funding comes as a levy from developers as a contribution to benefit the area in which a development occurs. The majority of authorities in the survey reported its use, typically for revamping of play areas or creation of play areas within new housing developments. However, several examples were encountered of Section 106 funding being used to create new parks adjacent to new housing development. Again attitudes varied between authorities. For example, **Doncaster** preferred to use the funding to improve existing parks or green spaces, rather than creating new green spaces which would become a maintenance liability in future years. In **Sheffield's Green Estate Programme (Case Study 9.5)** however this type of problem has been effectively overcome by charging residents a permanent annual ground rent levy to pay for on-going maintenance .

8.15   The sums involved can be highly significant. For example **Oldham** had raised £1 million over the past three years and **Doncaster** had accumulated £2.6 million of Section 106 funds to spend on urban green space (although, as explained in **Case Study 6.6**, these funds have not yet actually been allocated to green space projects, pending completion of the borough's green space strategy, which explains why Table 8.2 shows no use of Section 106 funds in Doncaster). However, there can be a rigidly formulaic approach to the allocation of the funding. For example, in **Sheffield**, Section 106 funding for parks is administered by the City's planning department, which often insists that the greater proportion of the funding has to be spent on formal sports provision in parks, or it will not be forthcoming. This can be in contrast to the views of community groups or parks officers, who may not always regard such provision as the priority for spending. The same problem was raised in **Lewisham**, where there was an apparent conflict between the needs of local communities as realised through extensive consultation, and what developers wanted to provide in terms of commercial attractiveness of new developments. In other local authority areas there is an insistence that funding must be spent as close as possible to the development concerned.

8.16   Nevertheless examples of a more flexible and creative approach to the use of Section 106 funding were encountered. These invariably occurred where a council had developed a strategic view of their urban green spaces. Examples included **Chelmsford**, where Section 106 funding was diverted to other parts of the town where under-provision of green space had been identified. In **Doncaster**, funds were not necessarily being allocated in the immediate vicinity of new developments, but were kept within the same ward. Green space trusts, working in close partnership with a local authority were able to negotiate Section 106 funds direct from developers, and then to use the money as they pleased (**Case Study 8.7, Glass Park, Doncaster**).

8.17 The **Single Regeneration Budget** (SRB) has become an important funding instrument in some areas for urban renewal projects. Funding is aimed at 'enhancing the quality of life of local people in areas of need', and is only available in certain specified parts of the country. It was cited as an external funding source by two thirds of the fifteen authorities in the survey. Uses and amounts involved varied, partly in relation to the amount available in any area. In some authorities SRB funding was used for maintenance for small scale works and maintenance in new housing areas. In others, SRB funding had been used, wholly or partly, to create new parks, for example **Stockport** have funded an officer to oversee the Brinnington SRB project.

8.18 For example in Newcastle two new parks, **North Benwell Nature Park** (**see Case Study 5.1 in Chapter 5**) and Gala Fields had been funded with money from SRB. In Sheffield, the Green Estate Programme (**Case Study 9.5**), which brought together a very wide range of new large and small scale green space projects, including new parks, was funded through SRB (although a partnership approach had also attracted major matched funding). Again in **Sheffield, Heeley Millenium Park** and the **Heeley Development Trust** (**Case Study 9.4**) were made possible through SRB funding. In these two Sheffield examples, SRB funding had enabled green space projects that were not driven primarily by the local authority to proceed, and in the case of Heeley Millenium Park, had allowed the independent Trust to be formed. SRB funding was also the primary source for another independent Trust, the **Glass Park Trust** in Doncaster (**Case Study 8.7**) In all these cases, SRB funding was possible because the green space projects were able to demonstrate significant community or employment benefits. The more recent **Neighbourhood Renewal Fund** (commenced in 2001), aimed at tackling deprivation through local strategic partnerships, has not yet made a significant mark, being cited by only two authorities as a funding source for improvements to urban green space.

8.19 European Union funding sources, administered primarily through the European Regional Development Fund (ERDF) and targeted at economically disadvantaged areas through **Objective 1** and **Objective 2** programmes, were not widely cited but this is largely a reflection of the spread of case study authorities in relation to eligible funding areas. Only in **Sheffield** had significant European funding been used for urban parks, again through the **Green Estate Programme** as well as other urban parks. However, a series of forward-looking district and neighbourhood park regeneration programmes had also been initiated since 2000, involving ambitious new master plans and community development work, mainly on the strength of new funding likely to arise from the City's designation as an Objective 1 area.

8.20 Other regeneration sources that had been useful in the past included **City Challenge**. Two authorities listed the **New Deal for Communities** as a potentially very important source – for example, in **Doncaster** an area of the town comprising of only 4000 households had been designated as a New Deal area and will receive £52 million in regeneration funding over 10 years. While the New Deal area itself does not contain any parks or other urban green spaces, the parks section has successfully argued that three nearby parks serve the needs of the New Deal population and these will therefore receive significant new funding.

No authorities had received support for urban green spaces under the **National Lottery New Opportunities Fund**, part of which is targeted towards green space regeneration, but this scheme is relatively new.

8.21   The major sources of external funding were therefore seen to be selective in their application, whether this was related to a focus on heritage objectives, to tackling severe deprivation, or to the amount of new development or house-building. This can cause problems both real and perceived . For example, the parks section at **Chelmsford** felt that the town's location in the south east and proximity to London meant that most significant sources of external funding would not be available to them. Similarly in any town or city the majority of parks or green spaces can also be 'left in the middle', not being of high enough heritage value to qualify for HLF funding or sufficiently deprived to qualify for regeneration funding, and perhaps lacking the advantages of an affluent and professional community to act as advocates. Yet green spaces in these areas can be equally in need of attention. Two other potential problems arise from reliance on external funding sources: how to fund maintenance in the long-term, and what happens to officer posts and staff once funding ceases. Sustainable long-term management, and developing exit strategies are two of the main concerns of the case studies in **Chapter 9**.

8.22   Another significant funding source that is less restrictive in its application is the **Landfill Tax Credit Scheme**, administered through ENTRUST. Funds are available to support environmental projects and projects that benefit communities in the vicinity of landfill sites, usually within a distance of 10 miles of the site. Landfill Tax monies can be used as matching funding for other grant schemes. While several authorities had used such money, in partnership with community groups, to create new and upgrade existing facilities, in some the requirement for funds to be spent within a specified distance of a landfill site meant that this benefited mainly country parks and urban fringe sites. In **Stockport**, however, the Greenspace Forum (**Paragraph 7.41**) has registered with ENTRUST as a body eligible for receiving grants, and the aim is to redistribute monies to community projects via groups affiliated to the Forum.

8.23   The final source of major external funding listed was private sponsorship. While many authorities are involved to some extent with business sponsorship, in most cases this cannot really be counted as a significant contribution in terms of overall budgets. However, it does enable features or facilities to be created or operated that would otherwise not be viable. A common example given was private sponsorship of a sensory garden within a park, or the running of a restaurant or café facility. The **Cheltenham in Bloom** scheme (**Case Study 9.1**) attracts around £20,000 in sponsorship each year. Other examples include one-off donations or deals with developers or companies. For example, **Bexley** obtained £30,000 from the technology company Fujitsu as a donation that paid for the resurfacing of all paths in a park, following the laying of a fibre optic cable through the park. However, very significant sums are potentially available through Private Finance Initiatives. These are a relatively new idea in financing of parks service delivery and were encountered rarely in the survey. They are discussed more fully below.

Making the most of resources: creative approaches to funding

8.24   A range of approaches were encountered that either increased the financial resources available, or made better or more efficient use of existing resources. Many of these approaches are discussed in greater detail elsewhere in this report.

PRIVATE FINANCE INITIATIVES

8.25   Private Finance Initiatives (PFI) have been used across the public services as a means of injecting private capital into, for example, the health, education and transport infrastructure, but have had very little application in urban parks or green spaces. In the initial profiling survey of 50 local authorities only two examples were encountered: in **Hastings** and **Lewisham**. **Lewisham** was one of the fifteen case study authorities and the details of its innovative and wide-reaching ten year parks management contract with the private contractor Glendale are given here (**Case Study 8.1**) On the evidence gathered it appears that such PFI style arrangements have potential for much wider application. In Lewisham, public surveys have indicated overwhelming support for the move and suggest noticeable improvements in maintenance and service delivery.

8.26   There appears to be a re-animation of parks-related activity in the borough and widespread optimism that the substantial programme of investment in parks over the first three years of the contract will yield positive results. The test of such initiatives will come in the later years of the contract, however, once the investment programme has finished and judgments can be made as to whether community aspirations have been met. In **Lewisham**, the bulk of the parks department has in effect been transferred to the private contractor, with remaining council officers having a contract and quality monitoring role, and retaining accountability through consultation mechanisms with park users and user groups.

8.27   The Private Finance style arrangement is one of the few avenues available to a local authority to produce an immediate improvement in the infrastructure, maintenance and facilities of parks that are not eligible for other significant amounts of external funding. It is, however, a form of mortgaging arrangement and therefore the annual payments back to the contractor exceed the amount that is paid to the authority 'up front'. However, **Lewisham** is happy with this arrangement, partly because of the visible effect that it has in the parks. But their satisfaction is also because, for the first time in many years, the parks budget has increased slightly to pay for the package, and the service will be protected to some extent from future rounds of budget cuts. Overall there has been no change in the numbers of personnel employed and, as yet, there has been no overall job loss, although personnel have changed with Glendale installing its own parks management team. While the overall effects of this private finance style arrangement may be positive in terms of investment and quality of green space, there are a number of concerns in terms of pay and conditions for personnel on the ground. The contractor pays lower rates for grounds maintenance staff than did the local authority. Although total numbers of staff have not changed, there has been a high turnover of staff in some areas – this can mean that relationships do not build up between the public and static grounds maintenance personnel. It is also unclear whether the momentum of change can be sustained after the initial years of such a contract when the initial up-front investment period is over. It is also essential that tight quality control (as is the case in Lewisham) is retained within the local authority to ensure quality of service and public accountability.

Case Study 8.1 Lewisham's Private Finance Initiative contract with Glendale

Lewisham entered into the contract with Glendale, which will operate for 10 years, in 2000. In effect the entire parks section was transferred to Glendale, with the company providing a combined parks management and grounds maintenance service for all the borough's parks (apart from Lewisham's largest park, which is still under council control), and a grounds maintenance service for other green spaces such as highways and churchyards. The work covers routine operations such as grass cutting, pruning and planting, litter clearance, cleaning, building and infrastructure maintenance, security, events and other aspects of parks maintenance. Glendale also directly manages the borough's 23 urban rangers.

Under the agreement, Glendale receives a *unitary payment* for both the service and the council's use of transferred assets. The payment is made in yearly instalments and varies from year to year as the service varies. In return, Glendale is granted a lease for the duration of the contract for those parks where there will be a significant capital investment. Glendale is only permitted to use the buildings for the purpose of providing the service, unless written consent is given for other purposes. As part of the agreement, Glendale will carry out works to an estimated value of £1.5 million in the first three years of the contract. The works have been agreed, but may alter following consultation with park users by both Glendale and the council. Although the figure of £1.5 million has been agreed, Glendale will have to bear the actual cost of the works, whatever they may be. If it is more than the estimate then they will bear the cost. If it is less they can keep the balance and are not required to account to the council for the difference. This arrangement places risk with the contractor. The outcome of the agreed works is and will be monitored to ensure that it meets the agreed specification. Penalty clauses within the contract impose fines if work is not completed satisfactorily.

The contractor, Glendale, bears most of the risks associated with the contract. For example, if the cost of labour increases then Glendale will bear the risk. However some risks are retained with the council. These relate mainly to certain legislative changes, changes to the investment programme following consultation with park users, or fire damage to buildings.

The lease technically constituted a disposal of open space and the council was legally required to advertise its intention to dispose in the local press. The contract is rigorously monitored: a random 10% sample of sites is taken every three months. Should any aspect of service delivery not meet the specification then a system of deductions from the unitary payment comes into play.

Glendale have been in existence for over ten years and were chosen on a competitive tendering basis, based 65% on price and 35% on quality. Until this partnership, Glendale were primarily involved in managing leisure facilities and running grounds maintenance contracts. Prior to the contract Lewisham had a multi-functional client team under CCT, which covered most of the borough's environmental issues. Subsequently the management structure has changed dramatically, with 'Parks and Community Services' now having responsibility for clinical waste, pest control, animal welfare and arboricultural and horticultural services. The involvement with the majority of parks now focuses on policy development and overseeing and monitoring the Glendale contract. Glendale brought in a new management team, although staffing on the ground has remained almost unchanged.

The contract has had immediate positive effects. The up-front investment has brought visible improvements, and has demonstrated a commitment to parks to local communities. The ground-breaking contract has also produced a high level of political commitment from the council.

Part of Glendale's remit is to increase community involvement and consultation – they have more than doubled the number of park user groups from 8 to 19 in the borough since the contract started and a member of Glendale staff aims to attend each meeting. Glendale is also contracted to run the parks events programme and there will be particular emphasis on engaging with all schools in the borough.

User satisfaction is regularly monitored, both by the council and a dedicated Glendale survey officer. Surveys of park users and feed back from user groups at the annual parks and open spaces conference is overwhelmingly positive, with the majority of responses reporting an improvement in service delivery over the first year of the contract and a noticeable increase in maintenance standards (it should be noted that, before the contract, budget cuts had previously driven maintenance standards down). The main negative comments were related to Glendale not being seen to achieve the goal of patrolling each park in the borough at least once a day. Interestingly the contract appeared to instil a sense of greater optimism in park users about the future, with virtually all respondents expecting the parks service to improve further over the next 12 months. The main potential problem with the PFI contract would appear to be related to this – peoples expectations have been raised and the next few years will test whether this expectation can be met.

CREATIVE RE-DIRECTION OF REVENUE SPEND

8.28   While much emphasis can be placed on partnership working and gaining external funding, it can be the case that internal re-direction of funds (rather than cutting budgets) can result in equal benefit or greater benefit. A clear example of this is Oldham's Park Refurbishment Programme (**Case Study 7.6**). This resulted from a review in 1994 of the parks service's winter works programme, which involved an annual spend of £400,000 to £500,000 per year on maintenance and small projects across the borough. Previously site foremen and charge-hands had put forward projects in an ad hoc and uncoordinated way. It was decided to pool all the resources, including materials and landscape development/design budgets involved in these works into a single coordinated investment in one park per year. Since

1995 some £2.5 to £3 million has been invested in targeted parks regeneration, a greater sum than is obtainable from most external sources. This revenue funding is matched with capital from Section 106 agreements and other monies (such as SRB, neighbourhood renewal). The advantage of this approach is that it gets away from a piecemeal, bitty and uncoordinated regeneration process and instead works with local groups to produce a masterplan, which is rapidly brought into reality. Of course, the revenue budget has to be sufficient to support this process in the first place and **Oldham** does appear to be one of the better funded authorities, at least on a per head of population basis.

OPPORTUNISTIC USE OF TARGETED GRANT FUNDING TO ACHIEVE WIDER STRATEGIC AIMS

8.29   While grant schemes, such as the Heritage Lottery Urban Parks Programme, may have specific purposes, wider strategic aims can sometimes be met on the back of such schemes. For example, **Glass Park, Doncaster** was funded primarily through SRB funding directed through Doncaster's Healthy Food Programme. While the park will serve as a base for Doncaster's Farmer's Market and will have areas set aside for local food production, much of the park is for amenity use. **Sheffield** has established a **Heritage Parks Programme** supported by a full-time Capital Projects Officer, as a result of a number of very successful applications to the Heritage Lottery Fund. Parks in the programme have local or national heritage listing. The role of the Capital Projects Officer is to secure the resource for and put in place landscape restoration management plans for eligible parks. Heritage is defined in terms of that special character, and not necessarily in purely historic terms. In the case of **Norfolk Park**, a Grade II listed heritage landscape, the most visible outcome of Heritage Lottery Funding is not a historical restoration, but a striking, contemporarily designed community centre and large-scale play area in the park. Funding here has been directed to meet needs identified for a 'City Park' as defined in Sheffield's Park Categorisation Scheme (**Case Study 6.9**) while at the same time ensuring the continuing care of an important heritage park in the heart of a deprived area.

FLEXIBLE USE OF SECTION 106 FUNDS

8.30   Several authorities referred to a flexible approach to the use of Section 106 funding as an example of creativity. As discussed previously, Section 106 monies can be used in a rigid formulaic manner or more flexibly. Flexibility in this instance meant achieving wider strategic goals by targeting the funding at areas of need, rather than, as happened in most cases, devoting funds to small scale facilities within developments to primarily serve the needs of those developments. For example, in **Chelmsford**, Section 106 funds had been amalgamated to provide two new parks and sports facilities that were too large to be sited within areas of new development. These new parks addressed deficiencies in provision identified in the authority's open space policy (**Case Study 6.7**) as lacking open space, but also catered for the new populations from new housing developments. As a principle, the new parks have been built to a high specification. The local authority will maintain the new parks, with revenue generated from increased council tax. It must, however, be acknowledged, that there can be conflict between the views of planners and the view of parks service officers as to where Section 106 monies should be allocated. One parks service that took a *'targeted approach to the use of Section 106 monies'* admitted that their planners were not wholly happy with this.

Partnerships

8.31 Earlier research[1] has suggested that local authorities will in future work more in partnership with independent environmental organizations and trusts. This has indeed proved to be the case and today many authorities are actively engaged in many and varied partnerships with a very wide range of different partners. Partnership working is now a fact of life, strongly promoted by the government, and many parks services take a 'cocktail' approach, mixing and matching partners with different things to offer in order to further their goals. In the profiling survey of 50 local authorities for this study all but two were involved in some form of partnerships relating to urban green space. **Table 8.3** shows the range of partners encountered, listing those mentioned by at least 4% of the authorities. A long and diverse list of other bodies were listed by only 1 authority (2%) in each case, covering: Wildlife Trusts, Housing Associations, the Fire Brigade, Film Crews, the Association for Public Service Excellence, British Waterways, Urban Forestry Unit, Heritage Society, Yorkshire Forward, Royal Parks, Crown Estates, Woodlands Trust, Ministry of Defence (MOD), Health Action Zones, Housing Association, Thames 21, Neighbourhood Renewal, Onyx Trust, ERDF, Parish Councils and Parks Trusts.

8.32 **Tables 8.3 and 8.4** perhaps gives a misleading image of the total range of partnership activity. There is certainly a sense that activity is not as vibrant or dynamic in the majority of cases as the relatively high percentages suggest. Much of the activity listed as partnership working could in fact be regarded as part of the necessary mainstream activity of a progressive authority, or that which is required for regeneration initiatives. For example, working with funding bodies such as the Heritage Lottery Fund or SRB is a requirement of obtaining that funding, and not really an equal partnership. One of the most successful authorities in obtaining external funding from such bodies stated that it had a piecemeal approach to partnerships and that partnership working had not been a priority until recently. In this case, external funding grants were not regarded as partnership working. Working with environmental organizations such as wildlife trusts or conservation volunteers is similarly a necessity on sites with conservation interest, and there will be statutory requirements to work with government agencies, such as the Environment Agency, for plans and policies when site designations or environmental regulations require it. So clearly terminology is an issue and partnerships mean different things to different people.

8.33 Many of the partnerships listed involve cross-departmental working within a local authority or within the public sector. The point here is that, while there was much evidence of creativity in bringing these partnerships about, there was less evidence of real innovation in terms of ground-breaking or far-reaching partnerships. While partnerships are in many ways a necessity to achieve goals, it should also be noted that, setting aside the major funding bodies, the results of partnerships generally had small site-specific outcomes. This was certainly true of the great majority of private sponsorship or business partnerships encountered. The above comments are not in any way intended to be negative or to belittle the genuine partnership working that was encountered. Rather, they seek to make the point that the search for partner individuals, organisations and institutions around green space issues is less developed in the UK than is the case in parks management in other countries

1 *People, Parks and Cities: A guide to current practice in Urban Parks.* Department of the Environment (1996).

and especially in cities in the United States. The Project for Public Spaces[2], gives a range of examples of cases where *"cities with small 'friends of the parks' groups were looking to more substantive partnerships mainly to increase funding and maintenance for their parks, as well as community involvement in them"*.

8.34 Five types of partnership were identified from this US experience: **Assistance Providers** help parks departments with education, programming and volunteers, and help with investment. Such groups are usually voluntary; **Catalyst** groups work with public agencies and others to initiate projects and provide financial support for new parks. These types of body are generally involved in advocacy, consultation, design and construction issues, and tend to be transitional in nature, moving on to new projects once earlier projects have been completed; **Co-managers** work in collaboration with parks departments by way of either a) a position jointly shared by the organization and the parks department that oversees park planning, design and capital projects and in some cases management and maintenance or b) by working jointly with a parks department to realize shared aims; **Sole Managers** for a park manage and maintain parks on their own, functioning as an independent entity with limited involvement of the parks department; and finally, **Citywide partners** are organized around an entire city or area park system, existing not to increase use and activity in a single park or green space but to raise the level and quality of open space and parks in an entire city, through neighbourhood organizations and park partnerships.

TRUST PARTNERSHIPS

8.35 It is much less easy to define such a partnership hierarchy for parks and other urban green spaces in England, with most activity occurring at the 'assistance providers' level in the form of friends groups (discussed in full in **Chapter 7**). There are of course clear cultural differences that promote greater potential external involvement in parks and green space management in the US. Catalyst-type activity relating to parks and green space creation and regeneration is perhaps most closely related to the work of Groundwork Trusts and certain Urban Wildlife Trusts in England (discussed below). These partners also play a co-management role in certain areas. An excellent example is that of the **Green Estate Programme, Sheffield (Case Study 9.5)** whereby Sheffield Wildlife Trust is coordinating a very wide range of green space projects in one part of the city through both shared posts and joint working.

2   *Project for Public Spaces (2000) Public Parks, Private Partners,* Project for Public Spaces, Inc. New York.

Table 8.3 The range of partners working with local authorities on parks and green space projects (Source: profiling study of 50 local authorities)

Type of Partner	% of Authorities Surveyed
Community Group	78
Environmental Organisation	78
Educational Establishments	78
Friends group	74
Local Business	70
Local Trusts	68
HLF	36
Sports Club	20
New Deal	14
Groundwork	14
Environment Agency	12
Sport England	10
Police	8
Sports Organisations	7
SRB	6
Countryside Agency	6
Allotment Federation	6
Probation Service	6
Landfill	6
Private Landowners	5
Health	5
Angling Group	4
English Nature	4
English Heritage	4
AGMA	4
Social Services	4
Health Authority	4
Football Foundation	4
Countryside Stewardship	4
Sports Facility Management Company	4

Table 8.4 **The main purposes of partnerships (Source: profiling study of 50 local authorities)**	
Purpose of Partnership	**% of Authorities surveyed**
Finance	76
Plans and policies	72
Management	72
Fundraising	72
Bidding	72
Combination of outcomes	58
Donations	48
Sponsorship/donations	39
General maintenance	36
Enhancing routine maintenance	24
Self-management	10
Funding	6
Sponsorship	2
Security	2
Volunteers	2
Promotion/Marketing	2
Consultation	2

8.36   In the current survey, a range of successful sole management operations for a wide range of types of green space was encountered in the form of Open Space Trusts. Again these are discussed in detail later in this chapter. The closest to a model of sole management for mainstream urban parks was that of the pilot in **Newcastle** to turn over Exhibition Park to an independent trust as a forerunner of wider sole management of parks in the city (**Case Study 8.6**). City-wide partnership around an entire green space network was not encountered. Probably the closest example was the partnership between Sheffield City Council and Sheffield Wildlife Trust to deliver community, park and green space regeneration projects across the city (**Case Study 8.2**). The areas of operation of this partnership are similar in coverage, although not necessarily in extent to those of a Groundwork Trust. However there are a number of differences notably that Sheffield Wildlife Trust is a city-based organization with a local membership and support from a wide range of local organizations and is also a long running organisation that can sustain a long-term local commitment to projects. This is somewhat different to a Groundwork Trust, which is usually set up from outside a city and whose future will depend on the availability of core funding.

CASE STUDY 8.2 City-wide partnership of Sheffield City Council with Sheffield Wildlife Trust

Sheffield Wildlife Trust (SWT) was formed in 1985 with the aim of making the city a 'better place for wildlife and for people'. Since that time SWT has grown to be the second largest wildlife trust in the UK (the first is the trust for the whole of Scotland). Up until 1997, SWT was one of many fairly small voluntary groups with which Sheffield City Council (SCC) worked in partnership to advance environmental projects throughout the city. However, with national backing from the Wildlife Trust partnership (Britain's largest environmental body), and by aligning SWT's agenda firmly with the regeneration of Sheffield, the trust has expanded rapidly. Now, with over 30 permanent staff and over 30 trainees, SWT has become a significant force in the regeneration of the city.

The partnership covers most aspects of parks and open spaces service delivery in the city. SWT co-sponsored the Sheffield's Parks Regeneration Strategy that underpins the work of the city's parks and open spaces service, runs land management, environmental education, community and training projects as well as chairing both the Park Users and Environment Forums. SCC pays an annual core grant of £30,000 to SWT and this is an extremely cost-effective partnership for SCC. For every pound that the council invests in SWT, a further £56 is levered into the city from the wide range of external sources that the partnership generates.

Four different levels of partnership can be detected:

Voluntary Sector Support. In this model, 'partnerships' arise when SWT gives support and credibility to an essentially SCC led project. In these cases SWT achieves its charitable objectives by helping SCC raise money to deliver environmental projects. Such support may include preparing business plans and attending meetings. While voluntary input may be high, the rewards may be significant. For example, SWT was involved in preparing the bid to HLF that secured funding for the regeneration of Norfolk Park, one of the flagship sites in the city's Heritage Parks Programme (discussed in **Paragraph 8.29**).

Voluntary Sector Led – SCC Managed. Here, SWT leads or coordinates projects although management control remains with SCC. This is achieved by having council officers on management committees, and by having council officers line managing SWT staff.

SWT – SCC Partnership. This has been the model for most of the recent environmental regeneration projects in the city. The objectives of both SCC and SWT are met and, crucially, SWT gains financial benefit for its long-term viability. Examples include: **The Urban Park Ranger Service.** A joint training programme with SCC has doubled the number of urban park rangers in the city; Manor and Castle Green Estate a partnership of many different organisations managed by SWT driving a very ambitious green space led social and economic regeneration programme (**Case Study 9.5**); and **Blackburn Meadows Environmental Education Centre** where SWT runs a community and education centre while SCC manage land reclamation and habitat management.

Partnership around a hub. SWT has a further role in developing productive partnerships between SCC and voluntary bodies through its role as chair of the Park Users Forum and Environment Forum, as convenor of the SRB5 regeneration area Environment Transport and Leisure Group, and as the environment theme manager in Manor and Castle.

8.37   While Groundwork Trusts are involved nationally in very many examples of good practice in urban green spaces[3], a mixed picture emerged of the working of partnerships with Groundwork Trusts in the case study local authorities included in this study. Five of the case study authorities included in the detailed survey described in this report had some experience of working with Groundwork. One authority was in the early stages of developing what was promising to be a fruitful partnership. Two authorities had experience of a Groundwork Trust based outside the immediate area coming in to work on individual projects and then pulling out at short notice before completion, leaving a community with raised aspirations and the local authority and the community to continue the project. Two others had worked actively with Groundwork in their area but reported that they had experienced some difficulties of communication and commitment.

8.38   These problems reinforce the importance, whoever the partner, of securing long-term local commitment and building a locally-based partnership founded upon open channels of communication and joint working. The great advantage of an increased role for Groundwork as an area-wide player in urban green spaces is that it is both a national organization with a lobbying and policy function, and the operator of a network of locally-based and community orientated trusts. However, the experience of the authorities in this study, which is probably not typical of the national situation, does clearly show the need for any Groundwork Trust to be firmly embedded in the town or city in which that work is taking place and to ensure that adequate resources are secured at the outset to see projects through.

8.39   Partnerships with those involved in the matters such as crime, health and youth are spread throughout this report. Two specific examples are given here, both from **Cheltenham**, of partnerships in a smaller non-metropolitan urban area aimed at tackling some of the issues relating to urban green space management, which featured in **Chapter 5**. The first, a partnership between the council and the RSPCA, addresses the issue of dog mess, which was found in the earlier part of this report to be a main deterrent to wider use of parks (**Case Study 8.3**); the second, Winston Churchill Gardens (**Case Study 8.4**), is a partnership to address concerns about standards of park and green space maintenance and is a fairly typical example of a 'cocktail' approach to using a variety of modest funding sources and partnerships to enable urban green space enhancement.

3   See '21 years of Rebuilding Communities'. *Landscape Design.* No 306, Theme issue on Groundwork. January 2002,

CASE STUDY 8.3 'Paws in the Park': Partnership against dog fouling, Cheltenham

Around 7 out of 10 households in the Borough own a dog and most of them use parks to exercise them. Dog fouling is considered a major problem and deterrent to wider use of parks. The council has embarked on an initiative to educate and persuade people to clean up after their dogs.

A partnership with the Royal Society for the Protection of Animals (RSPCA) was formed to further this educational aspect. An annual event 'Paws in the Park' was started in 1998. It is a one-day event in August, promoted as a family day out and is run jointly by the parks service and the council's dog warden. The event plays host to the regional heat of the RSPCA dog of the year competition, but it is not really a dog show, but rather an event to promote responsible dog ownership. Part of the show contains a good citizens dog test for good behaviour (the dog and the citizen!). The event secures a good deal of sponsorship from pet shops and veterinary practices and is hosted by a well-known TV vet. The cost to the council was £2500 in 2001. The parks service, as part of its educational effort, has supplied 1.5 million dog waste bags over three years free of charge to the public through 60 outlets in the town, at a cost of £9600 per annum. Before this they had a small 'poop scoop' scheme but this was more expensive because bulk buying has reduced the cost of each bag. Dog owners are able to use ordinary bins as well as dog bins for disposal.

The council has its own bylaw that enables fines of up to £500 for dog fouling – they don't use the 'Dogs Fouling of Land Act (1996) which only allows a £25 fine. Prosecutions have been effected for people who refuse to clear up or who are repeat offenders – the council's dog warden has the power to ask for offenders name and address and if they refuse the police can be called.

CASE STUDY 8.4 Partnership approach to regeneration: Winston Churchill Gardens, Cheltenham

Winston Churchill Gardens won a Green Flag Park Award in 1997. Work started on park refurbishment as part of an SRB funded regeneration scheme for the Lower High Street of the town, which identified the park as being of high value to the local community. However, residents were not happy with the park – the gardens were run down, with signs of neglect, and the maintenance contractor under CCT had not met the required maintenance specification.

The council worked in partnership with a steering group of local residents (now whittled down to a Sunday working group), including the manager of the Lower High Street resource centre, the head of the local primary school and 2 to 3 local residents. The entrance to the park was improved

through funding from the council's Housing Renewal section from their environmental enhancement budget. All footpaths were resurfaced from the Highways budget as part of a deal to put a cycle way through the park. A joint project, between the Lower High Street Partnership, the Parks

Section and Cheltenham Arts Council, was initiated for public art and outdoor furniture, designed by local school children as part of a parks fun day on the site. Private sponsorship for planting is input through 'Cheltenham in Bloom' (**Case Study 9.1, Chapter 9**).

The locally based steering group did not evolve into taking on a more active role in site management because they were happy with the improvements and felt "their job had been almost done". A public survey carried out in 2000 found that most people were very happy with the park now.

Ownership

8.40   As discussed in Chapter 7, it has been stated that[4] *'there are to date almost no examples of local authority parks being bequeathed into trust ownership'*. Those examples that were given were rather specialized and could certainly not be described as mainstream urban parks, being either based in London (which has a tradition of varied ownership arrangements) or in New Towns. Rather more examples of urban public parks owned and managed as trusts were encountered in this survey, which suggests that things may have moved on. While some cater for specialist users, such as **Scotswood Community Garden, Newcastle (Case Study 8.5)**, two described in this report could definitely be described as mainstream urban parks and both were bequeathed from local authority control. Admittedly, **Heeley Millenium Park (Case Study 9.4)** was a featureless 'Green Desert' created following demolition of blighted terraced housing in the late 1970s before a new, well used park was created under Trust status, but **Exhibition Park, Newcastle (Case Study 8.6)**, is the sort of urban park that everyone can recognize. Newcastle City Council is negotiating the transfer of the park to a 'community trust' that will operate on a self-management basis. If this pilot is a success, then trust status is seen as a model to be extended to other city parks, where appropriate.

8.41   **Exhibition Park (Case Study 8.7)** is an example of a community-led initiative that has received full support from the council. It demonstrates the potential problems that are encountered when transferring an established park from local authority control to self-management. However, there are potential advantages to the process. There is a reduced financial and administration cost to the local authority in the long-term, although the trust will receive a core grant. The main advantages will spring from the benefits associated with a high degree of community involvement, as outlined in **Chapters 7 and 9**. Access to additional funding, the energy of those involved, and the increased sense of ownership can, in theory, result in a more dynamic park than one which remains under local authority control. It remains to be seen how feasible it might be to extend the concept to a larger number of mainstream parks within a city. At Exhibition Park, a group of knowledgeable and experienced residents were able to drive the process along, and, through their contacts, were able to get together the appropriate professional back-up. It is this professional input that is essential to make sure a trust is protected legally and financially. Can this model be extended further across a city without the sort of city wide partnerships discussed earlier in this chapter?

4   *People, Parks and Cities: A guide to current good practice in Urban Parks*. Department of the Environment. (1996)

CASE STUDY 8.5 Scotswood Natural Community Garden, Newcastle

The community garden, situated in Newcastle's disadvantaged West End, was created in 1995 from former playing fields around one of the sites of Newcastle College, by a group of enthusiastic gardeners. The site is run as a partnership between the John Marley Trust, who manage the site, Newcastle City Council who own the land, and Newcastle College. An advantage for the garden initially was the presence of the adjacent Drift Garden Centre which was a community organisation, supplying cheap plants for local people. The 2 acre site acts as a demonstration site and a training resource for sustainable landscape design and management techniques and urban food growing.

Funding for the project came from City Challenge, and grants from environmental charities. A three-year grant from the National Lottery Charity Board supports two employees: a full time coordinator and a part-time administrator. The funding is tied to the garden reaching out to groups from ethnic minorities, disabled people and one parent families to increase their involvement with horticulture, gardens and landscape. Landfill Tax funding has supported infrastructure development, including an excitingly designed wetland scheme that takes excess water from the roofs and car parks of the college.

The garden is maintained by volunteers and trainees, and input from children through a junior garden club and schools programme, and runs a series of community festivals.

8.42   It is perhaps no coincidence that the majority of trust-managed public parks and green spaces were new entities, either creating a new park where none existed before, or changing the status of an urban green space from a recreation ground or playing field to a community park. In these instances there is less of a problem of conflict between new visions and traditional uses, as discussed in the case study for **Exhibition Park**. One of the most successful examples encountered was **Glass Park, Doncaster (Case Study 8.7)**. This park, created since 1999, on a 'post-industrial' site again demonstrates a significant achievement for a local community, but also entails a very creative approach to securing significant funding for a new park on the back of other objectives. Trust status was the only way that a park could be created to meet a significant shortfall in green space provision in the area, as indicated by **Doncaster's Green Space Audit (Case Study 6.6)**. At the core of the park is a 'Millennium Green', funded by the Countryside Agency's Millennium Greens programme in the late 1990s – a number of other examples of Millennium Greens operating as self-managed Trusts were found in the profiling survey of 50 local authorities. What is different about Glass Park is that the Millennium Green (although it is the largest in the country) forms only a small part of the total park. Glass Park shares some of the characteristics of case studies in **Chapter 9**. It certainly provides an alternative view of what urban green space is all about, providing environmental and wildlife benefit, recreation and amenity facilities to a local population, but also potential new business, enterprise and urban tourism opportunities, and making a contribution to city healthy living initiatives. The park has been created in partnership with the local authority, but it is difficult to envisage this level of activity occurring under local authority control alone.

Conclusions

8.43   The acknowledged decline in the quality of care of the urban green space resource in England can be linked to declining local authority green space budgets over the past 10 – 15 years. The majority of the case study authorities in this report had witnessed budgetary reductions over this period. Reduced budgets force hard choices which have manifested themselves in lower maintenance standards and failing infrastructure. These factors affect the perception that park users have of their local green spaces. However, calls for increased central funding for urban green spaces need to be matched with consideration of how funding is sourced and applied. The point was made at the start of this chapter that urban parks must be seen to be important in achieving wider policy aims in high profile areas such as education and health, in addition to their accepted aesthetic and environmental benefit to achieve funding in a competitive environment, urban parks and green spaces.

8.44   The creative approaches to resourcing of urban green space discussed in this chapter present a more complex picture than one of simple funding increase alone. The examples given (private finance arrangements, creative redirection of existing spending, partnership working) make creative use of funding to lever in additional resource, or make better use of existing resource. A constant theme of **Chapters 6, 7, 8 and 9** is that effective management of urban green space is linked with local authority culture and structure as well as levels of spend. However it would be wrong to make the link between severe financial pressure and increased creativity in acquisition and use of resources. Those involved in the more 'creative' of authorities emphasised that they would be able to achieve far more, in an equally creative manner, with less financial restriction.

8.45   This chapter, as well as others, focus on the added value that effective partnerships (whether it be with communities, organisations or agencies) can bring to base-line funding. Examples are given of how partnerships can achieve far more than would be possible by a local authority alone, and how partnership working can access otherwise unavailable funding. What is also clear from the case studies in this report is that the way local authorities may have to change radically to make best use of opportunities. It is also apparent that effective partnership working doesn't necessarily come on the cheap. Time and resources have to be put into forming and supporting partnerships. There is therefore a potential short and medium term financial cost associated with what might be a longer term financial gain. It also became apparent that, despite the very long list of partners that many local authorities can cite, there remains an opportunity for greater coordination of urban environmental regeneration initiatives at the 'city-wide' partnership level as well as promoting more individual site-based partnerships.

CASE STUDY 8.6 An urban park under Trust management: Exhibition Park, Newcastle

Exhibition Park is one of Newcastle's main parks, with a range of active facilities such as café, boating lake and model railway. The move to trust status was a relatively recent community initiative, in partnership with the City Council. The process started as a result of concern at the lack of local involvement in the park and the domination of the park user group by special interest groups and clubs without wider representation of park users. Independent consultants were commissioned to carry out research into what users felt about the park, the extent of current involvement, and to make proposals for the future, and in particular to stimulate increased local involvement.

The main results of the survey were that, although the park had suffered a decline in use, overall it was not vandalized and was viewed favourably by users and residents. The main proposal was that it was a priority to establish a user group that included a good representation of local people to work as a constituted charity in partnership with the council. The process created considerable interest in the park and demonstrated the willingness of local residents and most of the clubs to get involved and put forward exciting proposals for the park. It also proved the commitment of the council to form a partnership with them.

In parallel, and partly as a result of the above consultative process, a group of residents and interested parties generated a proposal for a trust to take responsibility for the park. An important driving force behind this move was the belief by some of the participants (who had backgrounds and previous experience of community work) that parks, unlike other types of public facility, had a unique potential in providing a focus for community engagement. A 'whole systems conference' was commissioned to bring together representatives of as many interest groups as possible to produce a shared vision for the park, with the theme of *'how can we make Exhibition Park a more accessible, welcoming and inspiring place with lots going on for everyone?'*.

The conference was held in the summer of 2000, with around 50 representatives attending over two days. A new community involvement and management structure was proposed. A *Community Forum* would operate as an extended user group, providing an opportunity for all local people to participate in decision making. At the conference a number of *Interest Groups* were set up that will continue to develop detailed plans and proposals. These groups cover areas such as landscape design; encouraging community activity in the park; management and maintenance; finance; and creating understanding between the park and its neighbours. A *Community Trust* comprising representatives from the Community Forum, the City Council, and a range of professional, legal and environmental experts and specialists will become the new managing body.

In October 2001 a planning weekend was held, again with a range of interested parties to set out ideas and themes for the trust to take forward. As part of the research for this report, discussions were held independently with representatives of special interest clubs (i.e model boats), council officers, local residents and key members of the group that originally proposed the trust. It was apparent that, although everyone was generally happy with the current situation and was very optimistic about the future, the process of developing the trust over the past three years had been a difficult one, with conflicts between traditional users and those who wanted to set up the trust. Such conflicts are perhaps bound to arise when a genuinely innovative process is embarked upon, without real precedent. There were two main areas where participants acknowledged that, with hindsight, the process could have been handled differently:

Managing change to maintain the involvement of committed local residents, while bringing in necessary skills and 'new blood' from outside. Managing a trust requires legal and professional input. The range of professional expertise embodied in the board of the trust is impressive, but is drawn from a regional base rather than a local base. This caused members of the original user group (mainly representatives of clubs associated with the park) to feel left out and isolated from decisions. The situation has now been resolved through many discussions, and all partners accept the evolving structure of the community forum feeding into the trust. It was essential that the additional expertise was brought in, and the backgrounds and skills of those involved will ensure that the vision for the park rises above the basic refurbishment of existing facilities, but will instead develop the potential of a dynamic cultural and environmental resource for the area. However, it is important that in such circumstances, traditional users, who through their commitment and voluntary input may have sustained park-based activities through difficult times, are fully included in the process of change.

Maintaining Momentum. Over the first three years of the process their has been a tendency to concentrate on strategic vision rather than on the ground action. In many ways this is to be welcomed. Most park regeneration schemes suffer because of a lack of coordinated and long-term vision, but instead focus on short-term piecemeal patching up activities. In particular, much effort was concentrated on debating methods to build 'capacity' in the local population so that subsequent physical development in the park catered for, and was well used by, an area with a heightened sense of community. However, this resulted in a conflict between two opposing views amongst those involved in forming the trust. One which favoured a 'social entrepreneurship' approach first and foremost, and did not wish to go down the standard route of 'planning for real' in the early stages, which they felt would lead to too much emphasis on physical site planning and discussions of infrastructural improvement. In contrast, the other group felt that the main activity should focus immediately on improving that physical infrastructure and responding to local needs, as identified through traditional consultation methods. Again, the conflict has been resolved in that now these two areas are to be developed in parallel, with members of the first group acknowledging that the process has perhaps been too slow, and that more physical improvement work in the park early on would have been useful in maintaining momentum.

These 'learning points' came the hard way, through experience, and it is to the credit of all those involved that these issues now appear to be resolved. Already the community group has secured investment of over £30,000 in partnership with Newcastle's Society for Blind People for a new community and sensory garden, to be built and maintained by the British Trust for Conservation Volunteers.

CASE STUDY 8.7 Public Park managed by an Open Space Trust: Glass Park, Doncaster

Glass Park was opened to the public in 1999 and is sited within a mixed residential and industrial area on the edge of the city. This mixed use is very evident around the park, with large areas of new housing being built on one edge, industrial units and factories on another, and the Doncaster canal running along another boundary. The park is not staffed or wardened.

The site was originally owned by Pilkington Glass PLC, which used the site to tip waste glass and materials from a nearby factory. In the mid 1990s several proposals were made to develop the site – these included landfill activity and/or extensive new housing. The resulting local opposition to these plans lead to the formation of a community pressure group to secure the site for local amenity and wildlife benefit. This was successful and the land was handed over by Pilkington Glass PLC under a 999 year lease for a nominal sum. The company has since been very supportive of the development of the park. Initial funding was obtained through the Countryside Agency's Millennium Green programme (the site is the largest Millennium Green in the country).

The site is now managed and administered by the Glass Park Millennium Green Trust, which has a board of 20 trustees. In order to sustain the site into the future, the trust formed a business arm: the Glass Park Development Company. This employs two members of staff who have the sole responsibility of raising funds for future development of the park. The two workers are in effect self-supporting because they have raised the monies to cover their positions.

The strategy that has been adopted has been to take advantage of regeneration funding sources, both from the national government and the European Union (South Yorkshire is one of the areas eligible for Objective 1funding to meet deprivation and post-industrial needs). The aim is to use this funding to develop the site so that, in time, it will be able to support itself from land-based enterprises.

The primary financial input has come from SRB funding. This has been administered through DOLFIN (Doncaster Local Food Network) which aims to promote healthy eating throughout the borough. The park is being developed in four phases, culminating in the opening of Doncaster's Farmer's Market on the site in 2003, providing a venue for food producers from across the region to sell their products direct to customers. The Trust negotiated directly with the developers of new housing estates around the edge of the park to have Section 106 monies paid direct to them, rather than to the local authority. This enabled them to have complete freedom over how the money was spent to benefit the local community.

Phase 1 of the development was limited in extent and served to provide a visual marker that something was happening on the ground, centering mainly around the planting of a new community orchard on the site.

Phase 2 involved the construction of the Millenium Green as a focus for community activities and events.

Phase 3 (currently underway) focuses on sports and recreational facilities, with an emphasis on youth activities. Facilities include new junior football and cricket pitches, a wheel chair games court, skateboard ramps and two 'watch tower' climbing and shelter structures.

Phase 4 (to be covered by EU Objective 1 funding) involves turning derelict buildings on site into an education and visitor centre, with arts and crafts sales, and an organic food growing demonstration site with café and hostel. A new canal-side pub with microbrewery is proposed to attract visitors and provide income. 85 acres of nearby farmland have been secured to grow local organically produced food, both for use in the on-site facilities and to sell on to distribution networks, again to generate income. The aim is for the park to eventually support employment of 50 – 70 people.

There was a high level of local involvement in site planning and implementation. Local schools were particularly involved in site design, producing artwork and sculpture for the site and in fundraising. 'Mother's Wood', was planted and funded by families of local children, at a cost of £5.00 per tree.

Not only has the wood and its longer term maintenance been paid for, but the majority of families and children in the area have a direct stake in the future of the park. According to trust members, the high level of local involvement is one reason why the park has had relatively little vandalism and damage. While local people were closely involved in the park's planning, professional landscape design and management assistance was also brought in. For both wildlife benefit, maintenance and cost reasons, the park was created along naturalistic, ecological lines. The environmental charity Landlife advised on suitable plant mixes and 'creative conservation' techniques. Already seed is harvested and sold from large-scale wildflower meadows for use in other landscape schemes. The park receives around 35,000 visits per year in its current state, and between 200 and 400 people are attracted to the regular events that are held throughout the year.

The two workers employed by the development company do not have environmental or horticultural backgrounds, but instead have experience in community working, fundraising, business and trade union activity. This has proved valuable in sourcing funds. Two additional factors have been important in their success. Strong political and council support has enabled the project to progress. The park is also a member of Doncaster Communities in Partnership (DCIP). DCIP has proved invaluable in providing training and networking to share experience in fundraising.

CHAPTER 9
A Role in Urban Regeneration

SUMMARY OF KEY POINTS

- There has so far been insufficient recognition of the role of urban green spaces as core elements of urban renewal, contributing more than just an attractive setting for other activity.

- Four levels of integration of urban green space into urban renewal can be identified, characterised by an increasing strategic synergy between environment, economy and community. They are:

  – attracting inward economic investment through provision of attractive urban landscapes;

  – unforeseen spin-offs from grassroots green space initiatives;

  – parks as flagships in neighbourhood renewal;

  – strategic, multi-agency area based regeneration, linking environment and economy.

- Parks and green spaces provide a unique focus for local community groups to achieve real change, acting as a catalyst for other initiatives that spin off into the wider community, and in so doing generate the sort of community contacts and cohesiveness that are considered an integral part of successful neighbourhood regeneration.

- From real case studies a wide range of social, educational and economic benefits can clearly be seen to be associated with community led green space renewal.

- Green space action plans should be inextricably bound into processes of economic, environmental and social regeneration.

- Raising awareness of the economic value of green space and its potentially key role in urban renewal represents perhaps the best chance for a significant increase in resources, investment and political attention to urban parks and other green spaces.

Introduction

9.1 Most research tends to concentrate on the environmental and social benefits of urban parks and green spaces. This perspective is as likely to come from landscape and green space professionals as it is from general members of the public. **Chapter 4** has outlined the wide range of potential benefits of urban green spaces and addressed the relatively neglected area of the economic benefits. It indicated that the off-site benefits of urban green spaces are notoriously difficult to quantify, but that those studies that have been carried out refer to the benefit of environmental improvement in attracting inward investment and raising land values. Less obvious, but potentially significant indirect economic benefits can also be associated with the health and education aspects of urban green space. There is a notable shortage of evidence about such benefits based on UK examples.

9.2 The Urban White Paper specifically refers to urban parks, play areas and public spaces having an important role in the urban fabric. Well-managed public open spaces are linked to improving the attractiveness of urban areas, promoting healthier lifestyles, benefiting wildlife and the environment and acting as an important educational tool. They are also seen as vital to enhancing the quality of urban environments and the quality of life in urban areas. Urban green spaces can certainly help to meet the challenges outlined in the White Paper – encouraging people to remain in towns and cities, tackling poor quality of life and lack of opportunity, addressing weak economic performance of some parts of towns and cities and reducing the impact of urban living on the environment, There has however been very little, if any, serious consideration of urban green spaces as core elements of urban renewal, contributing more than just an attractive setting for other activity. For example, the Social Exclusion Unit's 2001 Neighbourhood Renewal Action Plan makes no explicit link between urban parks and green spaces, and areas for priority action such as community self-help, local capacity building, arts, sport and leisure, and youth disaffection. It is therefore essential to demonstrate how green spaces can contribute to social and economic regeneration and to key policy areas such as health and education, as well as to environmental enhancement. At the same time it is vital to raise the profile of parks and green spaces in the array of neighbourhood renewal and urban regeneration initiatives. It is also important to note that there can be potential conflicts: quality of life issues associated with accessible green spaces can be jeopardised if pressure for high density urban development reduces the amount of available green space.

9.3 Local Strategic Partnerships (LSPs) are now being established across the UK with cross-cutting responsibilities both for preparing neighbourhood renewal strategies at the local level, and for preparing the new Community Strategies that local authorities are now required to make. LSPs are cross-sectoral umbrella partnerships, bringing together the public, private and voluntary sectors to provide a single, overarching local coordination framework within which other more specific partnerships can operate. Once again, the link between this initiative and urban parks, play areas and green spaces is not explicit. There is clearly a need for more work in this area, but the case studies included in this chapter make a strong case for this link to receive greater recognition.

9.4 From the range of examples found in the case study local authorities covered in this research, especially in the northern towns and cities where regeneration has such a key role, it is possible to recognise four levels of integration of urban green space in urban renewal, characterised by an increasing strategic synergy between environment, economy and community. These are listed below and discussed in the remainder of this chapter:

- helping to attract inward investment through provision of attractive urban landscapes;

- unforeseen spin-offs from grassroots green space initiatives;

- parks as flagships in neighbourhood renewal;

- strategic, multi-agency area based regeneration, linking environment and economy.

Helping to attract inward investment

9.5   Most towns and cities in the UK undertake some form of environmental enhancement through horticultural plantings as a means of producing an attractive image to visitors and residents. In many cases, however, this can be simply a cosmetic exercise, limited perhaps to bulb plantings or bedding schemes at 'gateway' entrances or routes into a city, or to hanging basket displays on a few streets. For most of the authorities covered in this survey, this was certainly an area that was first in line for budget cuts when financial pressures arose.

9.6   In relatively few cases was the quality of the urban green environment given a high political profile as a means for attracting inward economic investment and encouraging tourism. In the case study local authorities, **Cheltenham's 'Cheltenham in Bloom'** programme stood out as being the most co-ordinated and far-reaching scheme (**Case Study 9.1**). Although the town has a reputation for its floral displays, Cheltenham in Bloom as an idea goes well beyond the decorative. It is regarded as being highly economically important in attracting inward investment to the town. This may happen in a number of ways and particularly by:

- creating a high quality environment to encourage the siting of businesses;

- providing good outdoor recreational facilities and high environmental quality for those who will be attracted to work in such businesses;

- providing a very pleasant town centre to attract shoppers and encourage spending;

- providing a unique image and profile for the town to enhance tourism.

9.7   The scheme attracts substantial private sponsorship. Cheltenham in Bloom is linked to the annual Britain in Bloom competitions that many local authorities enter but what makes Cheltenham in Bloom so different from the traditional beauty contest that other authorities view these competitions as, is that in Cheltenham it is *'about the whole town and not just the judging route'*. Indeed Cheltenham markets itself as 'The Town within a Park'. The Parks service is relatively well financed, and has been able to protect itself to some extent against severe budget cuts because of the high profile of the scheme and the service and the adverse effects that any such cuts would bring to the image of the town.

CASE STUDY 9.1 Cheltenham in Bloom

Cheltenham in Bloom (CiB) has been in existence for 20 years and is run by an independent committee of 15 people. While the erstwhile purpose of the group is to promote Cheltenham's entry in the city category of Britain in Bloom, it has a much wider importance to the image and economic functioning of the town. CiB meets once a month to *'stress the importance to the town of trees and flowers in terms of economic investment through tourism and creating an attractive shopping environment, and contribution to local quality of life'*.

CASE STUDY 9.1 Continued

Although in the early days the main remit of the group was to raise awareness of the Cheltenham in Bloom initiative to traders and the public, a major function now is to fund raise and chase commercial sponsorship. The committee runs a series of competitions for private gardens and commercial premises. Although the focus is mainly on public landscapes and commercial premises, there is also community involvement in CiB from a number of schools, nursing homes and allotment holders and the council runs a tenants garden competition. Cheltenham Borough Council has its own nursery that grows and supplies all the plants (they also grow for three other authorities).

The organisation raises around £20 000 per year in commercial sponsorship. Smaller sums go direct to CiB, while larger amounts go direct to the council. The main long-term sponsor is Kraft Foods. Sponsors are given a dedicated site with a plaque and publicity in the local paper.

The committee is made up of representatives from the following groups:

- Chamber of Commerce

- Cheltenham Civic Society

- Traders Groups

- Kraft Foods

- Councillors

- Cheltenham Horticultural Society

- Cheltenham Flower Club

The involvement of council members results in a strong link with the council, although CiB is keen to maintain a public perception of independence from the council. The council has officer representation in the form of one of the Park Development Officers who administers the committee, takes minutes and organises the competitions.

Cheltenham has not won an award in Britain in Bloom since 1998 but this isn't necessarily the point. The Borough's Park Development Officer says that 'Cheltenham in Bloom is not just about the judging process – it's about making the whole town look good.' The annual report for Cheltenham in Bloom provides a review of most of the green space projects in the city and is regarded by the parks service as a surrogate annual review and progress report.

Cheltenham is still distinctive in its holistic approach, although many other authorities have caught up with the idea of floral decoration. There is a feeling, however, that it may be time for a review, in order to regain the initiative, given that the authority hasn't won for several years. There is also a definite feeling amongst officers that the high profile of the scheme does to some extent take time away from park development projects.

9.8   There are certainly few British examples of towns and cities that are renowned for the quality, innovation and creativity contained in their public landscapes, and which attract international tourists. This is in contrast to German cities such as Stuttgart and Munich that have gained a permanent legacy of high quality public parks as a result of the rolling programme of national and state garden festivals, or the modern public parks of Paris created in the late 1980s and 1990s. The New Town movement in the UK perhaps came closest to this ideal through the philosophy of siting housing and business in a very green environment. Interestingly, the parks service of the one New Town authority covered in the survey, **Milton Keynes**, was under great financial pressure because of the low relative political priority that the council currently places on parks and green space

9.9   Why is it then that so few authorities invest heavily in their green environment as a means of promoting a unique image for their town or city, and to enhance economic activity and quality of life? Of course, a town like Cheltenham has great advantages in that it already has a quality of architecture and a relative prosperity that in themselves encourage business investment. But similar thinking works in very different circumstances. For example, **Doncaster**, hit economically by the collapse of the mining industry in South Yorkshire, is looking to tourism as a way of increasing economic activity. In this instance, the Britain in Bloom process, and ultimately European competitions, are seen as very important as a means of putting forward a high profile for the town, not just within the UK but also within Europe. This is also seen as a way of ensuring a higher political profile for the parks section within the council.

9.10   It was noticeable from this research that where parks services in the case study local authorities were skilled at achieving a regular media presence and high public profile, as well as forging links with politicians, they were less likely to be hit hard by severe budget cuts. For example, Doncaster parks service has set out in the last couple of years on an unofficial policy to raise its profile to show the benefits of green spaces to the town and the effectiveness of the service in working with communities. Weekly press coverage, five television items and the staging of a number of festivals linked to the aviation and railway history of the town resulted in a significant budget increase in 2001 following ten years of budget cuts, and perhaps as importantly a clear commitment from the council to parks and other urban green spaces.

9.11   The main reason for the low profile of green space as a priority in urban development is, however, that in many authorities, parks and green spaces are seen as 'soft' issues and, as discussed in **Chapter 6**, verbal political commitment is not necessarily backed up by financial resources. It is certainly the case that, generally, parks and other urban green spaces are regarded as backdrops to economic activity and have a rather cosmetic and superficial role, and are certainly not seen as pivotal places in terms of urban regeneration. Cheltenham in Bloom, although well established, can still be regarded as innovative in the strategic view of green space that it embodies, but in essence it deals with the cosmetic view of landscape. The remainder of this chapter seeks to make a different case, based on evidence gathered in this study, namely that urban green spaces have a unique and under-publicized role in facilitating sustainable neighbourhood and urban renewal.

Spin-offs from grassroots green space initiatives

9.12   In **Chapter 7**, a number of examples were given of self-management of urban green spaces by community groups. In some instances, as at **Coalshaw Green Park, Oldham (Case Study 7.6)**, not only was a facility such as a pavilion and café run by a friends group, but also the operation of the facility led to other initiatives which had wider community benefit, such as lunch clubs and outings for young people. This tendency for successful community-led green space revitalisation to result in spin-off regeneration activities is recognised in **Oldham's** Green Space Strategy, in which the park friends group development strategy (**Case Study 6.10**) has enabled *'a community to gain experience, attract dedicated individuals and establish networks, thus developing the confidence to tackle wider social issues'*.

9.13   The key point here is that parks and green spaces provide a unique focus for local groups to achieve real change, and in so doing to generate the sort of community contacts and cohesiveness that is considered an integral aspect of successful neighbourhood regeneration. Two examples from **Doncaster** illustrate this with initiatives where active park Friends Groups have taken on these wider social issues, particularly with regard to young people. The two sites, **Grove Park** and **Manvers Park**, share a number of striking similarities in both their problems and solutions, although the first time that members of each friends group had met each other was during the interviews for this study. The role of the local authority in the development of both sites is a very supportive one, but, mainly through lack of resources, is much less hands-on than, for example, in **Oldham**. However, the fact that both groups have achieved so much is a credit to the parks officers who have enabled the groups to take the lead in the development of their sites.

CASE STUDY 9.2 Grove Park Gardes, Doncaster

Grove Park Gardens is a neighbourhood park that was created in the 1920s from an old limestone quarry. In its heyday up until the 1950s and 60s, the park was actively used and a real centre of community activity, with an impressive sunken bowling green surrounded by three terrace levels faced with dry stone walls. However, like so many other formerly thriving local parks across the country, the park went into decline in the 1980s and 90s and by the mid 90s the pavilion building was derelict, the park and play area were subject to continuous vandalism and the park was generally considered unsafe with prevalent anti-social activities and drug-taking occurring. This occurred in conjunction with successive budget cuts to Doncaster's Parks service – cuts which are now considered to have been extreme and to have caused a failing in parks infrastructure as well as a major deterioration in maintenance quality.

In 1996, local residents set up a group with the aim of preventing further decline. This was partly spurred by elimination of the bowling green as a cost-saving measure. Their primary objective was to re-open the pavilion as a community facility, to reduce vandalism and to provide a base for positive activities for young people. The group became the first of Doncaster's Friends Groups and were formally constituted as a registered charity. The Friends of Grove Park Gardens has 120 members and meets monthly. A dedicated committee, that has kept together since 1996, co-ordinates the activities.

CASE STUDY 9.2 Continued

The Friends Group have taken over the lease of the pavilion and have worked hard to gain funding from a wide range of sources, including Lottery funding, for the refurbishment of the pavilion, re-instatement of facilities and running of events and programmes. Their main purpose now is to provide as wide a range as possible of facilities and activities for local people to maximise the use of the park, with a particular focus on young people. This is partly because the group feels that a long-term process of rebuilding the park is required and that this requires engaging and involving the future users of the park. While it is also seen as the only way to eliminate vandalism and damage to the park, the main driving force is a strong local desire to provide activities and facilities for the young people of the area.

In terms of the infrastructure of the park and its use there is solid evidence of improvement. The group have revamped the park's tennis courts and put in a new play area. Surveillance and security have also improved with the active presence of the friends groups in a way that was not apparent before. There have been 5 prosecutions for dog fouling, and a 'park watch' scheme has been set in partnership with the police. Two members of the friends group undertake a litter pick and clean up of the park every weekend. But it is the range of activities and programmes around the park that is of particular interest here – community activities based around children and young people that could only spring out of a park because it provides a free continuously open gathering and focal place.

The emphasis on children arose because of the numbers that congregate and use the park at weekends, holidays and summer evenings. The Chair of the Friends Group says *'the park has the kids for more hours than they are in school'*. The activities organized by the Friends Group include:

- Parent and Toddler Group. This meets every week, including the school holidays. It is the only such group in Doncaster to remain open over the holidays. The group is the main user of the refurbished pavilion

- Football and Tennis coaching throughout the summer run in partnership with the police. Part of the idea of organizing these sessions was to involve children's parents. It had become apparent to the Friends Group that some of the damage in the park was being done by children as young as 9 and 10. In a bid to increase parental responsibility, the sports training sessions encouraged active participation by parents as well as children.

- Bulb planting by children – 5000 bulbs planted by the local primary school in 2000.

- Children's Christmas Party

- Bouncy Castle Hire – as well as being used for events in the park, the friends hire out their bouncy castle to generate income.

The Friends Group are now moving on to provide a welcome club for older people, based in the pavilion, in a bid to mix the generations.

CASE STUDY 9.2 Continued

The Chair of the group, who originally started the Friends of Grove Park Gardens in her role as secretary of the local Tenants and Residents Association, has gained greatly in terms of personal development from her involvement with the group. She has become very well known to the young people of the area, partly by being around in the park and talking to them, but also through the regular visits she makes into local schools to talk about the park. On the basis of this activity she was invited to be a school governor. She has become an advisor to other parks in Doncaster and also has been able to use the community work experience gained to get a job. Despite her work for the park taking up much of her spare time, this is willingly given because she gains satisfaction from the feeling of making a difference and seeing real results from the effort. In particular she is gratified to see the park bringing together different sections of the community. She feels the sense of the park being a centre for activities for young people is starting to return the park to the role it formerly fulfilled: a focus for community vitality.

CASE STUDY 9.3 Manvers Park, Mexborough, Doncaster

Mexborough is a township settlement near Doncaster that was hit hard by the collapse of the mining industry. Manvers Park is a significant piece of open space in the area that until recently was maintained as a recreation ground, but in practice was a large expanse of mown grass with no features or facilities.

Now the site has an active Friends Group with a high representation of young people and a notable number of wider spin-offs. Action around the park started in the mid 1990s when a group of young people went to see a local resident who undertook a lot of youth work, about what could be done with the park. She organised a petition to find out who else in the area was interested and approached Doncaster council in 1996 with a view to setting up a friends group. In conjunction with Dearne Valley

Groundwork, a six week consultation session was set up in the park over the following summer, with a range of events and activities to encourage local young people to get involved in the future planning of the park. The session was a great success and promoted a great deal of excitement and energy from the large number of young people who became involved. Unfortunately, at the end of the six weeks, Groundwork pulled out of the project. There was great pressure, however, from local young people for the meetings and the process to continue and, as a result a youth drop-in centre was set up in a community base next to the park. The centre was originally open one night a week and one afternoon a week in the school holidays. As a result, the group of young people along with two adults made a plan for the park along with council park development officers. As part of the process, the group travelled around Doncaster looking at parks to discover what they thought worked well. The plan included a large area of wildflower meadow, play areas for young and older children, and a skate park. However, funding was not immediately available to implement the scheme.

CASE STUDY 9.3 Continued

The drop in sessions resulted also in the group making and producing their own film, 'Estate Life'. It became apparent that many of the proposed park based activities were male orientated, and a lot of the outings of the group were to look at male orientated features such as BMX tracks – this had resulted in male domination of the group: finding non-sporting activities to attract girls into the group proved difficult. Eventually beauty sessions were started up on the weekday night sessions run by and for older girls and these have proved very popular. Because of the popularity of the drop-in centre at the community base, a second community facility was set up in the centre of the estate as a spin-off from the park: a one-stop shop advice and community resource centre that is open on weekday evenings.

In 1999 Groundwork again came back into the area and made contact with the Friends Group, who were initially dubious of further involvement because of their previous experience, and things were working well for the group anyway. However they have since found Groundwork to be very useful for their professional expertise in contract negotiation and sourcing funding. Sufficient monies have become available, notably through Section 106 funds, for the park scheme to be implemented.

The Manvers Park example is remarkable because of the long-term involvement of young people in the project: some of the original group are still involved five years later at the age of 18 and 19. As with Grove Park Gardens (**Case Study 9.2**), the driving force behind the project was to provide facilities and activities for young people in the area. As the co-ordinator of the group says: '*young people are losing the art of playing – they're turned loose early in the morning but are not allowed to play on the streets because of road safety. The park provides a safe environment*'.

Again, as with most of the other community initiatives described in this report, the group is driven by a committed individual. In common with the other initiatives also, the original impetus for the group was to make good a shortfall in local authority provision and to address the problem of lack of youth facilities. But it is also clear that such initiatives take on a life of their own and evolve to generate spin off activities that were not part of the original plan.

9.14   Although these two case studies are about community involvement they are included here with other regeneration initiatives because they illustrate the role of parks and green spaces in local capacity building and in generating community networks. Both were initially spurred on by a sense of despair at the decline in the quality of neighbourhood facilities, concern at the activities of young people and the facilities available for them, and a strong desire to do something about it. Both have been successful in achieving a rejuvenation of the parks in question, but they have also achieved something far deeper – a wider social attachment to the park for young people – one which it is hoped will sustain the park into the future. But there is also the sense at Grove Park that different sections of the community are being brought together through the activities being run at the park. At Grove Park, the key member of the friends group has gained employment as a result of the experience and is sharing her expertise with other parks groups. At Manvers Park, not only have youth development activities been sustained for a considerable number of years, but also a community advice centre catering for all sections of the community has been a direct spin-off of the park-based youth drop-in centre.

9.15   Both groups are adamant that none of this would have been possible if it wasn't for the park as no other type of community facility is able to generate such attachment or involve such a wide range of users. So, why do urban parks have such potential in galvanizing community initiatives and promoting spin-off effects? Those involved in the two Doncaster sites feel that it is because parks offer free, open and non-discriminatory access and are therefore quite different from most indoor venues, and also because they are open to so many different uses. Decline in quality and maintenance is also easy to see, but on the other hand, improvements can also be very visible. In the particular case of these two sites it was also considered that the parks were significant gathering places for young people (and also seen by parents as places for children to spend time in during school holidays). But there was also some sense, in the case of Grove Park, of trying to recapture some of the meaning that the park had once had to the community.

9.16   These examples are also similar in that the various community initiatives evolved in an unplanned way out of an initial desire to improve neighbourhood quality. They show the great potential of park-based groups to have spin-off effects in the wider community, but they also illustrate how much is dependent on having the right individuals involved. There are of course concerns that such individuals may be exploited to provide services 'on the cheap'. However, it is also clear from the **Doncaster** examples and others, that the voluntary activities enable individuals to realise creative or entrepreneurial skills that otherwise might not find expression, and it is also clear that the individuals can greatly benefit in terms of personal development. The remaining examples in this chapter take things a stage further: how can the latent potential of urban green spaces to contribute positively to urban renewal (as illustrated in the preceding case studies) be harnessed from the outset in a planned regeneration programme?

Parks as flagships in neighbourhood renewal

9.17   While the examples in the previous section were brought about by voluntary activity and to some extent the wider benefits were unforeseen, case studies are considered in this section of initiatives where parks and green spaces have been deliberately targeted as flagships or focal points for neighbourhood regeneration initiatives. They share some qualities with the previous examples: parks were chosen because they, more than any other neighbourhood facility, were able to act as a catalyst for other initiatives. There is also a great sense of local ownership: in the previous examples this was because of the supportive and permissive attitude of the local authority. In the examples that follow the sites are leased from the local authority and are self-managed by locally-based trusts. As a result, the trust has considerable control over what happens on the site, and perhaps more importantly in these examples, employs full-time workers to guide the development process.

9.18   The two examples considered here are both from **Sheffield**, which has major issues of historical economic decline and a need for regeneration, recognised by its European Objective 1 status. They are **Heeley Millennium Park** and **Longley Greens**. While both projects demonstrate the community strengthening aspects of the two Doncaster examples, they also show wider economic and environmental quality benefits. They also share what are emerging as common themes: local initiatives developing as a result of inadequate provision for community needs from the local authority, and a concentration on youth activities.

9.19 In the case of **Heeley Millennium Park (Case Study 9.4)**, a piece of land earmarked in the city plan for a neighbourhood park, in an area of the city where green space had been shown to be needed, had not been developed beyond a large expanse of featureless mown grass because of lack of resources. Through the local Trust's (Heeley Development Trust) development process, not only has a very popular local park been produced, but significant local employment has been generated, a range of youth and community development programmes initiated, new businesses have been set up adjacent to the park and a number of training and education programmes originated. Although it is notoriously difficult to quantify such benefits, the Trust believes that the new park and its spin-offs have resulted in economic stimulation to the area and has contributed to the area being seen as a more desirable place to live.

9.20 Most notable, however, in the context of this section, is that Heeley Development Trust is now a major player in regeneration of the wider area. This has involved them in revamping other parks and green spaces in the area to produce a coordinated green network through Heeley that not only improves environmental quality but also safety by providing off-road routes around the area. But more importantly the Trust is also now developing innovative housing and economic projects that aim to make Heeley distinctive within the city, but prevent a process of 'gentrification' by promoting affordable housing and local employment. As with the other case studies in this chapter, Heeley Development Trust is clear that none of this would have been possible without the park as the original focus for community development.

CASE STUDY 9.4 Heeley Millennium Park

The park was formed on derelict open land created after house clearance in the 1970s in anticipation of a new dual carriage way. A massive local campaign prevented the building of the road, but the resultant open space had no purpose and was topsoiled and put down to grass and left undeveloped for 17 years, under the control of Sheffield City Council Housing Department. Although the site was designated as local green space in the city's Unitary Development Plan, and the need for a park to service the local population was recognised, no resources were forthcoming from the council over and above the minimum required to keep the large expanses of open grass mown.

The introduction of the National Lottery in the 1990s provided the impetus for a community initiative to develop the site as a Millennium Park. A Steering Committee was formed in 1995, centred primarily around the adjacent and very successful **Heeley City Farm (Case Study 5.2)** which had already developed four acres of the site. The land was acquired from Sheffield City Council on a long-term lease with a peppercorn rent in the early 1990s, although the Trust had to pay a substantial up front sum to cover the council's legal and professional costs in securing the transfer. Although the submission to the Millennium Commission was not successful, the consultation associated with that bid proved beyond doubt the strong local desire for a park. In 1996 the Steering Group decided to set up the Heeley Development Trust as a constituted body that would be able to gain funding independently both of the City Farm and the City Council and which would stimulate enterprise and self-help within the area. The Trust has representatives from local schools, the council, business, training organisations and religious groups: all members of the Trust are locally based. The development of the park was seen as crucial to the wider economic and social stimulation of the area, and the Trust was set up to be the managing agency for the park. The aim was to create a modern park that would be the first in Sheffield to be conceived, designed and managed by a local community.

CASE STUDY 9.4 Continued

The initial ideas for the park were developed by two landscape architects: one from the city council and, crucially for the long-term success of the project, a locally based landscape architect working closely with the Development Trust and the community. They worked very closely with local youth clubs and schools, particularly the oldest years of the primary school, in drafting the early concepts for the park. This was partly because lack of facilities for young people had been the greatest issue arising from preliminary consultations about the park, and partly because it was felt that this was the most important group to bring into the development process for the long-term sustainability of the park. Between 1996 and 1998 funding applications were made and secured from sources such as SRB, ERDF Objective 2 and English Partnerships, and the park was constructed and planted between 1998 and 2000, at a total cost of £555 000. One border of the park was designated for light industry. Several new companies have located in the area and a number of adjacent buildings have been converted to manufacturing and business units, including two old chapels. In 1999 a Park Keeper was employed who is responsible for mowing the grass, picking up litter and keeping an eye on the playground etc. He is a local person, formerly long-term unemployed.

In the initial stages of Heeley Development Trust, the park represented the majority of the Trust's budget. Now it takes up only a relatively small amount. Very quickly the high degree of community involvement that went into the park's development led to expansion into related areas. The initial consultations with the local community about what the park should contain raised a number of issues that spurred the trust to raise funds to tackle these concerns. As a result the Trust now has a team that is involved in wider regeneration and community development. The Trust has a core team of 10 development workers including:

Youth team with one full time and three part time workers. In the initial consultation stages of the park's development, the major issue to arise was the lack of youth facilities and things for young people to do. The youth team was originally formed to undertake outreach work based around the park. For example an active programme of sports events was organized and all tree and bulb planting in the park was carried out by children. Now, although the same sorts of groups are targeted as in the earlier stages, the team attracts additional funding which means that is able to be financially self-supporting and is not part of the Development Trust's budget.

Community Development team with two workers

Local People into Jobs with one full time worker who provides advice and guidance on employment opportunities and runs training courses in conjunction with the youth team. Again the park has played a central role, with summer play schemes, a new area-wide child care co-operative and grounds maintenance operations being carried out by members of staff who have come up through the training programmes.

The Park is maintained by two staff, who each work 30 hours a week, along with 8-10 volunteers who undertake general grounds maintenance. Horticulture trainees based at Heeley City Farm also work on the site.

CASE STUDY 9.4 Continued

The Trust is now developing a large number of 'satellite sites': tackling areas of sterile incidental green space, and run down play areas and pocket parks within Heeley to produce a high quality green network for the area. But in addition to green space management and community development, the Trust is becoming an important local development agency. For example it is currently developing proposals for a 40 acre 'eco-village' mixed development with the aim of providing good quality rented accommodation for local residents.

A major focus of current activity is developing methods for generating income for the Trust once the main funding for the park runs out in 2003. Part of this is intended to come from the extension of the duties of the park grounds maintenance team to general street cleaning and maintenance of verges through out the area, partly through selling of skills to other agencies on a consultancy basis, and partly through diversification of activities beyond the park to take advantage of further funding opportunities.

There are a number of measurable outcomes of the development of Heeley Millennium Park:

- Improvement in environmental quality through the new park, the regeneration of the satellite sites and the proposed wider environmental face-lift.

- Provision of facilities and recreational opportunities, particularly targeted towards young people.

- Direct Job Creation through employment of development workers and maintenance staff associated with the park and the Development Trust

- Indirect Job Creation through economic stimulation and training schemes. Although this is notoriously difficult to quantify, the Trust can point to a number of concrete examples of businesses starting up or locating in Heeley purely because of the development of the park. These include a pub and retail units and light industry in the business park on the edge of the park. However, there has been some negative economic impact. Some established businesses have seen a fall in profits because of road closures as a result of the building of the park. While, on a positive note, local businesses have been willing to contribute financially to the park's development because of the potential associated increase in land values, the Trust is also mindful of a potential problem in terms of 'gentrification' of the area because of increasing house prices. The development of the new rented housing is a move to counter this effect.

- Building Local Capacity. Several of the full time workers on the project have come via the volunteer route, receiving training as volunteers, and being taken on when funding allowed. This has not only promoted employment of local people, but ensures a very high degree of commitment to the project itself. The skills gained have proved to be valuable outside of Heeley itself. For example, the Development Manager, who undertook much of the consultation and design development of the park, has now undertaken consultancy work on community consultation for other park regeneration schemes in Sheffield. The income from these activities is fed back into the Trust.

9.21 **Longley Greens** in **Sheffield** is not at such an advanced stage. The site is in one of the most economically deprived parts of the city and Longley Greens themselves were created when the Longley Estate was built in the 1930s, as central public gardens paid for through subscription by local residents. However, from the 1970s on, the greens became derelict and unmanaged under the control of the City Council's Housing Department, so that eventually they were no-go areas for local residents. The decline in the Greens mirrored a decline in the estate through the 1980s. Formerly the Greens were surrounded by shops and businesses, but gradually these disappeared, leaving empty and boarded up premises.

9.22 In the mid 1990s, a community initiative, developed through the local residents association, set out to reverse this decline and regenerate the area economically. A community trust was set up (LOCAL) which took over leases on disused premises around the Greens and on the Greens themselves. There were three major driving forces behind the initiative: in common with other case studies here, a strong desire within the local community to push for improvements as a result of the desperately poor state of the area; a strong desire to generate estate-based employment; and, in the case of some of the members of the group, a wish to return the Greens to being the focal point of the estate which they had been in the past.

9.23 LOCAL is a very good example of a community group working positively (rather than negatively and antagonistically) with the local authority to effect change. Council officers have been very supportive in facilitating action, but the impetus and initiative for change has come from LOCAL itself. Several of the former derelict buildings around the Greens are now in use – one as a community café, resource centre and base for LOCAL, from which is run a tool hire scheme for local residents. In 2001 a masterplan was drawn up for the Greens by consultants working in very close association with LOCAL and a wide range of community and youth groups. The scheme includes a large festival space and a site for a regular market and travelling fairs, as well as more traditional youth, wildlife and leisure facilities. Again, it is the presence of the Greens themselves that provides the focal point around which the initiative revolves. The group is clear that once the Greens have been invigorated and their use revitalized, then further buildings around their perimeter will be turned into positive use.

9.24 These two examples illustrate again the central role of an urban green space in stimulating wider regeneration. Both examples are site specific, in that they were, at least initially, based around a single park. The final section of this chapter considers larger scale strategic, area based regeneration programmes that link green space concerns with economic and social regeneration.

Strategic, multi-agency area based regeneration, linking environment and economy

9.25 It was suggested at the beginning of this chapter that for many regeneration schemes, 'landscaping' concerns may be seen as cosmetic elements of a programme, providing neat or attractive surroundings to the more substantial infrastructure or housing elements of a scheme. Recently, the idea of a stronger link between environmental regeneration, economic stimulation, job creation and education and training has come to the fore, partly as a result of emerging evidence from disparate local initiatives such as those already mentioned in the chapter. The main national agency involved in promoting this philosophy is Groundwork, which is formed from a series of regionally or city-based based trusts that enter into partnerships with local groups and local authorities to effect change. Issues arising from the experience of local authorities working with Groundwork are discussed in **Chapter 8**. Groundwork's Changing Places Initiative in particular, although focusing mainly on derelict, post-industrial land rather than urban parks, has the concept of linking economic development with environment as one of its key principles. Similar initiatives, more specifically targeted at urban parks, may also occur at local level with partners other than Groundwork.

9.26 The main lessons from the case studies reported in this chapter are that for effective and sustainable long-term regeneration a number of considerations need to be met (in addition to sources of funding and realisable goals). These certainly include professional expertise and help being made available to local communities, whether it be through partnership with an organisation such as Groundwork, or through the employment of workers through a Trust system, as with Heeley Development Trust. The various partners involved need to work on a basis of equality, without any conflicts of interest, and with clear and effective channels of communication. It is also very important that there is seen to be a long-term commitment to the process, that those involved have a real stake in the success of the programme, and that partners are seen to be locally based. In this study, one particular initiative – the **Green Estate Programme, Sheffield (Case Study 9.5)** – was encountered that fulfilled all these criteria and embodied a highly creative and innovative approach to neighbourhood regeneration. It is held up here as a model for working elsewhere.

9.27 The Green Estate Programme is an innovative environmental programme for the Manor and Castle Estates in Sheffield, that is led by the Manor and Castle Development Trust (MCDT). MCDT itself is constituted to receive UK Government and European funding. As a result it has been in the relatively uncommon position of leading funding bids (with Sheffield City Council facilitation) and retaining a much higher degree of local control over how the funding is used than is commonly the case. The Green Estate Programme complements the MCDT's approach to economic and social regeneration in the area. A strong partnership approach is at the core of the programme, involving MCDT, Sheffield Wildlife Trust, Sheffield City Council Parks, Woodlands and Countryside Service, the council Housing Department, the Youth Service, housing associations and the main housing developer, working with local residents, community forums and agencies. Sheffield Wildlife Trust (SWT) co-ordinates all the park and green space initiatives.

9.28 The Green Estate Programme and the renewal of the Manor and Castle area of Sheffield is a prime example of a Local Strategic Partnership that is delivering real results, and it is distinctive because environmental and green space concerns are at its core. It is effective because it demonstrates the real benefits of cross-agency and multi-disciplinary working. It also points the way forward because of the strategic area-wide view of green space as a central element in social, economic and community regeneration and the multitude of interconnected locally-based projects that address all levels and sections of the community. Although the Green Estate concept originated on the Manor and Castle estate, SWT have been invited to undertake feasibility studies to extend the concept to other parts of the city.

9.29   The Green Estate programme demonstrates a wide range of creative and innovative features and examples of good practice:

- a holistic approach to urban renewal with environmental initiatives at the heart of social and economic regeneration, and working strategically across an area with non-environmental disciplines. The area-based approach also enables resources to be re-allocated – if one project is delayed then funds can be directed elsewhere;

- a creative partnership between Sheffield City Council Housing Department, SWT and the main housing developer, opened up the opportunity for bringing in substantial Section 106 monies for the creation of pocket parks and the new district park. But through the charging of a permanent annual ground rent levy on each new house (paid by the resident to MCDT and ring-fenced for landscape management), funding was secured for the ongoing maintenance of the green spaces. Section 106 monies have also been used to part-fund the Project Development Officer for the creation of a new District Park within the area;

- job creation has been a major driving force with the creation of parks was seen as an opportunity for bringing in bigger regeneration gains using the Sheffield Rebuild model, employing local unemployed people (**Case Study 9.6**);

- the concept of productive land-use to provide a sustainable long-term future for the area endeavours to stimulate green or site based enterprises that will be either income generating or cost neutral. This includes acquiring capital assets, buildings and potential businesses that range from a pub on the park through to fishing ponds and cafes through to manufacturing enterprises;

- being able to take a long-term view (5 years at least rather than one or two).

CASE STUDY 9.5 The Green Estate, Sheffield

The Green Estate programme is an environmental action plan for the Manor and Castle Estate that aims to rejuvenate the parks and green spaces of the area, working with local communities to produce a sustainable, attractive working landscape. The Manor and Castle area achieved notoriety in the mid 1990s when it was dubbed by The Sun newspaper as 'the worst estate in Britain'. The estate suffered substantial unemployment following the shrinking of the steel industry workforce in Sheffield in the 1980s and 90s. A seriously deteriorating housing stock and an exodus of residents compounded the problems of the estate, which by standard economic and social indicators sits among the 15 most deprived estates in the UK. As is typical of many areas, social change and economic deprivation have been accompanied by wholesale environmental neglect. One of the characteristic features of the estate is its very high proportion of green space, once an asset when the estate was laid out as a model 'garden estate' in the 1930s-1950s, but now best described as comprising little better than expansive green wastelands, which do nothing for people and little for wildlife. A major rebuilding programme is under way, with large areas of unsafe housing being cleared for new residential development – this process in itself is creating additional open space.

CASE STUDY 9.5 Continued

'Environment' was one of seven strategic areas to address for the regeneration of the area, along with housing, health, economy, education and community, when the Manor and Castle Development Trust (MCDT) began planning a renewal programme in the mid 1990s. The idea for the Green Estate programme came about after funding was obtained to carry out a green spaces audit of the area. Sheffield Wildlife Trust (SWT) were contracted to undertake this. Following the audit, and the resulting recognition that the green areas represented a potentially valuable resource rather than a problem, SRB/ERDF funding was obtained for an 18 month partnership project between SWT and MCDT to develop the environmental action plan. The concept of the Green Estate was a result. The programme was launched in April 2000, with SRB funding for a five-year period until March 2004.

A key aspect of the total regeneration programme is that the environmental strategy has equal status to the other six programme areas, and the holistic nature of the regeneration process allows cross-cutting integration across all seven programme areas. There was no need for SWT to hard-sell the need for a high profile for green spaces within the programme. According to, the co-ordinator of the Green Estate programme, *'there was a willingness and critical mass of reasons to drive the landscape agenda, although the scale of operation has continued to take everyone by surprise'*.

The programme brings together a raft of individual projects that build together to help bridge the separation between communities and their immediate environment. The area-wide strategy has three major aims:

● To regenerate all the major open spaces, green gateways and corridors in the area, to release their social, recreational, environmental and economic potential;

● To encourage the integration of productive land use, with sustainable management techniques bringing diversity and value back into the urban landscape;

● To encourage the involvement of local people in their environment in any way possible, in order to help renew neighbourhood pride.

The programme, which currently employs 30 full time staff, is centred on three main delivery areas:

Capital works A programme of investment in regenerating existing green spaces, with particular emphasis on children and youth facilities, and major investment in new green space provision, including high specification pocket parks within new housing areas, and a new District Park, Deep Pits/Manor Fields. The new park at Deep Pits/Manor Fields has been chosen by the Urban Green Spaces Task Force as a national demonstration site, selected for the principles involved in its development, namely that it demonstrates good practice in consultation, innovation in design, conflict resolution, collaborative partnership working and innovative approaches to long-term management and maintenance. Other initiatives include a visitor centre and heritage farm, a 12 hectare national demonstration site for the greening of derelict land and numerous small scale community garden and incidental green space improvement schemes.

CASE STUDY 9.5 Continued

Community and Education. A very wide range of community-based activities for children, young people and adults is coordinated by SWT, working with all the schools and community groups of the area. Green Estate staff are based permanently in the area at two 'greenbases'.

Productive Land Use. The concept of productive land use is seen as the only means of ensuring long-term viability for the regeneration initiative, and the means for securing an exit strategy and continuation of the programme once SRB funding runs out. Productive land-use entails finding a positive use for all green spaces, and where possible, ensuring an economic return on that space. Specific projects include: implementing sustainable urban drainage schemes with developers using the green spaces to absorb and manage excess water; flower, tree, plant and seed production for use on city-wide planting schemes; market gardening, and crop and food production schemes; producing biofuels; paper production from Japanese knotweed; green waste recycling and community composting; and developing heritage and environmental tourism initiatives. A 'Green Estate Trading Company' has been developed to set up a separate trading arm and a portfolio of pilot enterprises.

CASE STUDY 9.6 Job creation through Sheffield Replant

Sheffield Replant is part of a parent company, Sheffield Rebuild, that was set up as a not for profit company and is a successful enterprise initially funded through SRB funding. Sheffield Rebuild employed local unemployed people from the estate on basic, but real wages and built the first of the new houses on the estate. A six year contract with the City Housing Department for garden refurbishment provided the impetus to launch Sheffield Replant. The contract was provided work for six months out of every year over the six year period. The need to secure the gap 6 month funding to sustain the initial team of 4 people and a supervisor for the remaining six months of each year led to a partnership project to be put formed between SWT and Wybourn Youth Trust. Additional maintenance contracts on sites within and outside of the estate mean that the company now employs 12 people, with further expansion planned as the new green spaces come on stream. Sheffield Rebuild and Sheffield

Replant between them now employ well over 80 staff. Not only does this stimulate economic regeneration, but it also gains local confidence and ownership in the initiative.

9.30   According to its co-ordinator, the success of the Manor and Castle programme can be attributed to a number of factors:

- being able to identify people's key needs though consultation and involvement (and being permanently based on site) and finding ways that environmental gains can be made in addressing these issues;

- a multi-disciplinary and multi-agency team that mixes landscape professionals with a wide range of other skills, enabling unique across the board 'ownership' of the project by all the key agencies involved;

- looking for partners everywhere – and working hard not to undermine other groups and organisations that would be better placed to deliver services in the long run. Around £1 million in matched funding was raised from around 30 partner organisations in 2001 to match core SRB funding;

- freely using the grant money available, but always focusing on the issue of when the grant money runs out – investing for the future;

- having an enabling approach: using the grant money, partners and local knowledge to take the risk out of problems for local groups and agencies, but handing back responsibility when appropriate;

- taking real risks – this would be impossible without a supportive and strategic partnership process;

- being very focused on long-term objectives and continually evaluating outputs with that in mind;

- matching small steps in capital improvements with incremental community capacity building – the aim has not been for rapid high profile impact but rather to generate long-term confidence;

- not promising too much to local communities and, as a result, delivering on what is promised. Pleasing people so that they want to work with you more is an important principle;

- finding every possible way to keep money in the area;

- using a 'scattergun' approach – developing a large number of small scale, locally based projects, not necessarily knowing which ones will succeed in a fast changing policy and economic environment;

- delivering new ideas as mini pilot projects in the field.

Conclusion

9.31   The case studies presented in this chapter begin to build an alternative picture of the contribution of urban green space to urban renewal. Firm evidence has been given that environmental enhancement not only makes places more attractive and pleasant (thereby promoting inward investment and increase in land values), but that green space initiatives can result in community strengthening and local economic stimulation as well as improvement to local environmental quality. But the argument is also taken further. It is suggested that urban green spaces can, uniquely, be the catalysts for these wider community and economic spin-offs in a way that other neighbourhood facilities or buildings are unable to achieve. **Case Studies 9.2, 9.3 and 9.4** (grassroots green space regeneration initiatives) share a common characteristic: in all cases, participants indicated that wider community and social spin-offs (i.e training programmes, neighbourhood centres, job creation, sports activities) would not have happened if action had not centred around an individual park in the first place.

9.32   The fact that parks offer free and open access all day, every day, non discriminatory access, and are visible representations of neighbourhood quality were identified as important reasons for the special role of parks. These points were raised specifically in connection with young people. Again, the availability and quality of facilities for young people and the extent of care of outdoor spaces by users is more obvious than with indoor facilities. The point has been made already in this chapter that it is perhaps no coincidence that the initiatives described in these case studies were driven by a clear need to improve neighbourhood resources for young people. Different levels of linkage between environmental, social and economic regeneration are indicated, culminating with the example of **Sheffield's** Green Estate Programme. This can be seen as encapsulating current best practice in the UK, demonstrating genuine holistic and sustainable urban renewal at a strategic area wide level, with urban green space tied inextricably into economic, environmental and social regeneration.

9.33   This can be a radically different view of the role of landscape than that traditionally adopted by economists and planners. Clearly, more work is urgently needed to further quantify urban renewal benefits. However, the central role that urban green spaces can potentially play in community strengthening and neighbourhood renewal makes a powerful argument for a much increased political profile and increased investment to meet local needs. Perhaps it is within this area that the greatest potential for an upturn in the fortunes of the urban green space resource lies. Elsewhere in this report the possibility of a national co-ordinating body or agency for urban parks has been raised. However, while the perceived benefits of urban green space are seen, in the public and political mind, to be primarily social and environmental (however important these may be) how likely is it that parks will rise significantly up the political agenda? It is surely recognition of the economic and regeneration benefits discussed in this chapter that will ultimately drive a further resurgence in interest and an increase in the resources directed at urban green space.

CHAPTER 10
Overview and Conclusions

Introduction

10.1 This final chapter provides an overview of some of the issues highlighted by the research and places them in a wider context, including reference to international comparisons.

The importance of urban green space

10.2 This research has confirmed the exceptional importance of urban green space to the future of towns and cities in England. It reaffirms and elaborates on the findings of earlier studies on the role that urban green space plays in the day-to-day life of urban dwellers, by virtue both of its existence – that is people simply knowing that it is there and seeing the contribution that it makes to the urban landscape – as well as its use for recreation and enjoyment. The sheer level of estimated use is in itself quite staggering, with the research estimating that some 33 million people make over 2.5 billion visits a year to some form of urban green space.

10.3 The range of benefits from urban green space covers the spectrum of social, health, environmental, and economic benefits. The range is well established and generally well supported by the available evidence, but deserves to be much more widely publicised and promoted. The economic, and to some extent the social, benefits of urban green space, have however been sadly neglected, in this country in particular. Most importantly, the research suggests that many policymakers have underestimated the role that urban green space can play in urban regeneration. Many still think of parks and other urban green spaces as just 'greenery' or 'landscaping' and far removed from what they perceive to be the real problems of urban communities. Although there are well known examples of major open space or park projects as flagships for urban renewal, in general major new initiatives, such as the Neighbourhood Renewal Action Plan and Local Strategic Partnerships, make little of the link between urban green spaces and other priority areas for action such as community self-help, local capacity building, arts, sport and leisure and youth disaffection.

10.4 And yet the case studies examined in this research, particularly in **Chapter 9**, provide an alternative picture of the contribution that urban green space can make to urban renewal. They provide strong, albeit anecdotal, evidence that environmental enhancement not only makes places more attractive and pleasant, thereby promoting inward investment and increases in land values, but that green space initiatives can also result in strengthening of community and social networks, support new training initiatives and provide local economic stimulation and additional employment.

10.5   The research has shown that urban green spaces can act as catalysts for wider community initiatives in ways that no other public facility seems able to achieve in similar circumstances. Again and again, people involved in these initiatives said that if it wasn't for the park (or other green space) nothing would have happened. The fact that parks are open every day for free entry and offer neutral ground with non-discriminatory access makes them completely different from many building based activities. A number of the initiatives that have been described are notable because they revolve around youth issues. Many have succeeded despite lack of investment so one can only wonder what the potential might be if they were to receive adequate funding.

10.6   This social, community and economic role goes well beyond the normal, somewhat blinkered view of the contribution of urban green space to the future of our cities. It needs to be given much greater prominence in promoting a higher profile for urban green spaces and in supporting the case for funding at both local and national levels.

Tackling the barriers

10.7   The research suggests that some 32% of people in urban areas are either non-users or infrequent users of urban green spaces, including many people from the under represented groups. The elderly and disabled people make up a higher than average proportion of the non-users while people from an ethnic minority background and young people make up a higher than average proportion of the infrequent users. Low levels of use sometimes result from personal circumstances, which the planners, designers and managers of urban green space can do nothing to change. But it is clear that many people are deterred from visiting these spaces because of the image that they have of them.

10.8   They are deterred by what they perceive as lack of facilities, including play facilities for children; the influence of other, sometimes 'undesirable' people; dog mess; safety and other psychological concerns; and concerns about environmental quality including litter, vandalism and graffiti. Tackling these issues and, equally importantly, letting people know that they are being tackled and publicising the resulting improvements, will do much to increase the willingness of people to use the green spaces which they may currently turn away from. None of these issues are new and no-one will be surprised by them. Yet although they have been recognised for some time and some steps have been taken to address them, it is still abundantly clear that many people have a deep concern that parks and green spaces are simply not what they used to be. This is not just nostalgia but a real concern about the perceived decline in quality of these community facilities.

10.9   In addition access issues are also significant, particularly to the elderly and to disabled people. They include concerns about: the proximity of and ease of access to urban green spaces, including the availability of convenient public transport; access to get into those spaces, including for example design of entrances and availability of suitable car parking for the disabled; and ease of moving around safely within them, including design of surfaces and provision for the visually impaired. The access concerns of disabled people take on added significance in the light of the 1995 Disability Discrimination Act and from 2004, service providers will have to make 'reasonable adjustments' to overcome physical barriers to access to their premises and facilities.

10.10   Social exclusion in society is mirrored by the under representation of some groups of people among users of urban green spaces. There is often lack of awareness and understanding within mainstream organisations, which can, for example, lead to failure to recognise fully, or to address, the particular needs of those groups who are most likely to be excluded in society. The research suggests that issues such as access for the disabled and the elderly, the cultural needs of different ethnic groups, and the changing lifestyles and needs of children and young people may all contribute to low levels of engagement with urban green spaces.

It's all about design

10.11   The research suggests that ordinary people, as well as many professionals, recognise that design often lies at the heart of what makes a successful urban green space. As one woman in one of our focus groups put it in describing her ideal urban green space *"Design, design, and design, someone needs to sit down and create it – it cannot just be thrown together"*. Design is also a key part of tackling many of the barriers to use of urban green spaces. It is not just a one-off process that happens when a new park or green space is created. Rather it is an attitude of mind and an approach to solving problems, which should also be an integral part of the ongoing management of urban green spaces, in the same way that thinking about management should also be a key part of the design process.

10.12   It is perhaps because of this recognition of the importance of design that some local authorities, notably **Oldham** and **Sheffield**, have given landscape architects a prominent managerial role in the parks department, putting design awareness and strategic planning and design skills at the heart of landscape management practices. They have played a role as leaders in relationships with friends groups, using the skills that more community focused landscape architects have in working on design and management issues with local communities.

10.13   Approaches to design do, however, have to vary to suit individual circumstances – covering the spectrum from facilitating community design at one level, to high-level innovative approaches to creating new urban green spaces at the other. Quality in design must always be the aim and designing with or for communities should not be allowed to produce a levelling down to mediocre end products, at the expense of originality and creativity. Designers need to find the right balance for each particular situation and site classifications, categorisations or hierarchies have a role to play here. District and local green spaces that are a community resource need to be designed with and for the community that will use them, requiring a different approach and different skills from the designer. On the other hand 'flagship' sites of city wide importance are likely to merit the highest level of design input and a highly creative approach dedicated to achieving the highest possible quality in either restoration or in creation of new open spaces, albeit also with involvement from the community. This approach takes significant capital expenditure and it is through willingness to invest that cities such as Barcelona and Paris have created modern park and open space systems that are the envy of many countries. The perceived lack of capital funds in local authorities in England is often an obstacle to developments of this type and needs to be addressed.

Working with others

10.14   Community involvement of some form is now a part of mainstream activity in most places. There are several different models for partnerships with communities and there are many successes around the country that show how much can be achieved, particularly in parks and other green spaces used for recreation. In Europe, similar approaches also show how partnerships with local communities can tackle many of the intractable problems associated with the vast areas of often barren incidental green space around housing areas. In England some of the most successful approaches seem to occur where there has been a real change in culture in the local authority parks service so that the emphasis on community involvement is core rather than partial or token.

10.15   Many of the issues come down in the end to questions of 'ownership', whether real or perceived. Creating greater 'ownership' by communities using urban green spaces results in greater levels of innovation, creativity, involvement, care and resourcing. Delegating responsibility to community groups and supporting their activities and decisions, can result in a high degree of initiative. It is also apparent that it is possible to manage the evolution of community groups so that ultimately they can take on real ownership of sites. This can happen in the more disadvantaged areas of the city as well as the more prosperous. There is therefore a need to find ways of supporting real or perceived ownership of sites by community organisations to enable varying degrees of self-management. Trusts are emerging as a very promising avenue for meaningful partnerships with communities in a variety of different situations. It must be noted though that effective partnership working doesn't necessarily come on the cheap. Time and resources have to be put into forming and supporting partnerships. There is therefore a potential short and medium term financial cost associated with what might be a longer term financial gain.

10.16   Beyond communities, the search for partner individuals, organisations and institutions seems less well developed in England than in some other countries, and notably the United States. There a range of different types of role for partners can be clearly identified, with many examples of organisations playing these different roles. In this country, however, it is much less easy to find examples across this range. Trusts (as above) and Private Finance Initiatives, of the type found in **Lewisham**, do, however, appear to be emerging as potentially fruitful ways of working to improve urban green spaces, provided that, in the case of the PFI approach, there are appropriate safeguards in terms of pay and conditions for personnel on the ground.

Breaking down organisational barriers

10.17   It is clear that fragmentation of responsibility for different aspects of urban green space management is a major hindrance to efficiency and community involvement. Bringing together parks policy and operations functions in the same department is just the beginning. Bringing together all responsibilities for green space strategy, management and maintenance within one section will foster a holistic view of the urban green space resource, of which parks are but one part. The distinction between town and country also needs to be blurred and ideas and working practices from one applied to the other where there are clearly likely to be benefits.

10.18   At the individual site level, dedicated on-site staff are clearly welcomed by the public and can do much to address the barriers to use that have been identified, by heightening feelings of safety and care for the environment as well as improving communication and support for users. The **Newcastle** model appears to have much to recommend it, with multifunctional park keepers providing the site-based presence in their community focused, area based structure.

10.19   Traditionally there can be a number of different people on the ground in parks and other urban green spaces usually undertaking strictly demarcated roles, for example as gardeners, wardens, park keepers, rangers, security staff, inspectors and cleansing staff. Breaking down barriers between these roles and instilling a sense of 'ownership' in everyone involved can not only be cost effective, potentially allowing more staff to be employed on-site, but can also encourage individual initiative and a culture of innovation in tackling problems.

10.20   Changing roles does, however, require new skills and a new breed of modern green space professional is clearly required. Landscape architects undoubtedly have much to offer, while the skills of rangers and countryside managers offer much in urban situations, to complement the skills of non-traditional park managers. But everyone working in this area needs a range of skills that cut across traditional professional boundaries and job demarcations, with the emphasis on community facilitation, entrepreneurial skills in fundraising and forming and managing partnerships, and design awareness and creativity in problem solving.

Strategic approaches

10.21   Many local authorities still take conventional strategic approaches to urban green space through development plan policies and parks strategies, as well, sometimes, as play strategies. On the whole, however, they do not take a broad integrative view of the whole urban green space resource, which recognises its vital contribution to the quality of life of urban dwellers. There is now a need for a more considered approach that moves beyond parks alone and seeks to address the full range of urban green spaces and the way that they can meet the needs of urban communities. Producing 'green space audits' which incorporate qualitative as well as quantitative information, and preferably involving communities in the assessment; formulating green space categorisation systems and typologies that drive policy; and producing holistic green space strategies and green structure plans that consider parks as just one element in a larger green space network, are examples of these developments.

10.22   This approach is given much greater emphasis elsewhere in Europe and current European initiatives demonstrate the importance attached to this area. The Research Group, under European Co-operation in the field of Scientific and Technical Research, COST Action C11 (Green Spaces and Urban Planning), which consists of thirty academics, professionals and public officials from 13 countries across Europe, is currently addressing the common issues related to green structure planning faced all over Europe by looking at case studies of individual cities, as well as innovative and experimental approaches[1]. The work is due to finish and report in 2004.

1   Chairman of the Group. Bernhard Duhem, French Ministry of Infrastructure, Transport and Housing, Paris.

10.23   A parallel cross-cultural study of people's understanding of green space (funded under the European Union's Fifth Framework programme under Key Action 4 "City of Tomorrow and Cultural Heritage" of the programme "Energy, Environment and Sustainable Development") known as GREENSCOM (Communicating Urban Growth and Green), is underway in the Netherlands, Finland, Sweden, France and Denmark[2]. It seeks to examine the way that the various officers who are involved in green space regeneration and management work with local people to bring about change on the ground. It aims to identify the barriers to the development of more effective and sustainable green spaces and should produce information on why some green space plans from the past worked well to improve the local quality of life and enhance biodiversity, while others failed. This group is looking at Utrecht and Houten, Helsinki and Tampere, Aarhus, Gothenburg and Cergy Pontoise as case studies, and will report in 2003. A further study under this Framework, known as the GREENSPACE project is looking at case study cities of Dublin, Eindhoven, Zurich, Aberdeen, Brighton and Hove and Barcelona.

Establishing the information base

10.24   It is already well-recognised that information on urban green spaces needs to be improved. This research has made suggestions about a typology for urban green space that could, albeit possibly with some modification, provide a basis for developing consistent records and estimates of the extent of different types of green space, both locally and nationally.

10.25   Surveys of the full range of green space could use either map techniques, similar to the National Land Use Database, or aerial photographic interpretation combined with some local authority data collection or field checking, of the type used in many rural land use surveys. The level of detail that can be achieved in such surveys (i.e. the level of the green space categories which can be reported) will depend on the survey methods used. If such a typology were to be adopted as the basis for an inventory of urban green space it would need to be tailored to the methods to be adopted and to be tested, consulted on and revised before putting it to practical use. If an overall approach can be agreed, however, then the typology could form the basis of some form of central guidance on definitions, identification of categories and methods of recording and reporting information.

10.26   Similarly a typology of users of urban green space by type of activity and type of person has been suggested as a result of the research. This too might usefully be taken forward as a starting point for model surveys of the use of the spaces and people's satisfaction with them. The Best Value surveys and the use of citizens panels or similar approaches is beginning to help in establishing better information about green spaces. To be really useful, however, such surveys needs to extend beyond the standard questions about satisfaction with parks and green spaces. A model questionnaire could quite easily be developed based on some of the local authority examples from this research, as well as the approach used in the telephone survey. Work in both of these areas needs to be further developed through consultation and pilot studies so that local authorities can be given guidance on a preferred approach.

---

2   Led by Alterra at Wageningen in the Netherlands.

Sharing good practice

10.27   Several of the case studies in the research, show how some local authorities are seeking to tackle the issues relating to urban green space, including barriers to use in imaginative ways. Undoubtedly many others elsewhere, but not covered in this research, will also have achievements to offer by way of good practice. Many different approaches have been shown by this research to work successfully in tackling some of the main problems, given the right level of support and commitment. They include changes in the structure and organisation of parks services; radical rethinking of on the ground staffing in urban green spaces, including new roles for rangers; partnership and educational approaches to dog issues; planned programmes of park redesign and refurbishment; and different ways of involving communities in developing and caring for parks and green spaces.

10.28   There is undoubtedly a demand at the grass roots level for some form of central agency to promote the cause of urban green space – virtually every local authority involved in the research mentioned this when asked if there were any matters they would like to raise through the research project. Such an agency is seen to be vital: to promoting the cause of urban green space; to sharing experience and providing guidance on good practice; and to developing experimental, innovative approaches to tackling the issues of urban green space, in the same way that the Countryside Agency, for example, is seen to work in rural areas. Whether this can be achieved through an existing organisation, or whether there is genuinely a case for some form of new Non Departmental Public Body remains to be seen. This is not a matter that has been considered in this research.

10.29   Whatever the outcome, however, there is a clear need to avoid duplication of effort and to ensure that where there are common interests with existing bodies, there is collaboration and not competition. To give just one example, the National Urban Forestry Unit and the Community Forest movement both have an interest in the economic effects of trees and urban green spaces on investment and property values, and a shared, or at least complementary approach to research may be one way of moving this topic forward.

References and Bibliography

Arnstein, S.R. (1969) A Ladder of Citizen Involvement. *Journal of the American Institute of Planners*. **35**. 216–224.

Centre for Leisure and Tourism Studies, University of North London (1997) *Survey of Islington Parks: report for Islington Council Leisure and Libraries Service*. London.

Centre for Leisure and Tourism Studies, University of North London (1992) *Survey of People Using St James's Park, the Green Park and Regent's Park*, London.

Chesterton and Pedestrian Market Research Services Ltd (1997) *Managing Urban Spaces in Town Centres*. Department of the Environment and the Association of Town Centre Managers. The Stationery Office, London.

Comedia and Demos (1995) *Park Life: Urban Parks and Social Renewal*. Stroud, Gloucester: Comedia.

Department of the Environment (1996) *People, Parks and Cities – A guide to current good practice in Urban Parks*. London: HMSO.

Department of the Environment, Transport and the Regions (1999) *Town and Country Parks Report of the Environment, Transport and Regional Affairs Committee*. The Stationery Office, London.

Department of the Environment, Transport and the Regions (2000) *Our Towns and Cities: Delivering an Urban Renaissance*. The Stationery Office, London.

Department of the Environment, Transport and the Regions (2000) Towards an Urban Renaissance, Report of the Urban Task Force. London: DTLR/Spon Press.

Department of Landscape, University of Sheffield (2001) *Improving Parks, Play Areas and Green Spaces – Interim Literature Review*. London: Department for Transport, Local Government and the Regions.

Department for Transport, Local Government and the Regions (2001) *Green Spaces, Better places*. *Interim report of the Urban Green Spaces Taskforce*. London: DTLR.

Harrison, C., Burgess, J., Millward, A. and Dawe, G. (1995) *Accessible Natural Green Space in Towns and Cities: A Review of Appropriate Size and Distance Criteria*. English Nature Research Report. No. 153. English Nature: Peterborough.

Holden, R., Merrivale, J. and Turner, T. (1992) *Urban Parks: A Discussion Paper*. Landscape Institute: London

Kit Campbell Associates (2001) *Rethinking Open Space: Open Space Provision and Management: A Way Forward. A research report prepared for the Scottish Executive Central Research Unit*. Edinburgh: Scottish Executive Central Research Unit.

Llewelyn-Davies/London Planning Advisory Committee and Environment Trust Associates Ltd (1992) *Open Space Planning in London*. Romford: LPAC.

MacFarlane, R., Fuller, D. and Jeffries, M. (2000) 'Outsiders in the urban landscape? An analysis of ethnic minority landscape projects'. In Benson, J.F. and Roe, M.H. (eds.) *Urban Lifestyles: Spaces, Places, People*. Rotterdam: Balkema.

Madden, K. *et al.* (2000) *Public Parks, Private Partners*. New York: Project for Public Spaces, Inc.

McAllister, S. (2000) *Institutionalised Racism in the Landscape: the exclusion of ethnic minorities from landscape processes* (Unpublished manuscript, University of Sheffield, Department of Landscape).

National Playing Fields Association (1992) *The Six Acre Standard: Minimum Standards for Outdoor Playing Space*. London: National Playing Fields Association.

Richardson, I. and Baggott, I. (1998) *Community Involvement in Parks*. ILAM Information Centre. Fact Sheet 98/6. Reading: ILAM.

Thomas, H. (1999) 'Urban Renaissance and Social Justice'. *Town and Country Planning*, **68**(11): 332–333.

Toronto Parks and Recreation (2001) *Understanding Personal Safety* [online]. New York, Project for Public Spaces, Inc. http://urbanparks.pps.org/topics/management/safetysecurity/toronto_safety_1

Urban Parks Forum (2001) *A Survey of Local Authority Owned Parks, focusing on Parks of Historic Interest*. London: DTLR, Heritage Lottery Fund, Countryside Agency and English Heritage.

Various Authors (2002) '21 Years of Rebuilding Communities'. Theme Issue on Groundwork. *Landscape Design*, 306.

Woolley, H. and Amin, N. (1995) 'Pakistani Children in Sheffield and their Perception and Use of Public Open Spaces'. *Children's Environments*, **121**(0): 479–488.

APPENDIX 1

Detailed Work Carried Out for Strand 1 and 2

Telephone survey of non-users

A1.1 The aim of this survey was to interview approximately 50 people in each of the case study authority areas who fell within an agreed definition of non-users or infrequent users of urban green space. The original intention was to conduct the surveys on the street in City shopping centres but it proved difficult to make sufficient successful contacts with people falling within the definition of non- or infrequent users to make this approach effective. As a result the British Market Research Bureau were then separately commissioned to carry out a telephone survey with the same aims. In this survey 1,588 successful contacts were made with people willing to answer questions about the frequency with which they used urban green spaces. From these, 515 completed interviews were carried out with people falling within the definition of non-users or infrequent users. No quotas were set for different groups of people, with the exception of young people, where early under representation of this group was corrected by a deliberate strategy of recruiting a small quota of teenagers.

A1.2 The questionnaire contained sections about: the things that put people off using urban green spaces; factors that would encourage people to use them more; measures that people think would improve safety in urban green spaces; and particular facilities, events, activities or landscape features that would encourage greater use; in addition the questionnaire was designed to obtain details of the gender, age, ethnic or cultural origin, employment status, accommodation profile and state of health of those taking part. The aim was to help in understanding the views of the sectors of the community who are under-represented as users of urban green spaces, that is women, young people, the elderly and people from an ethnic minority background and disabled people.

A1.3 During the analysis of the telephone questionnaire, and also in undertaking the focus group discussions (see **A1.5**), it became apparent that breaking the age groupings down further, would help in understanding of people's perceptions. The group of 'young people' is clearly not uniform in its views and so has been broken down into 12–15 year olds and 16–19 year olds because each group was found to refer to the other as 'older' or 'younger' kids. 'The elderly' have been broken down into 56–65 year olds, 65–74 year olds and those over 75 years of age. This is because the research suggested that the 'younger' elderly are, in general, more active both physically and mentally while the 'older' elderly, that is those over 75 years of age, tend to be less active.

A1.4   In identifying those from an ethnic background, the analysis of the results from the telephone questionnaire revealed that those responding included 74 people from non-European backgrounds. However, the numbers of people within each category of Black African, Black Caribbean, other Black, Chinese, Indian, Bangladeshi, Pakistani, other Asian and Mixed Race were so small (2–6 in each group) that further analysis between these groups was not possible. Thus one grouping of European, including English, Irish and other European, was used in the analysis with the 'ethnic' grouping, referred to in the analysis as 'Non-European', defined as including not only those mentioned above but also 40 people who declared themselves to be of 'other' ethnic or cultural origin.

FOCUS GROUPS

A1.5   To find out more about the views and perceptions of the under represented groups among users of urban green spaces, the research included a series of 43 focus groups spread approximately evenly across the ten Strand 1 case study local authority areas and covering, in roughly equal proportions, the elderly, young people, people with disabilities, people from an ethnic background and women. In response to concerns raised in some of the local authority interviews about their particular experiences and concerns, two groups of lesbian women were also added to the original list. All of the groups were organised in conjunction with established groups representing these sectors of the community, with assistance from the case study local authorities. Each group generally involved between 4 and 8 people, including both users and non-users of urban green spaces, meeting together for approximately one to one and a half hours (although generally two hours in the case of people with disabilities) in a local venue. The discussions were tape-recorded and separate notes kept. Time and resources did not allow for full transcripts to be prepared but tapes and notes have been analysed to extract the key messages from each one and then to compare different examples of the same group in different locations to identify common themes.

A1.6   Each discussion followed the same basic format and covered:

- whether, how often and for what reason participants use urban green spaces in their area and which types of space they have experience of;

- what benefits they think are gained by the community from urban green spaces;

- what they consider to be the good things about urban green spaces, which encourage their use;

- what they consider to be the bad things, which put people off using urban green spaces;

- thoughts about their 'ideal' urban green space environment and reactions to a series of photographs showing different styles of green space to stimulate ideas and discussion.

EXAMPLES OF GOOD PRACTICE IN URBAN GREEN SPACE MANAGEMENT

A1.7   In the ten Strand 2 case study local authorities, the initial discussions with senior local authority officers were followed up by more detailed discussion about aspects of good practice and innovative management. These covered details of approaches to community involvement, partnership working, and identification of good practice or innovation in urban green space management. These discussions led on to a further detailed look at individual initiatives or projects. Initiatives included issues like organisation, finance, strategic approaches and ranger services. Projects focused on examples of community involvement, partnerships and the contribution of urban green spaces to wider processes of urban renewal.

A1.8   The use of a structured sample of case study local authorities means that the work has 'dipped in' to practice across the country. It cannot, however, necessarily be claimed that the authorities or the projects examined necessarily represent 'best' practice or indeed the highest levels of innovation. Only fifteen of the over 350 authorities in the country were included in the sample and even the initial profiling survey only included 50 of them. Nevertheless the research does provide a good indication of the range of urban green space work that is going on in different parts of the country and in different types of authority. It was, for example, clear that in general terms there are real differences in emphasis and practice in the large metropolitan and industrial areas of the North compared with the towns and cities in southern England, although inner London areas like Lewisham, and large cities outside the sample, such as Bristol, demonstrate similar problems of deprivation and a need for renewal. Even within the sample of case study authorities one or two of the Strand 1 authorities also revealed good practice examples in management and where possible these were followed up.

A1.8   Across the ten Strand 2 case study authorities a total of at least three management initiatives and three individual projects have been reviewed in each case, and often significantly more. Not all of these are reported here, and not every authority appears as an example. This is not to suggest that they are not all doing good things – on the contrary, there is good practice across the whole range of authorities. The emphasis in this report is, however, on describing the innovative approaches, so that these can help to influence the spread of new ideas and the development of good practice for the future. It is not a comprehensive review of every area of activity in every case study authority, but a more focused look at the good practice and innovation which exists and also at the context in each authority which might generate these new approaches.

EVALUATING INDIVIDUAL PROJECTS

A1.9   In selecting individual projects for review the aim has been to cover a range of different types of urban green spaces and several major themes in management practice, including different types of community involvement, different types of partnership arrangement and different initiatives in relation to funding, management and contributions to urban renewal. Detailed discussions have been held with local authority officers involved in the projects and, where possible, with partners and community groups who are active in each. The aim in each case has been to establish details of the background and history of the project, its aims and objectives, the role and contribution of different partners and the views of those involved about the achievements, the benefits and the problems experienced in each case. From this attempts have been made to extract lessons for the future.

APPENDIX 2

Using the typology as a basis for reporting on the extent of Urban Green Space

A2.1   Typologies, definitions and classifications can serve several different purposes. In this research the emphasis has been primarily on their use in providing a reporting framework for information about the extent of different types of urban green space. The problems currently experienced in gaining a clear picture of how much urban green space of different types actually exists in urban areas have been outlined by the report of the Taskforce's Working Group One. Key issues are: lack of consistency in definitions; the risk of double counting where certain types of green space overlap, especially children's play areas, outdoor sports areas and woodland, all of which may occur within more broadly defined parks and recreation spaces; and concerns about the accuracy of returns and about lack of comparability between different local authorities.

A2.2.   Such problems are not confined to urban green space. Over the years there have been similar difficulties in surveying and reporting on other aspects of the environment that require both a broad national picture and comparison of smaller areas. This applies, for example, to: the annual Agricultural Census, which reports on specific categories of agricultural land use; the National Land Use Database and the Land Use Change Statistics; the National Woodland Inventory undertaken by the Forestry Commission; and the series of national Countryside Surveys funded by the Department of the Environment and its successors, and conducted by the Centre for Ecology and Hydrology, which audits, on both a census and a sample basis, the land use and broad habitats in the wider countryside throughout Britain. In every case similar issues have arisen about definitions and consistency of classification, as well as about cost-effective and repeatable methods of data collection. There are both top-down approaches based on national surveys and bottom-up approaches which produce national statistics from local returns.

A2.3   Urban green space reporting frameworks might be needed for three main purposes, namely to provide figures for:

- the extent of all urban green space, in total and by different categories, for all urban areas and for individual local authority areas;

- the extent of urban green space which is owned and managed by a local authority for different purposes and which might therefore be set alongside the costs of service provision to provide a standard comparison on the basis of expenditure per hectare;

- the extent of publicly accessible recreation green space which is owned and managed by the local authority and which can also be used to provide expenditure comparisons.

A TYPOLOGY OF URBAN GREEN SPACE

A2.4.　The first need is for a classification of urban green space that divides such land into a series of agreed categories, as discussed in Chapter 1 of this report. Surveys of the full range of land in the different categories could use either map techniques, similar to the National Land Use Database, or aerial photographic interpretation combined with some local authority data collection or field checking, of the type used in many rural land use surveys. The level of detail that can be achieved in such surveys (i.e. the level in the hierarchy of urban green space categories that can be reported) will depend on the survey methods used.

A2.5.　If a typology such as that shown in Tables 1.1 and 1.2 in Chapter 1 were to be adopted as the basis for an inventory of urban green space the categories would need to be tailored to suit the methods to be adopted. The typology would also have to be subject to consultation and piloting, and any agreed revisions made before putting it to practical use. If agreement can be reached then the typology could form the basis for some form of central guidance on definitions, identification of categories and methods of recording and reporting information. Table A2.1 is a hypothetical example that shows how information gathered through such an inventory, could be combined with local authority records of the area of land which is publicly or privately owned or managed, and the land which is used for public recreation. A proforma of this type, combined with clear and agreed definitions, would allow accurate and comparable figures to be assembled and for the problem of overlapping categories to be addressed, as shown in the example. A record of this type would allow reporting of a variety of quantitative urban green space indicators as shown below.

Possible reporting categories based on an inventory of urban green space as in Table A1.2

- Total Urban Green Space = 4947 Hectares
- Publicly Owned Accessible Green Space (a) = 2133 Hectares
- Publicly Owned/Managed Inaccessible Green Space (b) = 85 Hectares
- All Publicly Accessible Green Space (a+c) = 2597 Hectares
- All Publicly Inaccessible Green Space (b+d) = 2398 Hectares
- All Play Areas (Inside and Outside Parks) = 51 Hectares
- All Playing Fields (Inside and Outside Parks + Accessible School Fields) = 133 Hectares
- All Woodland (Inside and Outside Parks) = 757 Hectares

TABLE A2.1: EXAMPLE OF AN INVENTORY OF GREEN URBAN GREEN SPACE BASED ON PROPOSED TYPOLOGY

Ownership/Management and Access ⇒ Type of Green Space ⇓	Area (Ha)	Local Authority Owned/Managed Green Spaces		Private/Other Owned/Managed Green Spaces	
		Access for public recreation	No Access for Public Recreation	Access for public recreation	No Access for Public Recreation
Parks – Total	545	545	–	–	–
Play Areas (Included)	20	28			
Playing Fields (Included)	53	53			
Woodland (Included)	84	84			
Gardens	35	30	–	–	5
Outdoor Sports Areas – Total	78	78			
Golf Courses	48	30	–	–	–
Playing Fields	20	20	–	–	–
Other	10	10	–	–	–
Play Areas	18	18	–	–	–
Informal Recreation Spaces – Total	145	145			
Play Areas (Included)	5	5			
Playing Fields (Included)	15	15			
Woodland (Included)	36	36			
Housing Green Space	145	125	–	–	20
Other Incidental Greenspace	29	19			10
Domestic gardens	1569	362			1207
Remnant farmland	654	–	–	–	654
City Farms	25	15	–	10	–
Allotments	167	167	–	–	–
Cemeteries	56	56	–	–	–
Churchyards	38	–	–	38	–
School Grounds	145	45	60	–	40
Other Institutional Grounds	196	–	–	46	150
Wetland – Total	120	40	25	35	20
Open/Running Water	110	30	25	35	20
Marsh/Fen	10	10	–	–	–
Woodland – Total	637	330	–	200	107
Deciduous Woodland	230	230	–	–	–
Coniferous /Mixed Woodland	407	100	–	–	–
Other Habitats – Total	68	38	–	30	–
Moor/Heath	28	28	–	–	–
Grassland	20	10	–	10	–
Disturbed Ground	20	–	–	20	–
Linear Green Space – Total	345	120	20	105	100
River/Canal Banks	125	–	20	105	–
Road and Rail Corridors	220	120	–	–	100
TOTAL	4947	2133 (a)	85 (b)	464 (c)	2313 (d)